Why We Take Drugs

In older cultures, the use of intoxicant drugs was integrated into the rhythms of social existence and bounded by rituals and taboos that ensured their dangerous forces were contained and channelled. In modern western societies, by contrast, the state and the institutions of society have washed their hands of any responsibility for assimilating the desire for intoxication into social existence, and by doing so have sponsored a free-for-all that has often had disastrous consequences for individuals and communities alike.

Why We Take Drugs provides a timely intervention in the growing debate about the wisdom of the ongoing 'war on drugs'. Rather than adopting the assumption that drug and alcohol use is a problem that poses a threat to society, this book makes a case for the idea that society is a problem for intoxicant drug use and that it is society that poses a threat, by denying those who seek intoxication a legitimate and socially sanctioned space in which to experience these altered states. Scholarly yet approachable, it provides a new understanding of the meaning and role of intoxicant drug use in contemporary society, setting an in-depth phenomenological analysis of intoxication as an embodied experience within a wide sociological, anthropological and historical context. These ideas are brought to life by intimate and revealing accounts of ordinary drug users' experiences with a wide range of substances.

This book will appeal to a wide range of students and scholars throughout the social sciences, particularly in the areas of drug and alcohol studies, body studies, cultural studies, anthropology and philosophy.

Tom Yardley is currently working on a collaborative project looking at the changing boundaries and new convergences between prescription medicines, herbal remedies and legal and illegal recreational drugs.

‘In asking why we take drugs, Tom Yardley poses the question that is crucially excluded from the familiar discourse of drug control and finds answers that open the subject up in powerful and original ways. Intoxication, he argues, is not deviant or pathological but a quintessential component of modernity: a corrective to a risk-averse society, an unmediated experience in an increasingly virtual world, a technology for reclaiming control of time and creating a subculture of reciprocity and community. Combining lucid critical theory with vivid oral testimony, *Why We Take Drugs* provides a compelling framework for understanding the enticements, epiphanies and excesses of modern drug culture.’

—Mike Jay, author of *High Society*

Why We Take Drugs

Seeking excess and communion in the modern world

Tom Yardley

Routledge
Taylor & Francis Group
LONDON AND NEW YORK

First published 2012
by Routledge
2 Park Square, Milton Park, Abingdon, Oxon, OX14 4RN

Simultaneously published in the USA and Canada
by Routledge
711 Third Avenue, New York, NY 10017

Routledge is an imprint of the Taylor & Francis Group, an informa business

British Library Cataloguing in Publication Data
A catalogue record for this book is available from the British Library

Library of Congress Cataloging-in-Publication Data
Yardley, Tom.
Why we take drugs : seeking excess and communion in the modern world / by Tom Yardley.
p. cm.
Includes bibliographical references and index.
1. Drug abuse. 2. Substance abuse. I. Title.
HV5801.Y36 2012
363.29--dc23
2011037306

ISBN: 978-0-415-69610-4 (hbk)
ISBN: 978-0-203-12481-9 (ebk)

Typeset in Times
by Taylor and Francis Books

MIX
Paper from responsible sources
FSC
www.fsc.org
FSC® C004839

Printed and bound in Great Britain by the MPG Books Group

Contents

Acknowledgements vi

1 Introduction 1

2 Sacrificing the rational body: the transgressive economy of intoxication 9

3 Seeking the *impossible*: expenditure beyond necessity 24

4 Traditional time and modern time 42

5 From bodies in time to time in the body 57

6 Theorizing community 74

7 Intoxication liminality and community formation 92

8 Conclusion 118

Appendix A: How the interviews were conducted and interpreted: methodological and epistemological issues 131

Appendix B: Who was interviewed 141

Appendix C: Interview schedule 142

Notes 143
Select bibliography 155
Index 162

Acknowledgements

I want to thank my partner Lucy for her constant support and invaluable editorial input. I also want to thank Dr Ian Burkitt for his kind words and encouragement. Finally and most importantly I want to thank all the people I interviewed for giving their time so generously and sharing their experiences with such extraordinary candour.

1 Introduction

The desire to seek intoxication is one of the 'human universals', along with play, music and language, and has been a feature of every human culture.[1] Yet in contemporary western societies this desire is at best tolerated, and is often stigmatized or even criminalized when it is associated with the use of intoxicant drugs. Simply to possess certain plants or chemicals that other cultures have made use of and venerated for millennia because of their capacity to induce intoxication can incur severe legal sanctions in many jurisdictions. From the seemingly endless 'war on drugs' to the succession of moral panics about this or that substance or practice it seems that the possibility of intoxication always poses a threat to society, that the use of intoxicant drugs is always a problem that somehow requires a solution. It is as if we would really be better off without drugs and alcohol, and if they cannot be eradicated altogether then we must at least do our best to minimize their use and the harms they cause.[2]

But, maybe this is getting things back to front. Maybe it is instead society that has come to be the problem in relation to intoxicant drug use. Perhaps it is actually society that poses a threat to its citizens rather than the other way around, by denying those who seek intoxication a legitimate and socially sanctioned space in which to experience these altered states. In older cultures the use of intoxicant drugs was integrated into the rhythms of social existence and bounded by rituals and taboos that ensured their dangerous forces were contained and channelled. In modern western societies, by contrast, the state and the institutions of society have washed their hands of any responsibility for assimilating the desire for intoxication into social existence, and by doing so have sponsored a free-for-all that has often had disastrous consequences for individuals and communities alike. Unable either to successfully resist the use of intoxicant drugs, or to fully acknowledge and accept that they may meet intractable human needs and desires, our attitude to them as a society contains an unresolved ambivalence. The roots of this ambivalence can be traced to the rational and materialistic assumptions that are foundational for western culture. If the ideal of modernity is a competent, upright, bounded body that is under full rational control at all times, and engaged in purposeful activity, then intoxicant drug use poses a direct threat to this ideal.

It is for this reason that intoxicant drugs are often construed as an alien other that threatens to invade and disrupt our ordered everyday world.

Rather than viewing intoxicant drugs as an aberration that should be pushed to the margins of society, or if possible expunged altogether, this book will analyse their role in providing an experience of the self, the world and the other that lies beyond the endless chains of production and consumption which dominate our everyday existence. To ascribe this positive meaning to intoxicant drug use, and explain why modern western societies are unable to accept that such experiences could ever be a normal and even beneficial part of society's make-up, I have drawn on a wide range of sociological, anthropological, philosophical and historical sources. However, to really get to grips with the question of intoxicant drug use in modern society these theoretical ideas and factual accounts needed to be grounded firmly in the realities of lived experience. In order to relate these theoretical ideas, which underpin the book, to the everyday experiences of actual drug and alcohol users I asked a sample of people to describe in their own words what happens when they 'get high', get 'out of it' and get drunk, and analysed what they told me. It emerged from this process that to fully understand the experience of intoxication in contemporary society you need to comprehend not only what is happening when people become intoxicated, but also the effect it has on their relationship to time, and the specific social space that intoxication helps open up. These core themes, which might be called the 'what', the 'when' and the 'where' of intoxication, provide the basic structure of the book. Each of these themes is addressed in turn, first by considering it at a theoretical level and then going on to relate these ideas to the personal accounts of people's actual experiences of intoxication. At the end of the book I offer some conclusions about the nature and meaning of intoxication, and consider what implications these have for our understanding of contemporary society and its ambivalent relationship to intoxicant drug use. As part of this discussion, I raise questions about conventional understandings of what it means to be healthy, which define health simply in terms of the prolongation of life and the maintenance of functional capacity. I point to an alternative way of thinking about health and how it can be maintained in the light of what has been said about intoxicant drug use. I also ask what would be required to overcome the contradictions in society's attitude to drugs and alcohol that would allow for their integration into the normal rhythms of social existence, and offer some possible answers to this question. But for now, it would be useful to set the scene a little and introduce some of the key ideas and thinkers that have informed the analysis of intoxicant drug use presented in this book.

The making and *unmaking* of the modern body

The way we inhabit and experience our bodies has undergone profound changes in the transition to a modern industrial and post-industrial society.

From following a nomadic course in small social groups as hunter-gatherers, or living in fixed rural settlements in stable close-knit communities, we have moved to a mainly urban way of life where we now often live amongst strangers. While we may now be digitally connected, and are constantly on the move, we are typically not as intimately involved with one another as we were in the past. In this new urbanized setting our activities are largely organized through anonymous systems and governed by formal rules and these inevitably affect the way we interact with each other on a day-to-day basis. To fit in to the highly structured and fast-paced environment of a modern society requires us to adopt behaviours that are quite deliberate and controlled, and to carefully plan and monitor our activities at all times.[3] While we are generally safer, and certainly live longer than in the past, there has been a progressive distancing from each other, and from direct experiences of all kinds, as a result of these changes. There are far fewer outlets for the free expression of emotion now, and much less tolerance for physical spontaneity. If we think of how football, for example, has been transformed from a near riotous confrontation of local communities, when it first began, into the highly disciplined and professional spectacle we witness today we can see clearly how things have altered, and the direction that they are going in.[4] Other examples of how the new situation we find ourselves in, in contemporary society, has affected us can be seen in the way vision has become more important than the close senses of touch and smell in our everyday lives,[5] while at the same time electronic communication networks have tended to displace face-to-face contact as the importance of personal interaction has declined.[6] The generalized repression of expressive behaviours, at both a physical and emotional level, which these changes entail, is something we have come to internalize and accept as normal and even desirable.[7]

As well as encouraging a more restrained demeanour and a cooling of emotional expression, living and working in a modern society has also transformed the positive use we make of our bodies, and the way we perceive them. In the past, our time was occupied with activities that met our basic needs, for food, shelter and so on, or activities that fulfilled our aesthetic and spiritual needs, such as making music or engaging in religious rites. In modern and post-modern conditions these kinds of immediate intrinsically meaningful activities have been supplemented by a proliferating array of specialized fields of activity, such as sport, engineering or commerce, that follow their own, arbitrary internal logic.[8] To successfully participate in these specialized fields of activity requires the adoption of a rational and functional relationship to our body, whether in the pursuit of leisure, or in our working lives.[9] Our constant engagement in these specialized activities is often unavoidable and provides many satisfactions but can limit our awareness of the world as it exists outside and independently of these activities, and also leaves some of our deeper needs and desires unmet, and in particular our desire for intimate contact, or communion, with others.

Throughout history human societies have been characterized by an alternation between periods of mundane activity and moments of release from the normal constraints of work and routine. The purpose of these interruptions in the normal patterns of activity and interaction, which create a temporary, or liminal, social space is to exceed the limitations of everyday life and experience the world and being with each other in a new way, and to benefit from the sense of renewal that comes from this. Marcel Mauss, the French anthropologist, for example, describes the attunement of Eskimo culture to seasonal variations, where the labour and isolation of long winters is mitigated by the sociability and celebration of summer gatherings.[10] It is only in modern western societies that we have come to imagine that we can live without this rhythm of labour and renewal and devote ourselves exclusively to the necessary and the useful. By choosing to become intoxicated we reconnect with this ancient desire for renewal and release by deliberately stepping outside the boundaries set by our mundane activities, and transgress the imperatives for competence and control that are so pervasive in everyday life in contemporary society. In doing so, we open ourselves again to the possibility of experiencing the world and being with each other in ways that transcend the arbitrary divisions of society that go along with those mundane activities. The French philosopher George Bataille conceived of this setting aside of our competent and acquisitive everyday self, and all the benefits that self brings us, as a kind of sacrificial act. Bataille suggested that this kind of sacrifice was a vital part of human experience and that we cannot live a fully human life without it:

> Human energy does not exist to enable the function of economies. There has to be an expressive space beyond necessity or humans revert to animals or, with the assistance of technology, become wise machines.[11]

This idea of sacrificing the rational competent self of everyday life is central to understanding what we are doing when we choose to become intoxicated, because it is through this kind of sacrifice that genuine human needs are met – in particular, in modern times, the need to commune with others and to throw off the strictures of our normal routines.

Unfortunately, when we make this sacrificial gesture we also open ourselves to social disapproval because contemporary western societies are founded on, and valorize above all else, a rational and instrumental relationship to the body, the world and to others. In the next chapter, to illustrate what is meant by sacrifice in this sense, I will take the practice of gift giving among traditional peoples as an example and show how sharing states of intoxication with others has much in common with this ancient practice. Having explained, in abstract terms, what is meant by sacrificing the rational body of everyday life through intoxication, Chapter 3 will illustrate these ideas with some concrete examples drawn from the accounts that were gathered for the book of drug and alcohol users' actual experiences.

Time, modernity and intoxication

If the move to a modern way of life has changed the way we experience and use our bodies it has also fundamentally altered our relationship to time. In traditional societies the experience of time was closely bound up with natural patterns of recurrence, as the seasons succeeded one another, and attuned to the wider cosmos, as the stars, the moon and the sun passed through their various cycles. The passing and return of these different temporal phases was marked by rituals and rites that were shared in a lived present in the setting of an organic community. Human cycles of life were linked to these wider patterns through rites of passage that marked the body's transitions through the various stages of growth, maturation and decline. Rather than passing out of existence in a linear progression, as is the case now, time was recovered in all its fullness as the wheel of change turned. This cyclical experience of time explains why ancestors were felt to be present amongst the living in traditional societies, rather than being consigned irretrievably to the past.[12]

In modern societies time has been definitively separated from all natural cycles, and from the communal experience of a shared present. Instead, time has become a universal, standardized measure that is governed by a single ubiquitous machine, the clock, and its electronic successors. Rather than being cyclical in nature, time is now experienced as linear and continuous. Events no longer repeat and renew the past but instead are separated one from another and distributed along a single line of time. The effect of this shift to a linear conception of time has been to engender a sense of urgency, as we strive to make the best possible use of the time we have before it passes irretrievably from our grasp. This new urgency finds expression in the multiplying projects we plan and undertake, and in the gnawing anxiety that there will never be enough time to complete them all. Another new anxiety that accompanies this change in the way we experience time is that we will die an isolated death one day, and be left behind by time as it moves off into the future without us. A result of this intensified fear of death is that personal survival has come to be seen as the highest possible good in western culture. Conversely, any behaviour that might risk well-being or longevity is now viewed as being unacceptable, regardless of the value it may have in other ways. This is one of the reasons for our ambivalent relationship to intoxicant drug use because the use of drugs and alcohol is perceived as being likely to jeopardize our health and potentially shorten our lives.

As time is increasingly taken up with planning for the future, or dreading its arrival, the lived present has become less important in our lives. This tendency to displace experience from the present has also been compounded by other social and technological developments. In an oral culture, for example, communicating with others required their co-presence, whereas in a culture like our own that uses writing there is always a separation in time between the act of writing and the moment of reading.[13] This dislocating effect has been amplified further by other newer technologies, like television and the World

Wide Web. In these new media the distinction between what has already happened and what is happening now is blurred, and in any case we can always catch up with events later on so the significance of the present is inevitably diminished.[14] The overall effect of these changes is that time is now located outside ourselves as an objective reality that structures our lives while our experience of time is constantly displaced from the present.

Intoxication provides one means by which time can still be experienced as a lived reality, rather than as an impersonal fact. As a state of being, intoxication secretes its own sense of time and exists only in that moment of becoming that lies between the past and the future. The experience of time while intoxicated therefore resists measurement by the clock at a subjective level. When the lived present of intoxication is shared with others it can also be the basis for a profound form of communication that is ultimately founded in our mortality. By growing older together in the lived present of intoxication, a sense of time as something related to our natural existence is recovered. As one of the people I interviewed for the book put it:

> probably one of the stronger reasons why I continue to indulge would be the one of companionship … the situation when a group of people, being people that you know very well or a loose group of people that you've just met in whatever situation, but realizing you've got this sort of some kind of common, can't think what the word would be, acceptance, you know, of the moment. It doesn't need to be any sort of grand idea it's just sort of this acceptance of the moment and for that to be just what it is.

The importance to social interaction of human particularity, and the sharing of time together that is irrecoverable, will be crucial to our understanding of why people seek intoxication. In Chapter 4 the differences between time as it was experienced in traditional societies and time as we experience it now will be discussed more fully, and the implications of this for the way in which intoxication is seen in contemporary society will be drawn out. The temporal dimensions of intoxication will then be explored through an analysis of some drug and alcohol users' specific experiences in Chapter 5.

Intoxication and community formation

In tribal societies the community always already exists and people are simply born into it and occupy their allotted place. Ties to others, even including the dead who went before, are strong, binding and unquestioned. Members of the social group have the same understanding of the world, through a shared oral tradition, and are attuned to each other physically and emotionally through undergoing the same corporeal experiences. The individuals that make up the social group consequently acquire a singular identity that is at once possessed by each and is common to all.[15] Even in later agrarian societies limited travel and low population densities ensured that people typically lived with those who were known to them and with whom they had values, experiences and traditions in common.

In stark contrast to traditional societies, in contemporary western society, people may peacefully cohabit but their ties to each other are generally very much weaker. Social existence in the modern world is therefore often characterized by atomization and fragmentation. We frequently do not even know our neighbours, and are divided each from the other by countless markers of distinction, such as race, wealth or status.[16] Since the people we encounter are often unknown to us as individuals, and we have no strong common identity with them, most of our interactions tend to be fleeting, superficial and focused on the practical level.[17] In this context of relative anonymity, good self-presentation and the ability to communicate in the most universal terms have become valuable and much prized personal assets. This emphasis on the shallow but universal as the basis for interaction is reflected in the increasingly identical and interchangeable nature of the social spaces we inhabit, so that a shopping mall, train station or office block in Malaysia, for example, is much like a shopping mall, train station or office block in Berlin, Chicago or anywhere else.[18] While this impersonal environment can provide a high degree of freedom and autonomy for the individual, and rewards the enterprising who are able to adapt successfully to its demands, it tends to leave us without any real sense of belonging, and reduces the possibility of intimate contact with others.

However, while the organization and structure of modern societies may be at odds with a desire for community it is still possible to experience a sense of belonging with others under certain circumstances. The British cultural anthropologist Victor Turner,[19] for example, has suggested that entry into a shared state in which the activities of everyday life are temporarily suspended can induce an intense sense of belonging or 'communitas' with others.[20] This 'liminal' social space is created when the sensual reality of the participants is synchronized through shared physical experiences. During these liminal encounters, the differentiated relations that govern everyday life can give way to relationships of equality in which 'an essential and generic human bond'[21] is recognized by those who are present. Turner and Turner[22] have also stressed the significance of non-rational factors emanating from the body in the process of community formation by highlighting the crucial part played by shared physical ordeals during Christian pilgrimages. Separated from their normal environment and thrown together with others on a journey that is as arduous as it is free of all practical purposes pilgrims can find a common meaning in their shared situation that transcends their disparate origins. Temporary social spaces, in which a sense of community can briefly blossom through shared corporeal experience, may open up between the structures of society at any time. The two chapters towards the end of the book devoted to community formation illustrate how shared states of intoxication can be instrumental in opening up this type of temporary social space, and in some circumstances in the creation of enduring social bonds. In order to distinguish these experiences of community associated with intoxication from other ways of belonging, and to contextualize them in relation to modern society, consideration is given in Chapter 6 to the different ways the idea, and the ideal, of community has been understood by a variety of theorists. The role of intoxication in the formation of liminal communities, as revealed in the personal accounts of drug and alcohol use collected for the book, is then described and analysed in Chapter 7. It is now time to explain what it means to sacrifice the rational body of everyday life and how the idea of the gift can help us understand what we are doing when we make this sacrifice, and that is where we will begin in the next chapter.

2 Sacrificing the rational body

The transgressive economy of intoxication

We know nothing about a body until we know what it can do.
(Deleuze and Guattari, *A thousand plateaus,* 1988, p. 257)

Intoxication fundamentally alters the way we inhabit our bodies and relate to the world and to others and can be understood as a kind of *unmaking* or decomposition of the socially constituted body of everyday life. In this chapter I will seek to develop this idea by looking in detail at the mechanics and meaning of the sacrificial economy which is central to the experience of intoxication and to the *unmaking* of the rational body. It will be suggested, in abstract terms, that there are two distinct modes of engagement with the world: the first is founded on the meeting of *practical needs* and the development of *rational appropriations,* while the second is founded on the non-rational practice of *sacrificial expenditure.* Because the latter mode, sacrificial expenditure, finds its meaning in the context of practical necessity and rational appropriation, the characteristics of these everyday ways of being and doing will first be outlined, before going on to examine the nature of sacrificial expenditure as a non-rational practice. To elucidate the notion of sacrificial expenditure the concept of the gift, as it originated in the work of Marcel Mauss, will be explored.[1] The idea of the gift will be central to this discussion because the conditions necessary for the gift are the same as those that make any other sacrificial gesture possible. Consequently, to define the conditions necessary for the gift is, at the same time, to discover the meaning of intoxication as a form of sacrifice.

In the next chapter, this treatment of intoxication as a sacrificial economy will be expanded, and illustrated with material taken from the interviews I carried out with drug and alcohol users for the book. In later chapters, the implications of this sacrificial economy will be fleshed out by looking in turn at the temporal dimensions of the experience of intoxication and at its social location. Again, this will take the form of theoretical discussion followed by empirical analyses on the same theme. Finally, in the conclusion at the end of the book, the significance of this understanding of intoxicant drug use for the way we view drugs and drug users in contemporary society will be discussed.

Practical appropriation as a mode of engagement with the world

In all known societies, and in any conceivable society that could endure for any length of time, a substantial part of existence is, of necessity, taken up with activities that meet the basic needs for subsistence, shelter and, in the broadest sense of the term, reproduction; the 'self-preserving husbandry of everyday life' as Suleiman[2] has called it. Although sometimes labelled as 'Adam's curse', this burden of necessary activities is neither uniquely human, nor the sign of a fallen condition. As well as being needs that must be met if existence is to continue these practical necessities also present opportunities for the exercise of myriad human capacities. Meeting these needs provides both an outlet for our innate abilities and the means through which these abilities are developed and enhanced as cultural accomplishments in interaction with others.[3]

When we respond to these needs the world presents itself to our perception as more or less *useful* for their fulfilment, and when we appropriate elements of the world successfully action confirms our perception and the two are seamlessly joined. By appropriating and incorporating elements of the world in this way we discover in them a 'use value' that has a fundamental and universal referent. The limit of a use value in these terms is defined by the extent to which something that we appropriate from the world can be consumed without remainder in meeting a need that is unavoidable. When we eat fruit from a tree to satisfy our hunger, or drink water from a stream to quench our thirst, this is a perfect example of a use value. However, responding to the intractable needs of existence through the discovery of use values in the world does not, except in moments of great scarcity, fully exhaust human energies. There is typically a surplus of energy at both the individual and systemic level which, since it cannot be stored, must find other outlets. While we share with other species the necessity to engage practically with the world, and a surplus of energy over need, what has distinguished humans as a species is the extraordinary range and inventiveness we have displayed in finding ways to consume and produce with this surplus.[4] The remainder of this chapter will be taken up with contrasting two distinct ways in which this surplus of human energies can be disposed of that goes beyond the fulfilment of practical needs, rational appropriation and sacrificial expenditure.

From practical appropriation to rational appropriations

It has been an overwhelming presumption in western thought since the Ancients that human activity is, or should be, rational. In its strongest formulation this has meant that actions, to be fully human, must be guided by conscious and calculated intentions, and even in weaker formulations the assumption is made that actions are, or should be, rationally intelligible. From this perspective, what humans do makes sense because it fulfils a purpose that they are able to define or a purpose that others are able to discern.

Implicit in this view is a privileging of purposeful activity over other types of experience in which the world is meaningful only in so far as it is useful for human purposes and human acts are rational only in so far as they are useful. As will be seen, however, what is 'useful' from a rational perspective is not necessarily identical with that which has a 'use value', as that term was defined above.

By actively appropriating elements of the world for our own ends we confer meanings on them that are derived from our purposes: the earth becomes a farm or a city, the sea a place where we fish or navigate and the sky an arena for flight. To the unselfconscious pursuit of practical needs is increasingly added an ever more complex pattern of rational appropriations which stretch or even sever the link between need and activity. As a consequence, the unassailable logic of meeting unavoidable needs is superseded as a guide to action by the arbitrary constraints that are produced by our rationally conceived endeavours. While these new domains of action can never entirely eclipse the logic of basic needs, since they are secondary to and dependent on the meeting of these needs, they have come to attain the force of an unquestioned and independent reality in social existence. The radical French philosophers Deleuze and Guattari have described this process, which discursively constructs the world as an adjunct to human projects, as opposed to human needs, as 'the landscapification of all worlds and milieus'.[5]

An inevitable corollary of the privileging of purposeful activity which accompanies this 'landscapification' is an element of necessity, since possible acts exist in a hierarchy of effectiveness when judged by their outcomes in relation to a given intention. In other words, each appropriation of the world in these terms establishes what behaviours can count as rational: to play golf with a tennis racquet is patently irrational since it cannot lead to a successful outcome in the game. In the course of time these appropriations and the sets of rational behaviours which fulfil them have expanded, to a point where they have come, in modern western societies, to saturate existence almost entirely.[6] For Max Weber, the German sociologist, this emergence of distinct domains of rational activity that are divested of affective investments and operate according to their own self-referential logic, exemplified by science, art and the law, has precipitated a fragmentation of society in modernity.[7] Rather than a single common understanding of the world and society there are now a multitude of specialized knowledges and technologies that are incommensurate with each other and operate independently of one another; a jigsaw made up of pieces that can never fit together to form a single totality. The French cultural theorist Jean Baudrillard has described the cultural ascendancy of rationally ordered purposeful activity that has accompanied this fragmentation as a '[g]eneralized and permanent mobilisation' absolved of any requirement to be useful:

> Labour (even in the guise of leisure), like a primary repression, pervades every aspect of life in the form of a control, a permanent occupation of spaces and times regulated according to an omnipresent code.[8]

The rational appropriations that make up this generalized labour, in which 'the factory no longer exists because labour is everywhere', entails an experience of the world narrowed down to means and ends which, if they are to be successfully related to one another, require our absorbed attention.[9] All rationally ordered activities share this requirement, that an attitude is adopted by us that carefully differentiates only those elements of experience that are useful to the present purpose, regardless of whether the purpose itself is useful or not. It is of little consequence whether the tasks at hand are primarily physical in nature, such as those involved in building a house, or are largely abstract and conceptual, such as those that might be encountered while writing a book. It also matters little, as Baudrillard notes,[10] whether they are nominally categorized as work, leisure or fall into that ambiguous third category, charity, since they are all now governed by the same basic imperatives.

The accretion of rationally intelligible activities that has accompanied the development of industrial and post-industrial societies has then engendered a belief that all actions are subject to a necessity given in their purpose, and can therefore be judged rational or irrational. This belief has provided the basis for evaluative and moral categories which demand a body that remains fully under control and ready for rationally guided activity. Alphonso Lingis, the American philosopher, has suggested that this requirement that the body should remain under continuous control, announcing the individual's availability for purposeful activity, is manifested most typically in an erect posture: '[t]he body's verticality is that of an inner diagram of competence become habitual', as he puts it.[11] As the American sociologist Freund[12] has pointed out, postural attitude and inner state form a gestalt whose totality is expressed in the German language by the single word, *haltung*. For Bataille, it is not without significance that all other creatures, fish, birds and mammals alike, have a horizontal orientation in relation to the earth, while humans alone have adopted a posture that strains towards maintaining the vertical; a *haltung*, which, he believes, expresses our ambition to achieve control over ourselves and our environment and throw off natural limits.[13] By contrast, an uncontrolled body is a body that signals its inability to engage with the world in effective ways, forfeiting as a consequence its status as rational and therefore as fully human. While the competent and erect body passes unquestioned, other bodies that are unable, or perhaps unwilling, to sustain this attitude are always suspect and liable to being discredited. As the feminist scholar Margrit Shildrick has observed, any loss of physical self-control is readily translated as a loss of mental competence and moral agency.[14] Even in some phenomenological accounts, which seek to exhaustively describe the nature of being in the world, the default state is one of active and intentional engagement with a practical reality. For Merleau-Ponty deviations from intentional behaviour can only be accounted for as failures of the organism's orientation, as in disease states,[15] while Heidegger asserts that '[t]he kind of dealing which is closest to us is … that kind of concern which manipulates things and puts them to use'.[16] It is revealing in this context that the very term employed by Heidegger to designate the kind of beings that humans are (*Dasein*) is derived from a Greek ontology (Plato) and is most usually translated as 'the rational animal'.[17]

Rationality and experience

An important consequence of viewing existence from a rationalist perspective is that meaning is continually displaced from the particular moment as it is lived to the generic categories of discourse that are used to comprehend it. Since aspects of existence which are rationally intelligible can, in principle, be comprehended by anyone at any time, both events and those who experience them lose their situational specificity and are reduced to being instances of a type. By making the body and behaviour transparent to discourse in this way, rationality divests them of particularity and renders them identical with all other bodies and behaviours that succumb to the same intelligibility. Mortality, from this stand point, is no longer the passing of something absolutely irreplaceable but instead a common fate shared by all. Deleuze and Guattari have summarized the normative implications of this saturation of experience by discourse and rationally ordered activities in the following way:

> You will be organized, you will be an organism, you will articulate your body otherwise you're just depraved. You will be signifier and signified, interpreter and interpreted – otherwise you're a deviant. You will be a subject, nailed down as one … otherwise you're just a tramp.[18]

This incorporation of experience into discourse and its subordination to purpose produces a homogenization of existence and interaction that can only be overcome, according to Bataille, through acts of sacrifice that help to restore the world in its plenitude and particularity.[19]

Sacrificial expenditure as a mode of engagement with the world

While the need for purposeful activity may be a primordial given and the condition of our continued survival, this does not, in and of itself, establish it as the only or main reason for our existence. According to Bataille, purposeful activity can never be more than a necessary, but in itself insufficient, phase of existence: 'Men assure their own subsistence or avoid suffering, not because these functions lead themselves to a sufficient result, but in order to accede to the insubordinate function of free expenditure.'[20] What Bataille refers to when he speaks here of 'free expenditure' are those activities in which human energies and resources are consumed without remainder and so exist as an end in themselves, as opposed to productive activities that subordinate the present moment to the needs of a future goal. The meaning of free expenditure is found in the lived present whereas the meaning and success of productive activities is only discovered in their outcomes. Put differently, free expenditures are about the journey while productive activities are always, ultimately, about the destination. Only expenditures entirely liberated from necessity, whether this is the necessity of primordial need or the necessity inherent in rationally ordered projects, have the 'insubordinate function' of expressing genuine human desires. These free expenditures represent a pure use value that reconnects us with a world that is meaningful prior to all rational constructions and of which we are an integral part.[21] According to Georg Simmel, the German sociologist, expenditures of this kind, when they form the basis of sacrificial exchanges between individuals, are the foundation of all authentic social interaction.[22]

The elevation of rationality that has occurred in western thought, to the status of highest human function, is regarded by Bataille as a form of idealism.[23] An exclusive focus on rational activity diminishes human existence by yoking it to utilitarian ends and excluding any possibility of contact with the sacred, just as surely as the most urgent demands of material need:

> Human energy does not exist to enable the function of economies. There has to be an expressive space beyond necessity or humans revert to animals or, with the assistance of technology, become wise machines.[24]

This diminution of life is intensified when purposeful activity, no longer grounded in the relative certainties of use values that meet basic human needs, is subject to the endless displacements and deferrals that characterize the operation of exchange values in a modern society.[25]

The emphasis in western thought on the rational basis of action as the very essence of what it means to be human is precisely what lends intoxication both its social significance as a sacrificial practice and its transgressive potential. This is so because the two most fundamental characteristics of intoxication are that it is entirely *unnecessary* and that it is completely *without use*. There is no necessity that intoxication should occur in the first place and when it does occur it stubbornly resists insertion into the chains of purposeful activity that go to make up everyday existence in modern societies. These features perhaps endow intoxication with a special attractiveness in a society preoccupied with the necessary and the useful. As Baudrillard has remarked: 'In our culture, tethered as it is to the principle of utility, futility plays the role of transgression and violence.'[26] Because intoxication, like erotic activity, can never arrive anywhere but at the exhaustion and disgust which makes it impossible to continue, it offers, in this context, a peculiarly potent figure of futility.[27] For Klein, the American cultural historian, activities such as voluntary intoxication have a positive allure even beyond their value as alternatives to the principle of utility: 'A daemon is an old god, whose cult has been repressed but who's still haunting power to enthral the celebrant reverses its sign: what once was blessed now appears frightful and hideously tempting.'[28] By becoming intoxicated, the power of this old god is invoked and the world as something useful to human purposes, and the useful body that expresses our rational competence, is sacrificed.

To sacrifice the world as useful is always at the same time to sacrifice the body as competent, since the two are mutually constitutive and interchangeable. In the work of Pierre Bourdieu, the French sociologist, any distinction between a resource and the one who appropriates it is collapsed in the notion of the habitus. The concept of the habitus, as it is employed by Bourdieu, denotes a body that is simultaneously an agent of appropriation and the product of an appropriation. The body, from this perspective, acts as both a site for the accumulation of physical or social capital as well as the means by which this accumulation is accomplished.[29] However, by becoming intoxicated, it is possible to establish a different relationship with the world and with others since intoxication entails sacrificing this competent body and the social and physical capital accumulated in it, even if only temporarily and in part. The basis of this altered relationship is to be found in a passive opening to experience that stands opposed to the pursuit of purposeful activities. This opening to experience does not result from a volitional act, even if a decision to become intoxicated was made beforehand, but is instead the condition or state that is designated by the term intoxication. As is the case with sleep or changes in emotion, intoxication always takes us unawares no matter how much it was anticipated or desired. It is only after it has occurred that it is noticed, a mysterious transformation that lies beyond our will. For Deleuze and Guattari '[d]runkenness [i]s a triumphant irruption of the plant in us' rather than being an activity that we undertake.[30] By becoming drunk, or otherwise intoxicated, our identity with the world is manifested and the separation from the world that an appropriative stance affirms is, for a time at least, overcome. Avital Ronnel, the feminist literary critic and philosopher, conveys this abolition of the subject–object divide and the rational attitude that founds it by describing drugs as an 'outside already inside'.[31] This understanding of intoxication also coincides with Bataille's when he maintains that all states which violate the injunction which insists on bodily control and purposeful activity partake in some way of the sacred by re-establishing continuity with the world.[32] According to Bataille, events such as erotic activity freed from the goal of procreation, laughter, play and intoxication are all imbued with a sacred quality because they set aside the goods of the world in favour of a gratuitous expenditure that consumes human energies without remainder.[33] It is now time to consider in more detail the nature of this expenditure and the context of unlimited accumulation which gives it particular force and significance in modern societies.

The gift form and the conditions of its possibility

In this section it will be suggested that intoxication has important affinities with the gift form in that intoxication, like the gift, marks a transition from the realm of utilitarian ends and accumulation to that of immediate and wasteful expenditure. But before these affinities between the gift form and intoxication can be drawn out it is important to establish what is meant by this disputed term. To do this, it will be necessary to consider the long dialogue concerning the ontological status of the gift that began with Mauss and has subsequently been taken up in the work of Bataille, Derrida, Bourdieu and others.

In his seminal essay, *The Gift: Forms and Functions of Exchange in Archaic Societies* (1966 [1950]), Marcel Mauss describes practices of gift giving amongst tribal peoples that to a modern sensibility can only appear extraordinary. Whereas in modern societies a gift is an exchange of small and merely symbolic tokens which serves to mark significant dates, in some of the societies described by Mauss, such as the Trobriand Islanders, it is incumbent upon the giver that their expenditure should be unstinting, even to the point of ruination and death. Nothing less than a wholesale destruction of accumulated goods will suffice as a demonstration of the giver's generous intentions.

Given this potentially unlimited commitment on the part of the giver it might have been expected that the meaning of these offerings would have been seen to reside in the gesture of giving. However, from a social scientific perspective, focused on wider structural features and longer timescales, a very different explanation becomes possible. For Levi-Strauss, the French anthropologist and ethnologist, the meaning of the gift does not lie so much in the sacrificial gesture of giving as in the certainty that the gift will be returned with interest by the recipient in due course.[34] To receive a gift and fail to return it with a correspondingly lavish expenditure is almost unthinkable to the people whose customs Mauss records. This obligation to reciprocate, it is asserted, transforms the gift from an ostensibly disinterested act into a kind of challenge. Far from expressing generosity or a sacrificial desire, the gift is merely a stake in an ongoing agonistic competition whose real objective is to obtain the prestige that accrues to the most successful giver. The gift is not the end in itself that it appears to be, but rather the means by which an obligation is imposed so that the 'mutual challenges bring about a primitive system of contract and liability'.[35] Even if it is objected that the intentions or desires of the giver may, in principle or in fact, have been generous or sacrificial rather than competitive, they can still be dismissed as illusory by reference to the structure of exchange within which their act of gift giving occurs. According to Bourdieu the 'potlatch' or gift giving ceremony and the conventions that surround it are merely an elaborate charade that serves to deny the objective reality underlying this regulated exchange. This self-deception conceals the basic structure of reciprocity in order to avoid any mention of the gift's true price, which lies in the fact that it must be returned. A faint echo of this deceit is found in modern societies, according to Bourdieu, in the familiar practice of removing the price tag from a gift before it is given, while carefully scrutinizing the gifts we receive for their monetary value. Recalling his analysis of Kabyle society Bourdieu writes that:

> [t]his structural truth is collectively repressed … the giver and the receiver collaborate, without knowing it, in a work of dissimulation tending to deny the truth of the exchange, the exchange of exact equivalents, which represents the destruction of the exchange of gifts.[36]

Without in any way denying the structure of reciprocal giving initially identified by Mauss, or the agonistic element that this can entail, there may be good grounds for rejecting the interpretation provided by a conventional social scientific account, such as those offered by Levi-Strauss and Bourdieu, as a complete explanation for these ceremonies. The most obvious limitation imposed by this view of gift exchange is that it effectively evacuates any specific content from the concept of the gift by reducing it to a rudimentary form of credit and assimilating an essentially moral transaction to the realm of the contract. As the French philosopher Jacques Derrida notes, the very notion of a gift implies a break in the chain of reciprocity, an event whose meaning cannot be displaced to the future but lies firmly in the present:

> [w]herever there is time, wherever time predominates or conditions experience in general, wherever time as circle … is predominant, the gift is impossible … [t]hat a gift is called a present, that "to give" may also be said "to make a present," "to give a present" … this will not be for us just a verbal clue.[37]

The possibility of the gift is dependent on the possibility of discounting the future, whether this future is to be one of radical loss or one of complete restitution. The social scientific interpretation assumes that because reciprocity is almost certain the act of giving is therefore without risk and that because a failure to reciprocate attracts social disapproval the return of a gift cannot be entered into freely and have a meaning independent of its structural location. While the gift may be made in the almost certain knowledge of its return and reciprocated with a heavy and reluctant heart, there is nothing in the structure of the exchange as such which determines that this will be the case and so excludes the possibility of an authentic gift.

The temporal interval between a gift being given and its return, which Bourdieu sees as necessary for the dissimulation to be effective (since an immediate return would amount to a refusal) can equally be read as a demand for trust and risk taking since the possibility that the gift will *not* be returned, however small, is nevertheless absolute in this interval. This potential for the gift not to be reciprocated, it might be argued, ensures that it retains a moral significance that is ultimately dependent on the agency of the participants rather than on any structural determinants. In this interval, however great the bravado surrounding the gesture of giving, the giver stands symbolically naked and vulnerable before the recipient whom they now depend on entirely for the recovery of their position. Rather than imposing an obligation this could be read as a gesture of absolute trust; a trust whose betrayal is, as Mauss noted, tantamount to a declaration of war.

A further objection to a structural interpretation of the potlatch is that it focuses exclusively on the restitution of goods and the accumulation of prestige rather than on the *destruction* of goods and the importance which this aspect of the custom may have. If, as was argued above, setting down the goods of the world as something useful to human purposes opens the way to an encounter with others marked by the sacred then the potlatch can be viewed as not merely agonistic in its meaning but also festal. As Bataille has pointed out, in his analysis of the way profane and sacred moments succeed one another in social existence, 'the reserves accumulated during periods of work are squandered extravagantly at feast times'.[38] If the gift is not such an act of extravagant squandering then, as Derrida reminds us, it is no gift at all:

> The moment the gift, however generous it be, is infected with the slightest hint of calculation, the moment it takes account of knowledge [*connaissance*] or recognition [*reconnaissance*], it falls within the ambit of an economy: it exchanges, in short it gives counterfeit money, since it gives in exchange for payment.[39]

The economy of the gift by contrast is an economy that 'integrates the renunciation of a calculable remuneration, renunciation of merchandise or bargaining [*marchandage*], of economy in the sense of a retribution that can be measured or made symmetrical'.[40] The existence of the potlatch points to the presence of this latter type of economy, an economy that renounces calculation, if only because of its gratuitous character. If the true meaning of the potlatch lay in calculation surely it could be realized as easily through an accumulation of goods, as is so often the case when lavish displays of wealth are made in modern societies, rather than through an extravagant *destruction* of goods.

It is the destruction of goods that marks the potlatch as a sacrificial event whose essential meaning lies beyond the intentions, or illusions, of the giver. There is nothing in the idea of the gift, if it is understood as sacrifice, which demands a generous subject whose intentions guarantee the meaning of the act. It is rather the presence of a subject, a calculating subject who anticipates the future return of the gift that annuls the gift as gift. All that is required for a sacrificial event is that goods that could have been utilized are instead squandered or destroyed without thought to the future:

> For there to be gift event (we say event and not act), something must come about or happen, in an instant, in an instant that no doubt does not belong to the economy of time, in a time without time, in such a way that the forgetting forgets, that it forgets itself, but also in such a way that this forgetting, without being something present, presentable, determinable, sensible or meaningful, is not nothing.[41]

Even the form of the goods that are sacrificed is unimportant since, ultimately, what is sacrificed, as Derrida reminds us, is time or, more precisely, the future.[42] The only requirement for sacrifice is that the loss of this future will be irrecoverable and it is time in its passing which ensures that this will be the case. In older societies this meaning of sacrifice was well understood. When an animal is sacrificed by the community the solemnity and significance of the gesture resides in the fact that it is *this* animal that dies, reminding those who are present of the absolute heterogeneity of living things and of their own mortality.[43] Sacrifice communicates directly in such a way that to witness it is also to participate in it and so to be joined with the group. In the same way the potlatch, as sacrifice, has a direct meaning that exceeds any structural or symbolic interpretation of its significance.

Intoxication and the gift form

To illustrate the point that a regulated reciprocity, which includes an element of agonistic competition, can nevertheless transcend its structural constraints it is worth recalling Mars and Altman's contribution to *Constructive Drinking,*[44] where they describe the drinking customs practised at Georgian feasts. This example will also serve to make the connection between the gift form and intoxication, which so far has only been hinted at in passing, more explicit.

The Georgian feasts that Mars and Altman describe are presided over by a moderator or 'Tamada' who is charged with the task of ensuring that everyone present has a full glass before each of the innumerable toasts is offered, and that their glasses are completely emptied before the next round of toasts begins. To make this task easier, and to avoid any possibility of non-participation by the revellers in this prolonged ordeal by alcohol, only transparent vessels are permitted and these must be upended after each round. As the feast progresses the role of the moderator is supplemented by the toasts of the guests who use the opportunity to compete with one another in ever more demanding feats of consumption. However, by the end of the feast the strict regulation which prescribes that each separate individual shall consume the same amount as their fellows, or match them in competition, gives way to a communal sharing in which all eat from each other's plates and drink from each other's glasses. In a similar fashion, the careful seating arrangements that allocated each guest a definite place in the proceedings give way to a free circulation and random interaction as the feast progresses.

In their interpretation of these customs Mars and Altman concentrate on the wider social functions they are seen to perform, such as establishing and maintaining business and political connections. However, it could be argued that they are only able to accomplish these functions, paradoxically, through a setting aside of worldly goods and interests, in this case the goods and interests that reside in a rationally controlled and individuated body. Only as a result of mutually accepting the vulnerability and loss of control that accompanies intoxication is a trust established between the participants that can carry over into the profane dealings of everyday existence. From this perspective, what is important about these feasts is not the structural guarantee of equal shares imposed by the Tamada but the shared vulnerability imposed by intoxication. Bataille has described the significance of this shared vulnerability to authentic communication in the following way:

> [if] I thus consume without measure, I reveal to my peers what I am intimately: consummation is the way in which separate beings communicate. Everything is transparent, everything is open and everything is infinite among those who consume intensely.[45]

By freely surrendering individual control in a gesture of sacrificial expenditure the structural regulation of the feast, symbolized by the definite allocation of seats and the initial insistence on equal shares, is nullified and transcended.

To clarify further the underlying affinities between the gift form and intoxication, which both demand a sacrifice of worldly goods as something useful to human purposes, whether these goods are in the form of actual possessions or reside instead in the self-possession of the individuated body, it is worth considering another ritual of competitive drinking, that practised by the Mambila people. The customs of the Mambila combine the reciprocal structure of the potlatch with an agonistic competition centred on intoxication which permits entry into a sacred realm beyond the exigencies of purpose and rational intelligibility. At a young age the males of the Mambila are permitted, though not obliged, to form a friendship with a boy from another settlement. The conduct of this voluntary association is punctuated by periodic gatherings at which the two friends take it in turn to provide beer sufficient for the needs of all who are present. While gifts need not be reciprocated, if beer is offered it is a rule that it must be offered in greater quantities than at any previous gathering. In time, if the friendship is maintained, this leads to a massive provision of beer that can take days on end to consume and exhausts almost the entire grain surplus of the village, and, presumably, the energies and endurance of the villagers. On these occasions the host and guest enjoy equal status and 'the bonds of kinship and neighbourhood either do not exist or if they do are ignored in the context of the situation'.[46] According to Rehfisch, the anthropologist who studied the Mambila, the meaning of these voluntary practices of gift giving does not lie in their competitive structure, or in the obligations they impose on the participants, but instead in the contrast they provide to the profane concerns of everyday existence, a contrast that is obtained through a wasteful and unproductive expenditure of time, energy and resources. Although subject to customary and structural constraints, since they produce nothing and, according to Rehfisch, confer no additional status on either the friends or the villages who participate in them, the real purpose of these gatherings can only reside in a coming together with others that is liberated from the burdens of purpose.

Having suggested that intoxication has affinities with the gift form in that it involves a free and wasteful expenditure of resources, in contrast to the useful and productive activities of everyday existence, in the next section the limits placed on this expenditure will be explored through a discussion of transgression and the limits to transgression.

Transgressing the limit and the limits of transgression

It was suggested earlier that there are two distinct modes of engagement with the world, one founded on purposeful activity, accumulation and individuation and the other dependent on a wasteful expenditure that forgets the future and permits an experience of continuity with the world and with others. However, as opposed to each other as these two modes of engagement with the world may be, they do not exist independently of one another as alternative ways of being but rather as elements in a dialectic whose extremes can never be fully realized. As the British sociologist Jenks puts it '[t]ransgression is not the same as disorder; it opens up chaos and reminds us of the necessity of order'.[47] A wasteful expenditure that forgets the future is meaningful only because this same future is also recalled. If the future is forgotten entirely the event is deprived of the limit which endows it with meaning and allows it to be experienced as transgression. As the ethnologist Lowell Lewis notes, in a discussion of Brazilian carnival and the practice of *capoeira*, 'transgression loses its spice if the rules no longer have any force'.[48] If, on the other hand, the future is not forgotten entirely the experience remains within the realm of calculation and purpose. This point, where the taboo is simultaneously exceeded and accepted, has been defined by Bataille, with characteristic precision, as *the impossible.*[49]

Both the gift form and intoxication come into being at this impossible point somewhere between the ideal of a perfect rationality where everything is known and controlled and an absolute freedom where nothing is conserved. Neither the gift form nor intoxication aim for a final and definitive expenditure in which the dialectic between these two poles is destroyed, opening onto chaos and death, but rather a movement *towards* this limit. It is only on condition that a trace of the competent body remains that breaking the injunction demanding a controlled and purposeful attitude can be experienced by self and others as a sacrificial and transgressive gesture. Deleuze and Guattari describe what is required and what is at stake in this gesture:

> You don't do it with a sledgehammer, you use a very fine file. You invent self-destructions that have nothing to do with the death drive. Dismantling the organism has never meant killing yourself, but rather opening the body to connections.[50]

When, in this excerpt, Deleuze and Guattari mention 'dismantling the organism' this has nothing to do with an assault on the organs and flesh of the body but refers rather to an assault on the *organization* of the body that is produced by the discursive codes that regulate everyday existence.[51] While these 'self-destructions' may in practice involve violent procedures that do attack the organs of the body as such this is purely incidental to their meaning which is 'to recover the body from the violence that has lost and scattered it among signs'.[52] In a paean to cigarette smoking Klein evokes this moment when the body opens to the world and loses its organized and definite character:

> The smoke penetrates sharply, then exudes, softly envelops you in the experience of extending your body's limits, no longer fixed by the margin of your skin. Joining inside and out, each puff is like total immersion: it baptizes the celebrant with the little flash of a renewed sensation, an instantaneous, fleeting body image of the unified Moi.[53]

In a movement towards what Deleuze and Guattari have called a body that is 'not a collection of part objects but a living block' or the 'body without organs'[54] the smoker surrenders their body as something bounded and enclosed, upright and purposeful. This experience of the body, liberated from purpose and differentiation, is obtained through a sacrificial expenditure that suspends the principles of utility and conservation. The rituals of smoking crystallize a moment of existence outside time, according to Klein, by setting aside all instrumental relationships to the world and symbolically sacrificing the world and its interests to flame and smoke. According to Klein, the act of sacrificial giving embodied in smoking makes it akin to a form of prayer. Smoking is prayerful not because it is good or useful but precisely because it is the opposite of good and useful; a giving of the moment that does not benefit the giver. In the aesthetic gesture of smoking which, like laughter, is unique to humans a sacred and generous reality is briefly invoked. This ephemeral reality that is invoked by the sacrificial gesture of smoking is irreducibly localized and particular. The circumscribed reality of smoking, like the realities of play and the comic, stands opposed to the 'paramount reality' of the everyday that is shared by all and has the unquestioned force of the given, since all of our actions are oriented in relation to it. As for the implications of this sacrificial gesture Klein has no illusions, as is clear from his account of taking up smoking:

> Not for a moment is the beginning of smoking identified with positive tastes, good feelings, or narcotic distraction; it is vicious from the start, loathsome in anticipation, sickening in the process, and revolting and shameful afterwards.[55]

Far from disqualifying smoking as a worthwhile activity it is precisely these noxious characteristics that, for Klein, ensure that smoking can never be useful and so will always remain a suitable vehicle for communing with the sacred; a 'non positive affirmation', as the French philosopher Michel Foucault has described such transgressive events.[56] By transgressing the taboo on wasteful expenditure smoking, like other forms of voluntary intoxication, suspends the profane world of the everyday and its purposeful activities. The fact that this suspension can never be a final and definitive gesture but must always follow the shifting limit of the impossible in no way invalidates it. That the useful body will, in most cases, be fully recovered does not diminish the significance of its sacrifice, any more than the return of a gift automatically annuls the sacrificial gesture of giving.

Conclusion

In this chapter the concept of the gift has been explored in order to highlight some of the essential requirements of a sacrificial event. It was argued that both intoxication and the gift fulfil these requirements because they entail a free expenditure of resources which interrupts the cycles of purposeful activity and exchange that go to make up everyday existence. This 'forgetting' of the future, it was suggested, makes it possible to transcend, at an experiential level, both the exigencies of immediate need, and the second order necessities produced by rationally ordered projects. By temporarily halting the exchange of the present for the needs of the future such moments of sacrificial expenditure open the body to an experience of the sacred.

The essentially moral basis of gift exchange and of shared states of intoxication was also stressed. By renouncing calculation each of these events, it was claimed, entails a setting down of the goods of the world. Whether these goods are in the form of actual property or the goods amassed in a competent and controlled body, by abjuring them, even temporarily, the individual is left in a state of vulnerability that can, in certain circumstances, be read as a gesture of trust.

As has already been indicated, sacrificial expenditure has a different phenomenal basis from appropriative modes engagement with the world. Having outlined, in abstract terms, the key distinctions between appropriative and sacrificial modes of engagement the rest of the book will largely be taken up with exploring the implications of intoxication understood as a form of sacrificial expenditure. To do this, the temporal dimensions of the experience and its social location will be considered at both a theoretical and empirical level. But before these theoretical discussions and empirical analyses can be presented it is first necessary to extend the ideas put forward in this chapter by undertaking a phenomenological analysis of the interview material gathered for the book; the next chapter will be devoted to this task.

3 Seeking the *impossible*

Expenditure beyond necessity

In the last chapter it was argued that activities that respond to the fundamental needs of existence are foundational for society, and that society develops through a proliferation of rationally ordered activities that supplement these primordial necessities with their own second order imperatives. To the basic and universal requirement for sustenance, shelter and the conditions for reproduction is added an array of rationally conceived projects which have their own inherent logic and constraints, whether pursued under the sign of work or leisure. Meeting the manifold demands imposed by these different levels of necessity requires the adoption of an appropriative attitude towards the world that finds its most typical expression in a competent, erect and bounded body that is guided by rational intentions. The idea that intoxication can be understood as a kind of *unmaking* or decomposition of this socially constituted body was then examined. It was suggested, following Bataille, that purposeful engagement with the world does not exhaust either human energies or desires. Energies are expended and desires fulfilled not only through intentional goal-directed activities but also through the kind of free expenditure of resources, liberated from the claims of necessity, that are symbolized by the notion of the gift. Because intoxication entails a sacrifice of the world as something useful to human purposes and along with it the competent, erect and bounded body that expresses an appropriative attitude, and an individuated existence, it can be understood as a free expenditure of this kind. The sacrificial gesture of intoxication, in which the needs of the future are suspended or forgotten, can serve to re-establish a sense of continuity with the world and with others through a passive opening to experience. Although this passive opening to experience exists in opposition to a purposeful and appropriative mode of engagement with the world, it nevertheless takes its meaning in relation to it. There is an antinomy or tension between the necessities of everyday existence and the desire for a free expenditure of time, energy and resources, which transgresses the boundaries of these necessities. The necessities of everyday existence are at once exceeded and retained at the moment of intoxication, and it is at this *impossible* point that intoxication finds its meaning as a transgressive event. It is now time to discover how our embodied experiences are transformed by sacrificing the competent body of everyday life and the consequences of these transformations for our social interactions.

Since the very possibility of a sacrificial expenditure rests on the existence of a surplus that can be disposed of freely the first task will be to define the nature of the surplus that is expended through intoxication and to identify the opportunities that allow this expenditure to occur. Following this, the playful and experimental mode of engagement with the world which characterizes this form of expenditure will be contrasted with the planned and purposeful activities that typically dominate everyday existence in western societies. Having indicated the nature of the surplus that is expended through intoxication and the mode of engagement that characterizes this expenditure, the next task will be to define the fragile space between remembering and forgetting that delimits intoxication as an experience. Finally, the conditions that make it possible to experience intoxication as a transgressive event, and the limits to such transgressions, will be analysed.

Surplus energies and their wasteful disposal

In western societies that are predicated on an endless competition for supposedly scarce resources the very idea of a surplus that is not required for some other purpose is anathema.[1] Since this competition can never be definitively concluded the surpluses generated through production can never be realized but must continuously be reinvested in new cycles of accumulation.[2] This imperative is reflected in the ethic of deferred gratification, which was foundational to the growth of modern industrial society.[3] Despite the shift in emphasis from production to consumption, which has occurred in western societies since the inter-war years, this 'Protestant ethic' has not been diminished but simply extended into new areas. As Bourdieu reminds us, capital is no longer confined to the coffers of the industrialist but now takes many forms that are infinitely convertible one into another.[4] In these conditions, in which processes of accumulation pervade every aspect of existence, even the most apparently extravagant forms of conspicuous consumption can be read as merely another form of investment. Purchasing a mansion or a Ferrari has the function of enhancing social status and so opening the way to further rounds of accumulation, rather than being, as it might at first appear, a wasteful depletion of assets. A consequence of this insistence that every resource be put to productive use, and its enjoyment displaced or deferred, is that accumulation becomes synonymous with achievement and value, while unprofitable expenditures come to signal nihilism or inadequacy. Even, or perhaps especially, the body is understood from this perspective as being a form of capital that is difficult to maintain and easily diminished if it is not the object of careful and sustained husbandry.[5] However, while an ethic of endless accumulation and continuous labour may pervade contemporary western societies, the adoption or internalization of this imperative is never absolute or universal. As Deleuze and Guattari have observed, 'there is no social system that does not leak in all directions'.[6] Within the grid of rationally ordered activities that structure everyday existence in the interests of accumulation, gaps appear that can present themselves as opportunities for a wasteful expenditure of resources liberated from the exigencies of necessity. At such times, energies which are normally measured and channelled by purpose and necessity are dissipated in an undirected flow. In other words, resources that could be utilized for productive ends are freely expended without expectation of return. The greater the level of energy expended in this way the greater the sense of liberation from necessity it confers. Even expenditures that have a compulsive quality can be understood in this light as enacting a desire to wastefully squander resources and in doing so to sacrifice the competent, individuated and upright body of everyday existence. But before considering this latter point, which calls into question conventional notions of addiction, the gaps that permit wasteful expenditures to occur, and the nature of the energies they release, will first be examined.

The following excerpts from the interviews conducted with Geoff and Philip, which recall some of their very earliest experiences of intoxication, will serve to illustrate the point that free expenditures can commence when the grip of necessity is relaxed. In the first passage Geoff recalls the moment when he finished school, while in the second Philip describes completing his first stint of paid work. In the final short passage it is Geoff again who remembers a typical day taking amphetamine and smoking cannabis with some friends when he was 16:

> 'I'd finished school and I'd just finished and me and me mate were well we haven't got anything else to do today lets go and get some pot [cannabis] so we got some from someone we kind of knew … and smoked it and then just walked for ages you know talking and saying it isn't doing anything lets go and get something to eat because I'm really hungry … '

> 'I'd just left school and I'd just got paid for about three or four weeks work so I had lots of money in my pocket and decided that what we needed to do was go and buy some drugs and we went to clubs anyway you know I was taking drugs in clubs anyway you know speed [amphetamine] etc and just kind of went out to see what was about either some speed or some trips [LSD] or whatever and there wasn't any but bumped into someone that had some heroin so I thought well have some of that instead … there were three of us so we all had some injected it and then it's just kind of sat around chatting and smoking dope [cannabis] but you know it's one of those drugs that tends to make you not do anything if you see what I mean whereas some drugs are recreational for going out and for partying for dancing or whatever heroin is very much a sit down and do nothing kind of drug … '

> 'it was about 10 miles away and we'd do speed [amphetamine] and then cycle up there and then just sit around talking and smoking spliffs … '

At first glance the contrast between Geoff's and Philip's experiences could hardly appear greater. Geoff describes very active experiences characterized by continuous physical activity, walking and cycling, whereas Philip's account of his first encounter with heroin centres on doing almost nothing, sitting around talking with friends. However, at a deeper level what these disparate events have in common is that they each luxuriate in a squandering of resources to no obvious purpose. Once the obligation to engage in purposeful activities, exemplified in this instance by attending school or doing paid work, has been lifted their most immediate desire is for a wasteful expenditure of time, energy and resources. It is significant, in this context, that at no point is a reason or explanation for becoming intoxicated offered beyond the fact that the opportunity to do so was available. Becoming intoxicated does not appear to require an explanation, simply because it is not *for* something but is rather an end in itself that lies outside the logic of instrumental acts. The satisfaction of participating in events that are free of any discernible purpose and involve an unprofitable expenditure of resources is even more evident in the contributions of some of the other participants. In the excerpts below first Robert and then Edward describe their experiences with ecstasy and amphetamine:

> 'it's just that you had energy and you felt like the music was going through you you could feel the bass and the rhythm and so you were dancing … '

> 'there is that kind of energy factor that thing of suddenly it could be eleven, twelve, two, three in the morning and you're still sort of up for seemingly up for doing something still sort of something going on there's still to this very day I feel like that … yeah well I didn't realize at the time but I suppose more now I realize it you sort of do it to go off on a bit of a tangent to the sort of normality … '

To begin with it seems that the energies released by the drugs Edward reports using in the second passage will be harnessed to some goal, to 'doing something', but it emerges that the 'goal' has already been attained in the state of being intoxicated itself, that is, 'to go off on a bit of a tangent to the sort of normality'; a normality that is always recognizable as such by the rationally ordered purposes which constrain and channel it to specific ends.

If wastefully expending resources that might otherwise be put to 'good' use is one of the attractions of intoxication then it is to be expected that measures which will increase these resources are likely to be adopted with enthusiasm, as the following passage from the interview with Simon makes clear:

> 'we started meeting people in town that could like get us drugs to be able to drink more like and that's how I got like into doing drugs which was sort of like doing speed [amphetamine] so like we could go out and sort

> of drink more and stay up all night drinking and like simple as that really … '

The tendency to excessive consumption that is sometimes associated with intoxicant drug use may derive in part from this urge towards maximizing the energies and resources which are, or seem to be, available for a wasteful expenditure. It is significant, in this context, that many of the colloquialisms used to designate extreme intoxication, such as 'wasted', 'smashed', 'slaughtered' and 'annihilated', employ metaphors of uncontrolled expenditure and destruction.

For many of the participants the sensation of liberating energies that are undirected and free flowing is clearly central to the experience of intoxication; the 'floating energies that are not yet fixed or invested in techniques and signs' as José Gil, the Portuguese philosopher, has called them.[7] In some cases these liberated energies can manifest themselves in startlingly literal forms, as in this excerpt where George describes a positive experience with the drug LSD:

> 'This is quite a good experience because you could almost sense energy where it changed your perception it either distorts your brain in such a way that you think you can see energy and sort of an aura of the human body whether it does or not is a completely different by the by because you feel you can you feel you feel the energy coming out of your hands … because if you move in a really physical strong action and direct yourself in a certain way like pointing really really quickly and assertively you'd see energy coming out of your hand in the form of a white lightning bolt so they worked and that was a very good experience no negativity whatsoever … '

If the use of intoxicant drugs no longer provides this sensation of releasing free energies, here expressed in the very image of an unpredictable discharge, the lightning bolt, their use either tends to become aversive, or it is simply assimilated to the mundane. When this change occurs, the inability to continue with wasteful expenditures is likely to be regretted as least as much as is any squandering of past energies. In the following passage Simon laments the way his experience with intoxicant drugs has altered with the passage of time:

> 'as time's gone on I've got older I feel less and less inclination to do anything you know I'm just bored with the whole thing you know it's not about like it's about laziness now it's not about pushing at things and boundaries and danger it's just about sheer laziness and sloth you know and that's what I really don't like about it now.'

Where once the use of intoxicant drugs was associated with a release of uncoded energies which made it possible to push at 'things and boundaries' and to face dangers, now that these energies have dissipated the motivation to seek intoxication has been lost.

Even for those among the participants who understood their relationship with drugs in terms of addiction, their greatest anxiety was not that their perceived addiction would continue unabated but that their capacity for becoming addicted, and the free and wasteful expenditures this state entails, would be curtailed. In the following excerpts from Steven's interview he describes his experience of attempting to give up tobacco before going on to evaluate the desirability of a possible solution to his apparent enslavement to the drug:

> 'tobacco longest I've ever given up tobacco for is about ten days and I was a complete wreck at the end of it … you know after ten days I was absolutely crawling up the wall and driving everyone else up the wall as well so you know and I feel dirty that you know I've just put a spliff out and I've still got to roll myself a fag afterwards you know because my body says you know it wants the nicotine buzz you know and if I stop doing that I just my whole body just goes into a sort of don't know what can't really easily describe it but craving anyway and I will break into sweat and I will fall apart completely without it you know and about the only thing that can that I can do to you know offset that is stuff my face really eating a lot I can't afford to do that so I carry on smoking you know tobacco is the worst … '

It might be imagined that anything that could bring an end to this story of torment would be welcomed unconditionally. However, when the effects of a drug called Zyban that promises to halt such cravings is considered by Steven a more complex and ambivalent picture emerges of his 'addictive' behaviour:

> 'I just heard this morning actually [on the radio] they are talking about Zyban … it's supposed to be an anti-addiction drug and I'm a little bit concerned about that 'cos that's got like psychological implications hasn't it you know or think about it even psychiatric implications … if you're the sort of person who might get addicted I think it might I don't know alter something in your mind in your brain you know it must affect some part of your brain if it would actually stop you making the decision that you've got to have this or that whatever it is you know so my understanding of Zyban is it's a bit generalized you know.'

Having graphically described his uncontrollable cravings for nicotine and their deleterious effects on his health and well-being Steven finally remains unwilling to countenance the use of a medication that 'would actually stop you making the *decision* that you've *got to have* this or that whatever it is'. Whatever the accuracy of Steven's portrayal of Zyban's clinical effects his reluctance to surrender his bodily cravings would seem to confirm that, for some at least, desire is desired above all else.[8] According to Klein, the desire to consume without purpose or remainder is not, as it is often portrayed, an affliction so much as a reason for continued existence:

> Smoking a cigarette is … a "sacrificial ceremony" in which the disappearance of something solid, tobacco, is infinitely compensated by the symbolic gain I acquire in appropriating to myself the world around me. To give up smoking, therefore, effects an impoverishment of the world and of the self one is naturally reluctant to tolerate. Life without cigarettes is not worth living.[9]

Whether a life without cigarettes is worth living or not may be open to question but a life lived without the kind of desires that cigarette smoking signals, and the free and wasteful expenditures that give these desires expression, may indeed be one that is terribly impoverished. If humans are essentially 'desiring machines' then perhaps the greatest threat they face is not that their desires will remain uncontrolled but that they will be curtailed.[10]

The antinomies between the kind of encounters with uncoded energies released through intoxication that have been described above and the demands of everyday existence will be considered later, but first it is necessary to examine in more detail the implications for experience of inhabiting a world where the body as something useful has been sacrificed.

From labour to play

If the dominant paradigm for meaningful activity in modern western societies is the plan, intoxication, by contrast, follows instead the logic of free experimentation.[11] Whereas a rationally planned course of action effectively controls the future by moving in coherent steps towards a predetermined and clearly envisaged outcome, intoxication opens onto an unanticipated and contingent reality. As is the case with all experiments, and quite unlike the plan, intoxication is meaningful not only because the experiment can sometimes succeed but also because the experiment can always fail. This difference, between planning and experimentation, corresponds to the difference highlighted above between actively appropriating elements of the world for our own ends and an open process that passively awaits what will transpire; it also corresponds to the difference between looking and seeing. When we look we abstract objects from the environment as though they were separate from it rather than seeing that they *are* the environment.[12] As modes of engagement with the world, planned labour and the playfulness of experimentation both have in common that they initiate change. However, they do so in an entirely different manner, as Deleuze and Guattari have observed:

Work is a motor cause that meets resistances, operates upon the exterior, is consumed and spent in its effect, and must be renewed from one moment to the next. Free action is also a motor cause, but one that has no resistance to overcome, operates only upon the mobile body itself, is not consumed in its effect, and continues from one moment to the next.[13]

Intoxication has the character of a free action in these terms. It restores the world to an undifferentiated condition in which objects that are rendered serious and separate by labour take on a playful and indeterminate character. These objects include the human body. In the following passage from Steven's interview he recalls a party he attended where the combined effects of alcohol and cannabis overwhelmed both his competent and upright demeanour and the apparent certainties of familiar objects:

'shortly after smoking it I remember I had to go outside and get some air then I started throwing up I had to lie down and I distinctly remember this garden 'cos it was kind of rounded it was like being on a ball lying down on the edge of a ball … you know it was just strange the whole thing was shaped like the corner of a ball with a house sat on top of it but I remember there were trees and fences and things but I couldn't get up anyway I sort of found myself lying down because I felt so ill and throwing up I couldn't even move when I was throwing up so I was throwing up all over myself … '

While there can be little doubt that this would have been a very unpleasant experience at the level of physical discomfort it was also an experience in which the world is *seen* in a new and refulgent light divested of many of its everyday meanings. This is not the world of gardens, fences, trees and houses that are recognizably made in our own image but rather a world that is *found* in all its uncanny splendour when the grip of these abstractions is loosened. In seeking this other world, whose meaning precedes the rational and the purposeful, the potential for adverse side effects, such as illness, did not prove to be a serious deterrent to further experimentation for Steven or for most of the other people I interviewed. Indeed, as will be seen, the presence of unexpected and uncontrollable sensations, both pleasant and unpleasant, is a hallmark of intoxication without which it would have little meaning or allure as an experience. The following excerpt, from Geoff's interview, also vividly conveys this sense of encountering a familiar world that is rendered new and unfamiliar once the rational purposes that order everyday existence recede from perception:

'we did big lines of ketamine [anaesthetic] and then went off to the off licence to buy some beer and kind of came up on it as we got to the off licence and it was just the situation of picking up beers and just staring at

> the can and just thinking what am I doing here again and again just putting it back and it just seemed to take forever to buy you know a few items of alcohol … we did succeed in the end and kind of walked back stopped slowly and then I bumped into a Muslim girl that I knew from college quite strict Muslim all in full dress and I tried to have a conversation with her and I don't know to this day what she must have thought of me but I felt like I was acting really strangely … it wasn't like when you'd usually go to the shop and buy some beers … it wasn't like that it was kind of more like it was happening in a dream you know I think that's the best way I can describe it but I've always found ketamine a bit indescribable … '

Again, as in Steven's account of his experience with alcohol and cannabis, Geoff attempts to convey in words an experience that remains irreducible to discourse. In an effort to evoke his experience more fully Geoff eventually employs the metaphor of a dream but is forced to dismiss even this as somehow inadequate. Finally, Geoff characterizes the effects of ketamine as 'a bit indescribable' giving lay expression to the insight that experience both precedes and is excessive of all discursive constructions that render it intelligible and coherent. As Gil has observed '[l]language is never exhaustive about the world which symbolic thought appears to encompass – there is always a surplus',[14] a surplus that is sometimes made strikingly apparent by intoxication.

When the world is no longer composed of objects that have a meaning and purpose that is definite and fixed the way is open for the familiar, now rendered malleable, to be playfully reinvented. In George's interview, after taking LSD with some friends, it is language itself that becomes the object of such a reinvention:

> 'we were making a radio programme sort of later in the evening … filling in with different characters different subjects but as we were tripping these different characters and different subjects were completely different and didn't really make any sense which is quite hard to describe we did tape it and listened to it the next day we listened to it after we did it and it was hilarious it all made sense and we were all very very funny but the next day it made no sense whatsoever we were just gibbering fools and what we'd written down as like headers on a piece of paper demonstrated quite a strong level of dyslexia I think which none of us really suffer from the words actually the letters didn't make words.'

In this parody of collective endeavour a playful world of shared meanings is created in the space opened up when everyday imperatives are no longer being enforced.

However, it is not only the world as an object of perception and the objects that we encounter within it that appear in a new and playful light during intoxication but also the body as a resource for purposeful activity. In the passage below Karen recalls an evening in which the taken-for-granted competencies of everyday life, such as walking, give way to a playful enjoyment of the body, albeit one that ends, on this particular occasion, in minor disaster:

> 'we did five one after the other you only do Aftershock when you're really drunk anyway … and we skipped from the pub it was quite early we'd been drinking from three and it was only about eight o'clock and we kind of came out of the pub we'd been to D's for loads and then went to the pub for another couple and then we skipped from the pub home Brian in the middle and Jenny and I either arm the momentum started building and we got faster and faster 'cos Brian's legs are longer than ours and then we were going down the subway and it was just getting faster and faster and faster and faster and I felt my legs going and we crashed and we all flew over head first and that's when I nearly pulled my ear off when I whacked my head my ear my shoulder all down one side and Jenny did it on the other side with all her knee Brian carried on running for a couple of paces more than us and fell on to his shoulder … '

In this incident, by forfeiting the controlled body of sobriety Karen, Brian and Jenny, for a time at least, moved beyond a mundane world governed by intention and rendered predictable by necessity to enter a playful realm of unanticipated and unplanned events. In a society that is increasingly saturated with images, objects and 'experiences' that are mass produced and identical, where even 'danger' and excitement are typically calibrated in advance and infinitely repeatable (as in a fairground ride or bungee jump), such encounters with the genuinely unexpected, however trivial they may seem, perhaps have a particular value that may sometimes appear to outweigh the risks involved.[15]

Having considered the mode of engagement that is typical of intoxication, where the planned and the purposeful are sacrificed to the playful and unexpected, it is now time to define that impossible point where transgression occurs. This impossible limit, where both the gift and intoxication come into being, exists in the space between forgetting and remembering. Some of the tensions and difficulties created by seeking to inhabit such an impossible space will then be examined.

Intoxication and forgetting

In the last chapter it was noted that western thought takes rational self-possession to be the model of authentically human behaviour. However, as was also noted, phenomena, such as religious ecstasy, erotic investment and of course intoxication, call this presumption into question. Human experience is not only a matter of remembering at all times what we are doing and who we are but also of forgetting these things on occasion in order to transcend the individuated existence they express. While identity and purpose provide a means of going on in the world that is indispensable they do not, in themselves, exhaust human capacities or desires.[16]

Intoxication as a consciousness that forgets itself reaches its limit at the moment the necessities of existence are recalled. To seek the moment of forgetting that is intoxication is to seek an impossible point between these necessities. It is impossible because the crucial question of the dose can never be decided with any certainty in advance. This indeterminable quality is summed up in the Greek word *pharmakon* which means both medicine and poison, an ambiguity that can only be resolved through the administration of the drug.[17] If the dose is too high the primordial necessities of existence will reassert themselves, or be ignored with potentially fatal consequences, as in this passage from Michael's interview:

> 'did a stupid one with the magic mushrooms that I regretted well yeah I did regret that involved eating loads before walking back to D from F and that was about a 10 mile walk along the A 29 I think it is it's a busy road and that was just like a bit of an ordeal really it was fine at the start you know but I came down really really suddenly because I nearly got run over … and I sort of blacked out for a while but I could hear this loud roaring noise which I think was an engine of a lorry and I don't really know what I did somebody told me that I'd walked out into the road without looking or anything … '

Alternatively, if the dose is too low the point of forgetting will never be reached and the experience will remain within the confines of the everyday. To take a sufficient quantity of any intoxicant drug to get beyond the realm of rational calculation is, by definition, to enter a state where, in the absence of calculation, too much may be consumed. First Philip and then Tony illustrate this dilemma in their interviews when recalling some experiences with ketamine [anaesthetic] and temazepam [tranquillizer]:

> 'well I mean you get to the point where you don't notice that you've actually done the last line [of ketamine] so you do the next one.'
>
> 'I mean I've done similar things but I came home once and my two mates are ripping the flat apart because they're looking for the drugs I point out to them that they've actually taken them they don't believe me so then accuse me of stealing them I keep trying to point out to them that no they definitely took them this is why they're so stoned and this is why they think that they haven't its just that they've forgot taking the second lot and they're basically tearing the whole flat apart accusing me this isn't unusual.'

But as Tony also indicated, getting to this point of forgetfulness is central to the experience of intoxication – its defining characteristic:

> 'I suppose that's the great thing about when the drugs do work you don't tend to actually know what happened and kind of maybe that's the idea.'

To move beyond calculation as a basis for action is both a condition for intoxication and the greatest danger of intoxication. The dilemma this poses, between wanting to retain control and the desire to be liberated from calculation, is one that can never finally be resolved. However, more often than not the consequences of surrendering control are likely to be farce rather than tragedy, and may also, on occasion, be an experience of sublime transcendence. In this excerpt, Tony describes an experience with the drug LSD in which the farcical, the near-tragic and the sublime rapidly succeeded one another:

> 'it was almost blowing maybe must have been force eight nine wind was absolutely howling and we'd sort of got up to the beach and that and it's freezing cold it must be November December and the girls the three girls are straight down the beach and into the sea and we literally had to run after them and grab them back because they were I mean the drag back down at sort of D and that is incredible you can get sucked right under … they just walked in going "oh this is wonderful look at the water" and we just had to like some moment of sanity took over sort of me and a mate and we just literally had to run in and grab them out of the water and I mean we were lying on the beach lying on the gravel and just watching the stars just sort of pulsating and swarming around each other and it was the pure intensity of the whole experience for the whole night that made it so memorable because it was there wasn't any kind of little sort of paranoid edge at any time and it was one of the times that I can actually remember where although everything was completely confused and messed up it was absolutely perfect if you were able to kind of let go of trying to sort of make something you know understandable out of it.'

While intoxication may be defined by a forgetting it is also demarcated as an experience by the boundaries which enforce remembering. The point of remembering, which marks a diminution in the state of intoxication, is not inherent to intoxication as such but is rather a product of interactions with the environment in which intoxication occurs: drunkenness will become apparent far more quickly in a library or a church, for example, than it would at a Christmas party. At the point where intoxication is recognized as intoxication it enters the realm of discourse and is subject to definition in relation to the necessities and norms of everyday existence. The possibilities for intoxication are therefore conditional on the environment in which it occurs both in terms of how safe it is from primordial threats and in terms of how rationally ordered it is. Many of the participants recalled moments when the boundary between intoxication as a pure forgetting and the self-consciousness of remembered necessities was crossed. A couple of examples, from the interviews with first Michael and then Joanna will suffice to show this passage from one state of being to another and to indicate its origins:

> 'it's like you remember them if they were interrupted I remember one being interrupted when me and my friends were all bouncing around his friends bedroom and I remember shouting something like "I feel really great" over and over again until his mum burst in through the door and said "I'm sorry to make you all feel really really bad can you not take drugs in Steve's bedroom" and we all sort of went thumph' [gestures downwards with hand at this point to indicate the sudden deflation of the moment]

> 'the first thing he [Joanna's father] said to me was "you're drunk" which I felt terrible about because to be perfectly honest I didn't know that I was drunk I'm not sure that I really knew what drunk was and I was a little bit unclear about how you ended up drunk in the first place but I knew it was like I knew that he was really disapproving of me and then I did realize that all the time that I'd been walking to the station I'd been sort of falling over my heels I was wearing these wedge heels at the time and I hadn't been able to walk properly and I kept stumbling and like that and I thought oh that's 'cos I was drunk so I was terribly ashamed and that was my first experience with actually being drunk as I now know.'

These passages make clear the extent to which intoxication as something recognized and defined comes into being through encounters with the demands of social existence. As an innocent forgetting intoxication is constantly vulnerable to the imposition of social necessities that can radically discredit it as a legitimate way of being. In the excerpt below, from the interview with Simon, the countryside of his youth is invoked as a place of apparent freedom from both social necessities and primordial threats:

> 'where it was all like rural it like you could take like loads of trips [LSD] and get totally off your nut and do whatever you wanted and you had none of the threat of violence that you get in town.'

However, it remains unclear to what extend this idyll existed in reality and to what extent it is simply remembered in this way.

Transgression and its limits

Although intoxication may have the effect at times of turning the world of the familiar and the everyday upside down, it is not a condition that seeks a revolutionary outcome. There can be no question of a finality in which intoxication as a permanent or absolute state supplants the world of the everyday. Even if oblivion is sometimes the consequence of intoxicant drug use it is never the aim. On the contrary, it is only through the continuing presence of boundaries which delimit the world of the everyday that intoxication can be recognized as intoxication and experienced as a transgressive event.[18] Transgression, in this context, is not a matter of breaking or ignoring rules that exist 'out there' and can therefore be dispensed with, although it can certainly involve this. Rather, transgression is primarily a question of initiating transformations which violate boundaries that exist 'in here'. While these transformations may push against the limits of our social and material existence they can never accomplish a definitive liberation from these necessities. These material and social necessities define the very conditions for our continued being: 'the domain of constraints without which a certain desiring and living being cannot make its way' as the feminist scholar Judith Butler puts it.[19] Although loosening the grip exerted by social and primordial necessities can be an exhilarating experience, it can never be one that is entirely without cost. The competent and useful body of everyday life is sacrificed in order to commune with the sacred, but this sacrifice requires both a degree of commitment and a certain generosity. This is so because the results of this sacrifice are inherently unpredictable and the losses it entails can never be recovered. Time, energy and resources that could have been put to productive use are freely surrendered to a future that it is hoped will be fruitful but which in reality remains unknown and unknowable. Intoxication remains an ambivalent experience because, like the gift or sacrifice, it unites giving and receiving in a single gesture.

Seeking the point of transgression where the useful body is surrendered and the world received involves the testing of boundaries. If these boundaries are exceeded by too great a margin the necessities of existence can reassert themselves, interrupting the forgetful moment of intoxication. Boundaries may be those of physical endurance, social expectation or even those of remembering and can come into play both at the moment of intoxication and over time. In the following passage Philip describes a situation where carefree expenditure almost turned into radical and absolute loss:

> 'She was sat on the end of the sofa and I actually injected her she had put it in her arm I just pushed the plunger sort of normal I was getting mine ready turned around looked at her and she was blue checked pulse checked breathing wasn't happening so put her on the floor did artificial respiration cardiac massage for about five minutes and she then came round I collapsed into a heap shaking and crying was fine up until the moment she came round 'cos I was busy doing something and then I was just a complete mess ... she came round and had a go at me 'cos her chest hurt I'd been pumping her heart for her that wasn't very nice.'

Rather than attaining a sense of playful release from the necessities of everyday existence by the use of intoxicant drugs the force of these necessities was instead simply redoubled and given greater immediacy in this case. As Deleuze and Guattari have observed: 'It's a very delicate business, these intensities: the finest intensity becomes harmful if it over taxes your strength at a given moment; you have to be able to take it.'[20] However, it is not only the primordial boundaries of physical existence that may be challenged, if transgression goes too far the complex and changing boundaries that traverse social space may also be exceeded, as in this account of a birthday celebration taken from the interview with Karen:

> 'we just got more and more and more drunk everybody but then you know everybody just ended up well Linda ended up getting so drunk she got her tits out and you know and everybody but I encouraged her I was so drunk I was "go on Linda get them out" and I'm not like that at all but 'cos she is a bit like that I remember quite a scenario that it was awkward and it was just like "O.K. great, she's got her tits out" and all these strangers looking at these massive pair of tits and oh it was just weird.'

At the point where intoxication becomes self-aware a limit is reached and the spell is broken. When this will occur may have as much to do with the social context in which intoxication occurs as with the level of intoxication understood in purely physiological terms. As Jenks has noted: 'transgressions are manifestly situation-specific and vary considerably across social space and through time.'[21] A loss of control that in one context is instantly stigmatized may be the very mark of unselfconscious freedom in another. When asked to recall some of his best experiences of intoxication David produced an image of Bacchanalian abandon that went far beyond the boundaries encountered by Karen and Linda:

> 'I don't know all get together and have a party and everyone is throwing up everywhere and shagging on the front room carpet.'

If intoxication reaches a limit point when it is remembered it is also subject to the opposite limit, a forgetting that is too complete, as the following passages from the interviews with first George and then Geoff makes clear:

> 'I'd say probably the worst experience is not being able to remember what's happened due to the fact probably drinking too much too regularly for too long it's quite annoying me at the moment … I mean I've probably had conversations with people about serious things that I have no recollection of.'

> 'I obviously started coming up on the Largactil [major tranquillizer] felt sick so I can remember going up the stairs and getting to the landing

> I got up to the landing and then the next thing I knew I was on my back at the bottom of the stairs and it was really quite a psychedelic experience of kind of colours and that kind of thing going on I was kind of thinking oh what's going on heading towards the light or something and then I could kind of see in the middle of all the colours like people peering over me and then just kind of gradually came out into that with everyone kind of leaning over me going are you alright you alright apparently I'd had a bit of a fit or something … I completely lost control of myself and passed out at the top of the stairs you know anything could have happened … on acid all the time that I was off my head I still knew that my friends were around me whereas on the Largactil fucking I was in another world.'

The limits of forgetting and remembering that delimit the possibility of intoxication, as an unselfconscious moment outside the primordial and social necessities of existence, are not only those of the immediate situation but also come into play over time. In the excerpts below first Steven and then David recall moments when it was no longer possible to forget the necessities of existence after prolonged periods of regular intoxication:

> 'I stopped doing that 'cos at least with the coke [cocaine] you don't sort of have to well I don't think you have quite such a come down well you don't really but you know whiz [amphetamine] is always a price to pay you know you always feel like shit later and it really really breaks me out you know I'm covered in zits after I've done some whiz you know I don't really need the whiz to get zits as it is so you know it really doesn't help and I just looked at myself one day and I just felt so disgusting I looked filthy dirty greasy spotty yuck you know I felt like complete shit I had no energy for anything you know but that's after like months of prolonged use you know but … you know I had a big taste for speed but eventually I you know knocked it on the head 'cos it wasn't good.'

> 'I was living down K and my intake must have been a bit high and I give me self bronchial pneumonia didn't I week in hospital … yeah that give me cold realization I didn't want to do drugs for a while after that just really didn't want to do any of them quite happy to just be living that's doing too many bongs and hot knives and things like that very debauched at times.'

It is a paradox of intoxication that the greater the forgetting the less likely it is that it will be sustained free of the limits imposed by primordial and social necessities. In the passage below Michael contemplates what it would have meant to forget the world of the everyday in order to explore more fully the possibilities of intoxication:

> 'I had the feeling that there was a magical side to nature which … taking the magic mushrooms enabled me to walk up to the door and that I'd

> then have a choice that I could walk into that and never come back or just kind of peek round the corner and I sort of peeked round the corner a few times but was quite conscious of like I wanted to go back to the normal world I didn't want to which maybe also showed on a rational level a desire not to become a person who lived in a homemade tent on a hill 'cos that was what the magical world would have meant socially I had no interest in doing that at all and the whole thing and I never really got into them again after that.'

While this passage perhaps overdramatizes the alternatives as an all or nothing choice between a sacred and profane world of experience it nevertheless contains the essential ambiguity of intoxication as a sacrificial economy. To attain the sacred entails freely giving up the competent body we live through – but this surrender can never be completed or the sacred itself will be forfeited. In *Politics of Friendship* Derrida asks the question: 'how many friends should one have?' and after much musing on the topic concludes that one should have enough friends but not too many.[22] If the people I interviewed for this book were to be asked how many intoxicant drugs one should take it is likely that many of them would give a similar answer, 'enough but not too many'. Searching for this point between enough and too much, both at the level of the particular episode and over the course of time, ensures that intoxication always remains an essentially experimental enterprise.

Conclusion

As we have seen, intoxication can be understood as a kind of sacrificial gesture in which the body as something useful to human purposes is freely given up in order to open ourselves to new experiences and commune with the sacred. This understanding of what it means to become intoxicated was illustrated by tracing some of the consequences for embodied experience and our social interactions that result from intoxication. It began by showing how energies that are normally harnessed by necessity and purpose to specific ends are liberated by intoxication and flow freely. These undirected energies are manifested in a playful and experimental mode of engagement with the world that contrasts with the pragmatic endeavours of everyday existence. This change in orientation is exemplified by the shift from looking at a world that is differentiated and fragmented by our interests and projects to seeing a world whose meaning precedes these concerns. The alteration in perspective and mode of engagement wrought by intoxication is not one that is absolute but exists in a fragile space between the primordial and social necessities that circumscribe our existence. These necessities, which allow us to go on in the world, are at once retained and exceeded in the moment of intoxication defining it as a transgressive event. Having considered the shift in orientation that results from sacrificing the competent body of everyday life it is now time to explore these issues in more detail and to draw out their implications. To do this, the temporal dimensions of the experience of intoxication and its role in community formation will be analysed and discussed. In the next chapter, the temporality of traditional societies will be contrasted with the temporality of modern societies at a theoretical level. The points raised by that discussion will then be illustrated and amplified in Chapter 5 with examples drawn from the interview material gathered for the book. This pattern of theoretical discussion followed by concrete illustration will be repeated in subsequent chapters which will examine the role of intoxication in the formation of liminal communities. Finally, in the discussion which concludes the book the cumulative import of these various analyses for an understanding of the experience of intoxication in contemporary society, and how drug use and drug users are viewed, will be assessed.

4 Traditional time and modern time

We began by examining the role of intoxication in the unmaking of the modern, rational bounded body. The sacrificial economy which underpins this unmaking of the socially constituted body, and defines intoxication as a transgressive event, was discussed and these ideas illustrated with material drawn from the interviews conducted for the book. It is now time to explore the temporal dimensions of the experience of intoxication. Since time is one of the basic parameters of all human experience any adequate account of intoxication must include the experience of time associated with intoxication among its considerations. In order to understand the significance of time to the experience of intoxication, and the significance of intoxication to our experience of time, it is necessary to consider the way our perception of time is conditioned both by the particular temporal schemas that prevail in society and by our embodied experiences. The experience of time while intoxicated becomes intelligible only when it is related to a wider context of temporal experience that has social, historical and primordial dimensions. We will compare the way time was conceived and experienced in traditional societies with the way time is experienced now in order to uncover the relationship between *Aeon* and *Chronos,* duration and becoming, structure and immediacy in the experience of intoxication. The relationship between these different aspects of temporal experience will be explored initially by looking at how the experience of time in traditional societies has been understood from a social scientific perspective. Experiences of change and recurrence in the setting of traditional societies, and the body's role in these processes, will be outlined. It will be suggested that temporal experience in traditional societies is constituted both through the cyclical reproduction of existing features and by the constant renewal of these recursive elements in a lived present. The locus for this relationship to time in traditional societies is the body which at once contains the past and allows for its transformation in the present. The following section will then describe the distinctive temporal context of modernity, against which intoxication in contemporary society finds its meaning. The effects that these different temporal schemas have on the experience of time, and in particular their implications for the relative importance of the present and the future, will then be discussed. It will be argued that phenomena such as intoxication point to the body as a continuing source of temporal experience despite changes that have tended, in the conditions of modernity, to locate time definitively outside the body. A view of temporal experience will be put forward that sees the body not only as a site where socially constituted temporal schemas are reproduced but where time is also transformed, annulled and secreted, and where novel and unanticipated events such as intoxication emerge into social existence in a lived present. In the next chapter, the role of intoxication in reconnecting the experience of time with embodied existence, and the importance of sharing irrecoverable time with others while intoxicated will be examined through an analysis of people's temporal experiences while intoxicated as revealed in the interviews conducted for the book.

The experience of time in traditional societies

In traditional societies the diachronic and synchronic elements of temporal experience are intimately fused. The series and cycles of life which connect different moments and place them in a relationship one to the other, and the immediate experience of these moments, are not distinct at the level of experience in these cultures.[1] As a consequence of time being experienced in this undifferentiated manner the same events can be read as both the latest in a series of related episodes, and as being entirely of the moment and without precedent. The nexus for this organic experience of time in traditional societies is the body, which acts as both the repository of a tradition and as the focus for immediate experience in a lived present.[2] However, in social scientific explanations of traditional temporality these two facets of temporal experience have often been separated out and the importance of one emphasized over the other. Some accounts which foreground the diachronic aspects of temporality in traditional societies will now be considered, before going on to look at how the synchronic dimensions of temporal experience in these societies has been analysed. A means by which these apparently incompatible perspectives on temporal experience may be reconciled will then be suggested. Later, the implications of this discussion for an understanding of the temporal dimensions of intoxication in contemporary society will be drawn out.

Temporality and recurrence in traditional societies

Time and change have been theorized using a range of different temporal models, to the point where conceptions that are fundamentally incompatible have been propounded. For example, some have proposed a fixed teleology (Marx), whereas others envisage an open future whose features are yet to be determined (Mead).[3] Given this conceptual diversity there is a surprising degree of consensus regarding the nature of temporal experience in 'traditional' societies, that is in those societies that existed before or exist outside modernity.[4] People in traditional societies are typically understood as inhabiting a form of time that is collective, cyclical and intimately bound to the sacred. This produces a temporal environment that is effectively 'timeless' because it is overwhelmingly oriented to the reproduction of existing structures and established patterns of behaviour.[5]

There is, it is believed, an organic unity between the experience of time and the routines of the social group in traditional societies. In classical conceptions of traditional temporality this implies a close affinity between social time and natural time, with activities that are governed by routine being linked to seasonal and other cyclical patterns of recurrence. Mauss, for example, details the attunement of Eskimo culture to seasonal variations, such that they have 'two social structures, one in summer and one in winter, and that in parallel they have two systems of law and religion'.[6] The natural and the social are also seen to dovetail in the rites of passage which simultaneously mark the succeeding stages of life for the individual and the group, and relate the passage of time to wider patterns of recurrence and the rhythms of the cosmos.[7] Rather than being autonomous of individual or group life, time is woven into the fabric of existence and operates in concert with the other elements of collective activity to form what, in Mauss's terms, would be designated as a 'total social fact' in these accounts. Time, in effect, is produced and owned collectively as a by-product of the group's activities and social arrangements, and time exists in harmony with the cycles of life to which these activities and social arrangements are in turn synchronized.

The mechanism which facilitates the appropriation of time in this way by traditional social groups is found in the use of collective rituals which serve to fix time, 'bringing to it an order, a regularity, and a reiterative rhythm that stem the flow of the temporal wound'.[8] These magico-religious ceremonies 'join the present to the past and the individual to the collectivity'.[9] Rather than being performed *for* the collectivity these ritual ceremonies are performed *by* the collectivity so that those who carry out the rites and those who witness them are one and the same. The celebrants make a past present again through the form of the ritual, since they carry out the same movements as 'those the ancestor made in the same circumstances'.[10] This 'implicit eternal permutational conception of time', the view that time is universal, durational and characterized by rhythms that change in form while remaining essentially identical in content implies a continuous alternation between sacred and profane periods within an overall 'sacred time environment'.[11] This sacred time environment renders not merely events that occur in time as sacred but, in specific circumstances, time itself. This is so because the sacred 'seeds itself within time through a symbolic time-environment in which critical dates begin and end durations, the particular dates and durations concerned are equivalent and there is a linkage of multiple series, cycles and orders of duration'.[12] From the perspective of Emile Durkheim, the French sociologist who developed these ideas about time in traditional cultures, the key to understanding ritual activities and their role in the production of a temporality that is both cyclical and sacred lies in their recursive nature and in the integrative functions they perform through the arousal and channelling of emotion. The source of the sacred is traced to society itself and the awareness of it that the experience of 'collective effervescence' evokes: 'Religious forces are in fact only transfigured collective forces, that is, moral forces; they are made of ideas and feelings that the spectacle of society awakens in us, not of sensations that come to us from the physical world.'[13] Ritual performance establishes an identity and equivalence between different moments of collective 'effervescence' and is the basis for a universal temporality founded on the alternation of sacred and profane durations. The experience of time in traditional societies, in this view, is one where the same temporal patterns are consistently repeated in succeeding generations and their significance is derived from the social.

The Durkheimian view of time also concentrates on the recursive dimension when it comes to conceptualizing the role of the dead in traditional societies. Ancestors are understood as being reincarnated in succeeding generations rather than as being fully present in the world of the living. This implies that every generation is a repetition of that which preceded it without development or change. However, this emphasis on the diachronic elements of temporal experience and on the reproduction of order over time represents only one aspect of traditional temporality as it has been understood from a social scientific perspective. In some accounts the synchronic dimensions of temporal experience are also fully acknowledged.

Temporality and change in traditional societies

In contrast to the view of traditional temporality described in the previous section, which sees it as predominantly cyclical in nature with the body acting as a repository of established gestures that reprise past events, the experience of time in traditional societies has also been understood as focused on the lived present and as opening onto an unknown future.

The recursive aspect of collective rituals which lends them the *appearance* of simply reproducing that which existed before may be misleading, making the exclusive focus on identity found in the Durkheimian view of traditional temporality questionable. In particular, the significance of spontaneity in the release of sacred forces during ritual performance is neglected by their assimilation to a tradition.[14] Evidence for this can be found in the very form taken by many of these rituals. Ritual ceremonies, of the kind described above from a Durkheimian perspective, are often conducted with a degree of informality that would be unimaginable in contemporary religious practice. The British social anthropologist Edmund Leach, for example, has documented ritual performances where 'shrines are constructed *ad hoc* and abandoned as soon as the ritual is over'.[15] These ceremonies are conducted in this way not because of any lack of reverence for the sacred nature of the rites being performed but because the sacred is experienced as a lived reality in the present, rather than as something that requires enduring monuments that attest either to its commemoration or its anticipation. In other words, the sacred is evoked in the uniqueness of the present as well as through an iterative gesture. It might be speculated that if ritual performance in traditional societies is often the same in form it is also always different in content, having the character of an event as much as an activity. As José Gil has observed, rituals:

> 'signify' particular actions and gestures, and not symbolic 'meanings'; they designate realities, they set forces into motion, they are 'in the present' … the essential role of rituals in the question of power relates no doubt to the possibility of capturing the free forces that traverse bodies.[16]

The effectiveness of these ritual ceremonies in transcending the profane order of existence depends on their character as something that happens *to* the participants as well as being something that is simply undertaken by them in a mimetic relationship to an established past.[17] While these magico-religious ceremonies may indeed integrate past and present, group and individual, this may be accomplished, paradoxically, through the abolition of time and the dissolution of the individual in an ecstatic present, manifested through dance, music and the intoxication of the body.[18] From this perspective, ritual performance can be defined not only by its place in a temporal structure but also by its de-structuring and de-temporalizing effects. These two aspects of temporal experience are vitally manifested in the body since at each moment the body is both the culmination of what has gone before and the place where what has yet to come comes into being.

A focus on the importance of the present and the body is also sustained by attending to the mode of cultural transmission in traditional societies where a limited fund of myths and stories is imparted in their telling. Again, the importance of this resides not only in the fact that it re-enacts a tradition, as a Durkheimian perspective might insist, but also in the fact that this telling exists *only* in the present and opens onto an unknown future. A clue that myths and stories in traditional societies are dynamic rather than merely recursive in nature is provided by the insight that these stories and myths are not fixed, but fluid, undergoing constant mutations as they accommodate change by reinventing the past in an ever new present.[19] The significance of the present is further heightened by orality because sound, which conveys the spoken word, is transient and exists only in the now of lived experience. As the American cultural and literary historian Walter Ong has noted, sound 'exists only when it is going out of existence. It is not simply perishable but essentially evanescent, and it is sensed as evanescent'[20] in an 'oral–aural event world'.[21] The transition from an oral to a chirographic and ultimately to a typographic culture has radically altered our experience of time. In societies whose culture is predominantly oral there is no temporal dislocation between the production and consumption of communicative acts since co-presence is required for their realization. This implies the location of meaning in the body, and in the present, since meaning is given in real time through words and gestures rather than being stored in the mind, or in exterior artefacts, for formulation or decoding at other moments. It is for this reason that, according to José Gil, 'tribal people have no need to interpret the unconscious meaning of signs and symbolic acts – they carry them in their bodies'.[22]

When it comes to the place of the dead in traditional societies an alternative to the Durkheimian model also exists. In traditional societies the dead are present in the world of the living, according to some accounts, so that the past is not merely reproduced in each generation but actually endures.[23] The living and the dead do not occupy separate temporal locations from this perspective. Rather than ensuring that all links between the living and the dead are irremediably severed, time allows active connections to be maintained by folding back on itself. The living and the dead are cohabitants, albeit with different rights and powers, of a single time environment, in which the dead are 'guarantors of life and sources of power',[24] and 'beings with a full role to play, worthy partners in exchange'.[25] It is this quality of temporal reversibility that, above all else, is seen to distinguish traditional temporal experience from that which succeeded it in modernity in these accounts. In contemporary society the dead are definitively absent and we are waiting to join them, not as partners, but in an absurd and final annihilation.[26] This inclusion of the dead in the world of the living radically affects the relationship of traditional peoples to the future as much as to the past. They are not embarked on a journey that points only in the direction of the future, and culminates in a singular death, but instead face backwards as they move forward in time, incorporating what passes into the present rather than simply leaving it behind. As Gil puts it, 'because their vector of the future is turned toward the past – toward the dead, toward ancestors – [they] have history ('stories') without historicity'.[27]

These differing perspectives on traditional temporality suggest that it can be understood as cyclical in character, with an emphasis placed on the importance of recursive features, but it can also be viewed as resting on a dynamic relationship to time in a lived present in which the body plays a vital part. It will be argued below that the experience of time in modernity also rests on a continuous interplay between structure and immediacy centred on the body, and that understanding this is crucial to understanding the temporality of intoxication. However, before drawing out these affinities between temporal experience in traditional societies, temporal experience in modern societies and the temporality of intoxication, it is first necessary to highlight the distinct temporal context that modernity has given rise to.

The experience of time in modernity

It is widely accepted, in both the classical canon and in more contemporary theorizing, that our relationship to time has undergone a radical transformation in the conditions of modernity.[28] What has proved less easy to agree upon is the significance and scope of this transformation. However, on one point there is a degree of consensus and that is around the characterization of time in modernity as linear rather than cyclical. This implies an experience of time in which events are radically separated from one another at different points on a single line, a line that runs from the past to the future and is in a state of continuous extension. The source of this new form of time has been identified both with the aspirations of post-Enlightenment culture and with the artefacts that this culture has given rise to. It is seen as the product of a rationalist ontology that has endowed time with an objective and independent existence. In more concrete terms, it is a product of the devices, clock and machine, which facilitate the measurement and maintenance of this newly constituted reality. This new form of time has variously been construed as an alien and alienating imposition and as an opportunity to make the future in new ways freed from the shackles of tradition. These differing interpretations of modern temporality will be considered in turn.

The experience of time in traditional societies is intimately bound up with bodily existence, attuned to the wider cycles of natural recurrence and linked to the sacred. In contrast, time in modernity has been re-imagined as a universal and standardized environment that is liberated from both tradition and the cycles of nature. As Anthony Giddens, the British sociologist, has observed, modernity has led to the 'creation of a standardized "past" and a universally applicable "future"' that ushers in a single shared temporality for the whole of humanity.[29] An important consequence of this systematic objectification of time is that the body has been occluded as a potential source of temporal experience and temporal meaning. Time now lies beyond embodied events of change and recurrence and is often experienced as an abstraction. Conceived of in this new way, time has become available for contemplation and manipulation at a cognitive level and has been reified as the ultimate measure of all things. The existence of this uniform temporal framework has been foundational for the proliferation of rationally ordered projects that define the enterprise of modernity. As well as meeting a technical need for ever more precise quantifications of duration, this new form of time also fulfils social and organizational tasks. From the vast durations of the geologist or astronomer to the infinitesimal intervals of near-instantaneous electronic communications time has been brought within the realm of the known and assigned a definite place. This way of appropriating time has facilitated an accelerated pace of existence in the conditions of modernity and post-modernity as ever shorter intervals are accounted for and put to use. Once time is amenable to easy and accurate measurement in this way its role is also assured as a boundary for the manifold 'finite games' of society within which rationally ordered projects are undertaken. This is so because it is only when the game is known to be over that a winner can be declared and the next game begins. Most activities in contemporary society are conducted between exacting temporal limits, whether these are set by the ninety minutes of the football match or the longer cycles that govern the electoral process.

The existence of these 'finite games' and the overlapping deadlines they set imposes a compartmentalized structure on temporal experience in contemporary society.[30] The implications of this new temporality for the ways in which time is perceived will now be considered before going on to assess the limits to these effects posed by embodied experience.

Machinic temporality

Time in modernity has been understood as being at odds with both the living and the dead.[31] It consigns the latter to an irretrievable past, while it enslaves the living – who had formerly been attuned only to each other, to nature and to the cosmos – to the rhythms of the machine. Modernity runs on a machinic temporality. From the monstrous steam-powered threshing machine in Hardy's *Tess of the D'Urbervilles* to the French philosopher Michel Foucault's prototypical modern institutions (the prison, the school, the factory and the hospital) the functioning of a machinic temporality is evident.[32] All modern technologies and social arrangements operate on a mechanized clock time and would be inconceivable without it. The fundamental role of the machine in the production of this temporality is described by José Gil in the following way:

> the machine, and machines generally incorporate time. Pulleys, wheels, pistons, rods – their mechanical movement reduces subjective and collective temporality to a homogeneous quantitative time, by scanning and secreting a linear time.[33]

The spectre of humanity subjugated to blind mechanized forces has haunted the modern imagination from the dawn of the industrial era. One of the most potent symbols of this anxiety is found in the idea of a temporality that is impervious to human concerns. The machine and the clock provide interchangeable symbols for an inhuman social order that threatens to supplant the natural rhythms of life.[34]

The clock transforms time into an object that occupies space, opening the way for its assimilation to a law of general equivalence that renders everything identical and interchangeable. This change replaces quality with quantity as the principle measure of existence.[35] This assimilation of time to a generalized equivalence finds its apotheosis in the maxim 'time is money' with all the promise this formula holds for a future of devalued and objectified human interactions. When time itself succumbs to commodification in this way it becomes something that people wish to hoard. As the French cultural theorist Jean Baudrillard puts it, the 'infinity of capital passes into the infinity of time'.[36] However, while ultimately time may be the only thing we have, it is certainly not something we can possess.[37] As Heidegger reminds us, '[a]long with the certainty of death goes the indefiniteness of its "when"', mocking any ambitions we might have to control time and postpone this 'when' to a moment of our choosing.[38] Nevertheless, the struggle to control and extend time continues, manifested in the proliferating regimes of diet, surgery, exercise and cosmetics that promise to maintain, or even increase, our stock of time.[39] When time is experienced as a resource that should be accumulated or preserved it loses its savour as the passage of the unique or the return of the familiar and becomes instead a series of identical segments.

As well as taking on the character of a possession, time in the context of modern life operates as a rigid discipline that is simultaneously external to the individual and at the same time necessarily internalized.[40] To be attuned to the accelerated rhythms produced by this modern temporal discipline requires a bodily attitude that is characterized by constant attention and continuous fine-grained adjustments to environmental cues, particularly in urban settings. The activities of driving a car or shopping at a supermarket are only the most obvious examples of a ubiquitous temporal demand exerted by our surroundings. This demand takes the form of needing to continuously monitor and respond to a rapidly changing environment. Even to watch television successfully requires a degree of steady attention and relative postural stasis, however minimally engaging the actual content of the programmes may be. Television continually emits linear narratives that prompt our attention; because it is only through knowing what has just 'happened' that the endless succession of images remains intelligible. Responding to these kinds of cues does not so much involve the exercise of rational decision making at a conscious level, since, according to Merleau-Ponty, the French phenomenologist, these responses are semi-automatic, but instead requires a degree of availability, an openness to occupation.[41] The rapid oscillations of the modern environment constantly seize our attention and occupy our time with a sense of frenetic urgency. Stimuli that exist without any discernible connection to our needs have come to supplant the temporal rhythms of nature which formerly structured the organic experience of time in traditional societies.[42]

The 'filling' and 'emptying' of time in modernity

If the transition to modernity has involved the replacement of 'recurrent social systems' with 'changing social systems' this move to incessant change has affected the experience of time in two important respects.[43] First, it has 'filled up' time, because continuous change requires continuous activity for its realization and this leads to a 'constant sense of busyness, of never being unavailable, of always being on message … [which] is accompanied by an intolerance of waiting'.[44] A second, and even more distressing, consequence of the permanent innovation that has come to characterize contemporary society is that the volume 'of what remains to be done and the possibilities which cannot be realized far exceed what can be fitted in'.[45] This superabundance of available tasks makes it impossible to assimilate the culture we inhabit, and, according to Simmel, lends a tragic character to modernity.[46] Davies, writing in a medical context, has speculated on the effects of these twin pressures on the modern individual in the following terms:

> Rooted deep in the psyche of people living in advanced industrialized nations is a conception of time that encourages its protagonists to exercise control over its 'passing', make plans for its presence, and find activities and thoughts to 'fill' it in order that it will not be 'wasted'.[47]

This transforms time into a scarce resource that must be utilized as fully as possible before it passes out of existence. The activities that fill time come to occupy consciousness to the exclusion of time itself, making it something we do rather than something whose passage we witness and inhabit. As Walter Benjamin, the German cultural theorist, has remarked, 'the time has passed when time did not matter'.[48]

However, time in modernity is not only 'filled up' with activity, with anxiety and with the anticipation of death, it is simultaneously emptied of experience and meaning. Since labour 'as pure and simple presence/occupation' has become all pervasive it is no longer possible to distinguish between work and its opposite, 'free time', since both imply the 'same mobilisation and the same investment'.[49] Time in these circumstances loses its connection with distinct experiences and becomes a single undifferentiated mass. In relation to this development, Ahmadi has perceptively noted the semantic shift which has occurred in the connotations which the term 'experience' can evoke. Previously experience designated a slow accretion associated with an individual's maturation whereas now it is linked to the 'intense moment' that can break through the 'monotony of novelty' which characterizes everyday existence. Experience has become definitively associated with the energies of youth rather than the wisdom of age and a search for extremes and intensities that, it is believed, can re-establish contact with an authentic core through the body's sensations.[50] Participation in extreme sports, the restless urge to travel to exotic locations and the desire to use ever more potent psychoactive drugs can all readily be attributed to the emptying of time in everyday life. With all narratives of progress now discredited, and the past offering no guide to the future, people have been left becalmed in a featureless sea of time where change certainly occurs but any sense of meaning or direction is entirely absent.[51]

The promise of an open future

The advent of a conspicuously modern temporality has not only been associated with a dystopic vision of loss and alienation but also with the promise of an open future whose eventual character can, in part at least, be determined by our own endeavours. Influenced by the American philosopher

G.H. Mead's work on time and change, theories that foreground the role of choices 'made in the present by individuals in interaction' have been propounded by theorists such as Anthony Giddens.[52] The loosening of ties of custom and tradition opens the way to a future that is actively created rather than being largely inherited from previous generations from this perspective. Instead of being taken up with reproducing the past the present is now to be taken up with inventing the future. Through the action of 'disembedding mechanisms' this future can no longer be derived from the past so its eventual form must remain uncertain. In these circumstances an ability to reflexively adapt to new information becomes of paramount importance. This view of our relationship to time is predicated on the idea that 'people's reflections upon the circumstances, rules and consequences of their actions can have an impact on their future lines of conduct'.[53] With failure to adapt adequately to incessant change as an ever present danger, the era of 'life as a planning project' commences.[54] The burdens and opportunities that this new open future brings are summed up in the idea that risk has replaced fate in the human imagination as the principle that governs our relationship to the future. While the project of 'colonising the future' may mean leaving the past behind it 'emphatically does not mean succumbing to the allure of the present',[55] which is to be entirely taken up with 'self reflexive narrative production and lifestyle choices'.[56] This emphasis on the role of the future in assigning meaning to the present marks the ascension of linear time from the status of ontological reality, which this discussion of modern temporality began with, to that of normative ideal.

The idea that projective activities focused on the constantly receding horizon of the future are the only legitimate occupation effectively evacuates the lived present of any independent meaning. In addition, because time is apprehended only at a cognitive level in this model, and only as a projected future, the body is effectively de-temporalized. The significance for temporal experience of both the past and the present is discounted in this one-way street to the future in which the body is understood as being merely the instrument of a self-present consciousness in pursuit of rational objectives.[57] Nevertheless, by emphasizing a future that is inherently unknowable in advance and the role of the individual in its creation this approach is valuable in a number of respects. It suggests that people are actively engaged with their environment and that they recombine elements from it in novel ways as they move forward in time. In addition, it maintains that the outcome of this process cannot be fully deduced from what is already in existence. Finally, if these points are conceded, it could be argued that this approach also implicitly acknowledges that there are some limits to sociological explanation.

Modern temporality has been understood as both a source of alienation and as affording new freedoms, but it has invariably been conceptualized as linear in nature and as universal in scope. This implies a radical discontinuity between temporal experiences in modern societies and those in traditional societies. Some theoretical difficulties raised by this assumption will be outlined below before going on to propose a more embodied conception of temporality that connects the experience of time in traditional societies with that in modern societies, without assuming their identity.

The antinomies of sociological time

The temporal perspectives which have been considered in this chapter provide valuable insights into the origins and nature of temporal experience. However, by linking temporal experience to particular forms of society in a historical time frame they risk producing a simple binary that suggests one experience of time for traditional societies and another for modernity. The cyclical time of traditional societies and modern linear time are defined by the enumeration of mutually exclusive characteristics in these accounts. This has the effect of consigning certain temporal experiences (such as contact with the sacred or the co-presence of ancestors) to non-western forms of society, while simultaneously denying other temporal experiences deemed to be more typical of modernity (such as change and development) to previous or other societies.[58] When the presence of temporal features that are characteristic of one era or type of society are acknowledged in the 'wrong' place they can only be understood as a residue of what existed before or as an intimation of what is to come. In other words, such events can only be interpreted in relation to a different temporal moment and never in their own right.

The significance of this temporal dichotomization is that it tends to overlook the body as a continuing source of temporal experience and meaning. If a more embodied conception of time is adopted, traditional and modern temporalities can be seen as contiguous rather than incommensurate, without effacing the very real changes that have occurred in temporal experience. So far we have focused on the temporal characteristics that differentiate traditional and modern societies. By locating time in the body it is also possible to discern important continuities in the way temporal experience is constituted.

From bodies in time to time in the body

By making time linear, measurable and universal, modernity has also made time useful. The price for this usefulness is that time is often experienced as both arbitrary and relentless. Time no longer refers either to the body or to the world but only to itself. As an abstract conception it orders existence by distributing objects and events in a uniform manner to points on a single all-encompassing grid. However, as pervasive as the influence of this new objectified linear time may be it is never manifested in an absolute form at the level of embodied experience. Linear time in practice is constantly relativized by embodied events of change and recurrence. The material conditions of our existence and the temporal representations that prevail in our society are in a state of continual interaction centred on the body and the present. In traditional societies the influence of the past reaches its limit and is remade by embodied events in a lived present. In modern societies the influence of linear time also reaches a limit in the body and is remade by events in the lived present. The cyclical temporality of traditional societies and the linear time of modernity both structure temporal experience by making it universal. The body particularizes time by sedimenting a past that is its own and by opening onto an unknown and eventful future that is unique.

Evanescent events that occur in a lived present are constantly assimilated as part of wider temporal structures by being assigned a meaning as part of a tradition or assigned a place in the grid of linear time. Conversely, elements that figure in a tradition or occupy a specific place in the flow of time may be experienced at any moment as a unique event in a lived present. According to Deleuze and Guattari the experience of time in all periods and under all social arrangements is composed of elements that are structural or recursive in nature and elements that come into being on the threshold of the unknown.[59] These complementary elements of temporal experience which exist in a state of continual transformation one into the other in the body are labelled by them as *Aeon* and *Chronos*. *Aeon* refers to that impossible moment of becoming when the lived present is experienced in its plenitude, but only on condition that it is experienced without awareness, while *Chronos* is the time of knowledge that assigns each moment an identity and places it in a relationship with other moments. *Aeon* is characterized as:

> the indefinite time of the event, the floating line that knows only speeds and continually divides that which transpires into an already-there that is at the same time not-yet-here, a simultaneous too late and too early, a something that is going to happen and has just happened … the time of the pure event or of becoming which articulates relative speeds and slownesses independently of the chronometric or chronological values that time assumes in the other modes.[60]

Chronos, by contrast, is defined as: ‘the time of measure that situates things and persons, develops a form, and determines a subject’.[61]

In the context of the sacrificial economy of intoxication that was analysed in chapters 2 and 3, *Aeon* describes the moment of forgetting on which the possibility of the gift depends, whereas *Chronos* marks the calculated duration that allows the contract to be enforced. By focusing on the interplay between *Aeon* and *Chronos* in the body it is possible to relate the experience of intoxication in contemporary society to the experience of time in traditional societies. However, this does not imply an equivalence or identity of temporal experience between the two. Temporal experience remains essentially heterogeneous in character due to the temporal situation of the individual body. An embodied temporality resists any final reduction to either diachronic or synchronic explanation. Between that which already exists (structure) and that which is yet to exist (becoming) is 'the space of the life of the body'.[62] For José Gil structure and becoming are represented at the extreme by the caricature and the figure of the monster. The caricature 'reduces the expressiveness of the body to a single sequence of gestures … and presents the despotic sign monopolizing the body' while the figure of the monster 'shows nature – the body – setting itself up as a signifier without the help of (and against) culture … the irruption of the individual asignifying body in social space'.[63] The caricature is the image of the body divested of temporal change and subject to an endless recurrence while the figure of the monster depicts a pure becoming in the present that resists all structural influence. The caricature and the figure of the monster mark the unsustainable limits of temporal experience, *Aeon* and *Chronos* in pure form. In contemporary society these limits find exemplary expression in the practice of science (structure) and the desire for intoxication (becoming).

The scientific predilection for a de-temporalized body is graphically illustrated by Twine in a fascinating account of the practice of phrenology and its related pseudo-scientific disciplines. The 'science' of physiognomy, which maintains that the underlying character of a person is revealed by fixed facial characteristics, was pioneered by Lavater. Lavater established his discipline in opposition to pathognomy, which is concerned with the dynamics of facial movement and expression as indicators of emotion. The use of a limited set of features to designate an equally limited set of character traits ensured that interpretation remained firmly in the hands of the physiognomist who could skilfully decode all facial expressions according to a predetermined pattern. This method was later refined still further with the use of the silhouette, whose advantages Lavater described with enthusiasm:

> Silhouettes alone have extended my physiognomic knowledge, more than any kind of portrait … We see in it neither motion nor light, nor colour, nor rising nor cavity … The silhouette arrests the attention: by fixing it on the exterior contours alone, it simplifies the observation, which becomes by that more easy and accurate … The silhouette is positive and incontestable proof of the science of physiognomics.[64]

In case it might be thought that these physiognomic procedures are confined to a field that has long been discredited as unscientific it should be pointed out that to still and de-temporalize the body, in the interests of science, is common in even the most venerable disciplines. In medicine, for example, first the autopsy and later the scan have been employed to produce order and intelligibility where once the mysterious and the unknown reigned.[65]

In contrast to the scientific ambition to free the body from time and change so that it might be known in its entirety and without remainder, intoxication expresses the opposite desire, to be liberated from knowledge and structure in a moment of pure becoming that leaves no discernible trace. Between the cadaver and the monster lies the temporality of the living body and the time of intoxication. In the next chapter the interview material gathered for the book will be analysed to draw out some of the interactions of *Aeon* and *Chronos* that intoxication gives rise to in the body.

5 From bodies in time to time in the body

In the last chapter the temporality of traditional societies was compared to that of modern societies. It was suggested that in traditional societies the body acts as a locus for temporal experience and that people in these societies collectively produce and inhabit a singular temporality. This singular temporality is invoked through ritual performances that serve to integrate social and natural patterns of change and recurrence. As a consequence of this harmonious relationship to time, distinctions between past and present, structure and immediacy, sacred and profane durations remain fluid and indistinct at an experiential level in these societies. This organic experience of time was seen to contrast sharply with the temporal demands and assumptions of modernity. In modern societies time is understood and often experienced as something that exists independently of bodily existence and of natural patterns of change and recurrence. The sense that time is recoverable has given way to a belief that time moves inexorably forwards leaving the past in its wake and primordial rhythms have been replaced by a superabundance of arbitrary alternatives. Time has become useful in the regulation and coordination of activities in the conditions of modernity but only at the cost of being emptied of all intrinsic meaning and value. However, it was also argued that the organic temporality which prevailed in traditional societies can never be entirely supplanted by the linear and segmented temporality of modernity, despite its pretensions to both universality and objectivity. The body remains as a source and measure of temporal experience, both by incorporating the past through embodied memories of gesture and sensation and by opening onto an unknown future. Embodied events such as intoxication restore temporal experience to the body and by doing so reconnect it to the rhythms of the world and the presence of the sacred. The significance of intoxication for our understanding of temporal experience will be explored by analysing the interview material gathered for the book from a phenomenological perspective.

The body at once articulates the past and transforms it in a ceaseless becoming that is manifested at an experiential level through events such as intoxication. While the past always presents itself in an organized form, whether as habitus, memory, cycle or sequence, the present is experienced as something particular that remains to be organized and assigned a definite meaning. In everyday life in contemporary society the temporal schemas that serve to organize experience predominate and the present is constantly assimilated to these categories in a more or less seamless fashion. Intoxication, by contrast, tends towards the interruption of this organized condition by making the unprecedented nature of the lived present fully apparent. However, this experience of becoming in the lived present can only ever be ephemeral. Even the most heterogeneous experiences of becoming are assimilated in time at a structural level by being assigned a place in relation to other events. The meaning of intoxication as an embodied event is to be found both in the uniqueness of the lived present and in the relationship of this present to a wider temporal context that has social, historical and primordial dimensions. Each of these temporal aspects of intoxication, the moment of becoming and the relationship of this moment to wider temporal structures will be considered below, and their interactions described.

Sacrificing the future in the present

Alterations in the way time is perceived and inhabited are central to the experience of intoxication and to its social meaning in contemporary society. Intoxication is an embodied event that occurs only in the lived present and is always unanticipated at an experiential level. This is so because the transition from sobriety to intoxication marks an abrupt change from an everyday world of meaning to a different 'finite world of meaning' that is incommensurate with the everyday. The passage between these distinct worlds of meaning is not a gradual transformation but rather has the character of a leap that can only be recognized as such after it has already been made.[1] While intoxication may be carefully planned for and expected at a specified hour its presence as a sensual reality remains impossible to anticipate. As an embodied event intoxication is therefore to be understood primarily by reference to a lived present and the momentary transformations that divide the future from the past.[2] As event, intoxication occurs in and is oriented to the lived present, as opposed to the tasks of everyday life which are oriented to the future.

The temporal changes that have accompanied modernity have tended to defer experience to the future and to displace it from the body. By making time linear and calculable the importance of a past that is simply left behind is diminished while the future takes on a new allure once its presence can be planned for effectively.[3] As the future has not yet come into existence it can be envisaged in an infinite number of different guises, any one of which may, in principle, be brought into existence through planning and labour. This temporal orientation towards the future forecloses experience in the lived present by making it merely the first step in a projected sequence of actions that has a determinate outcome. A consequence of relating to time in this manner is that experience is subjected to constant deferrals. The present is given over to activities that can only come to fruition at some more or less distant point in the future, a point that is likely to be endlessly postponed as new futures are imagined and new projects begun.[4] As well as deferring experience to the future these imagined alternatives and adopted projects create a cornucopia of possibilities, commitments, deadlines and schedules that tend to fragment temporal experience in everyday life. Whatever we do, the spectre of all those things we could or should have done instead haunts us, giving the present an aura of incompleteness and insubstantiality. We strive to overcome the sense of existential unease this situation produces by working towards the completion of our projects, little realizing that it is precisely our projects that give rise to our unease.

In contrast to the way in which the present is typically experienced in contemporary society, as a series of displacements and deferrals, intoxication allows the present to be inhabited in its plenitude. It is only when the present is given up as something that is ours to possess and utilize that it can be experienced as something that has an existence and meaning beyond our conscious intentions and desires. By sacrificing the present as a resource that serves a real or imagined future, and surrendering to the embodied temporality of intoxication, the presence and passage of time can be witnessed as a palpable reality. The recovery of the present that is engendered through intoxication is evident at a number of different levels in the accounts people gave of their experiences. These clues to the way intoxication is oriented to the lived present will now be outlined, in this section, and then illustrated in the following sections with material drawn from the interviews.

First, immersion in the present is manifested as a forgetting, of both the past and the future. This forgetting becomes apparent only at the point where self-conscious awareness returns and efforts are made to locate and account for time that has elapsed. The point when the temporal limits of everyday existence enter consciousness is often a harbinger that the forgetting of intoxication is coming to an end and that a return to relative sobriety is imminent. Second, the behaviours, both passive and active, that are characteristic of intoxication demonstrate an attunement to the present. Those who are intoxicated generally eschew purposeful activity and so, by implication, a concern for the future. A passive or aimless demeanour and a predisposition to spontaneity typically replace the active and directed activities of everyday life. When those who are intoxicated do engage in identifiable activities they are likely to be within those realms of experience that have an affinity with the present, such as dancing, music or forms of play that are 'infinite', that is without temporal boundaries.[5] Third, since intoxication is experienced and communicated only through the body and in the present, in order for it to be shared co-presence is essential. In contemporary society there is a growing trend toward disembodied and delayed communicative exchanges that is exemplified by the use of the telephone, a poignant device which both facilitates contact between people and implies their separation.[6] This dislocating effect has been amplified by other newer technologies, like television and the World Wide Web. In these media the distinction between what has already happened and what is happening now is blurred, and in any case we can always catch up with events later so the significance of the present is diminished.[7] The overall effect of these changes is that time is now located outside ourselves as an objective reality that structures our lives while our experience of time is constantly displaced from the present. As a social and embodied experience intoxication resists the temporal dislocations that are characteristic of so many communicative acts in modernity.

The centrality of the lived present to the embodied experience of intoxication appears, then, in people's accounts as a forgetting, in the affinity of intoxication with evanescent activities and in the requirement for co-presence. These markers that intoxication is oriented to the present will be considered in turn. Once the significance of the lived present to the experience of intoxication has been established, the role of the body in sedimenting a past, and the importance of this to the experience of intoxication, will then be examined.

Intoxication and forgetting

To be absorbed in the immediate sensations of the lived present is a forgetful condition. Conversely, at the instant the present is remembered and becomes an object of conscious attention that present has already been consigned irretrievably to the past, as Alfred Schutz, the Austrian phenomenologist and sociological theorist, explains:

> the whole present … and also the vivid present of our Self, is inaccessible for the reflective attitude. We can only turn to the stream of our thought as if it had stopped with the last grasped experience. In other words, self-consciousness can only be experienced *modo preterito*, in the past tense.[8]

Intoxication fulfils a desire to move beyond a self-consciousness that fixes existence as something already known and allows it to be experienced in the 'present tense' as a state of becoming. Rather than events being experienced as something that happened *then* from a separate vantage point that is *now,* in other words in a linear fashion, intoxication invokes the present as something that is simultaneously *now* and *always.* In the following passage, in which Geoff recalls an experience with the drug ketamine, the centrality of the lived present to the experience of intoxication is made explicit:

> 'Once on it I thought that I was a very small person controlling a very large body … you just think that's the way it's always been … you forget that you have a normal life and a normal sized body that you control in a normal way.'

The complete falling away of the past and the future that is implied by 'that's the way it's always been' and 'you forget' is particularly striking in this case as ketamine is a drug that is very short acting, with its effects typically lasting no more than thirty to ninety minutes from onset – as measured by the clock that is. This immersion in the lived present in which time becomes singular, now and always, is a possibility of our embodied existence that lies beyond conscious intentions. The lived present of intoxication allows a unique conjuncture to be experienced, where the history of an individual body is transformed as it interacts with its environment. This point of becoming, which is at once the culmination of the past and a new beginning, effectively abolishes distinctions between past and present at an experiential level. However, while the moment of intoxication may be experienced as now and always it is nevertheless also transient. In the following passage Michael describes an experience with magic mushrooms that captures the transition from absorption in a vivid present in which 'you forget' to an awareness that the moment of forgetting has already passed:

> 'I was able to look down into the earth and it was made of patterns coloured patterns geometric patterns that I could see down through like diamonds it was like a jewel and I saw right inside it until somebody spoke to me and then it went [clicks fingers] and then it had gone and it was just muddy earth … '

The shift in tone as Michael's hallucinatory vision suddenly vanishes in a return to earth, that is at once literal and symbolic, marks the transition from a world that is being discovered anew to a world that is all too familiar. In other words, it is the transition from the realm of the sacred to a profane order of existence, from a lived present to a present that has already been organized by the past. When an interruption in the flow of time such as this occurs the lived present is transformed into a remembered past. An event that is now in the past can enter into history through language in the form of narrative and so take its place in relation to other events. The recognition that an event has passed can take the form of nostalgia, as in this excerpt from Joanna's interview where she recalls categorizing an early experience with the drug LSD in this way:[9]

> 'I remember at the time sort of having tears in my eyes and saying "I'm never going to be this happy again" so I labelled that at the time as being my best ever drug experience and I certainly haven't ever been happier than that.'

While forgetting is an essential prerequisite of intoxication it must be a forgetting that also remembers. Again the figure of the *impossible* appears in the need for a forgetting that is absolute but nevertheless retains at some level that which has been forgotten. Intoxication is a forgetting that can forget itself and in doing so can move beyond forgetting towards oblivion. Rather than time merely passing unnoticed in an absorbed present, in which 'hours can pass in what seems like seconds', as Tony put it when describing his experiences with LSD, a forgetting that is too complete can lead to a sense that time has instead been lost altogether. In the following passages first Peter and then Steven describe occasions when seeking to recover the present through intoxication actually ended in their losing all sense of the present:

> 'I woke up just outside L in a field with a policeman shaking me and I'm cut to pieces naked sitting down in the middle of a field going "Ahrr?" and that's the only time I woke up and I thought "what the fuck" and I'd lost twenty four hours so in twenty four hours I'd gone eight miles from where I was and even to this day I still haven't got a clue how I got the eight miles or what I done in-between.'
>
> 'I don't remember blacking out anywhere but I must have because I remember you know there was definitely a hole between the party and back to his place.'

The limit point of forgetting, which jeopardizes the present as an experience that can be recalled, even coincides at times with apparently purposeful activities, as the following passage from Philip's interview, where he describes an occasion when he was using opiates and the tranquillizer Temazepam, suggests:

> 'a two hour chunk just completely missing walking all the way to B got some more drugs out of the chemist sold them somehow spent the money as well because I didn't have that much more cash on me and then gone all the way back to G and knew absolutely nothing about it … '

As well as forfeiting the present as an experience that can be recalled, a forgetting that is too complete can also lead to real practical dangers, as Simon confirmed when recounting some of his early experiences with alcohol:

> 'hanging off the bridge by my fingertips … pissed as a cunt couldn't walk and a couple of my mates pulled me back over … '

More prosaically, the forgetting in the present that intoxication can engender may result in the boundaries that demarcate the obligations of everyday existence being exceeded, as Robert and Karen discovered after devoting time to the lived present of intoxication. In the first excerpt Robert describes waking up on a Monday morning after a weekend of intensive heroin use while in the second passage Karen recalls an impromptu 'crack session' with an old friend:

> 'I came to in my bed before the morning just still absolutely fucked but knowing I'm meant to be at work.'

> 'you know hundreds of pounds worth of rocks we did that night and yeah I had to be at work at ten o'clock in the morning and at quarter to ten I was still round his house at F and we still had a little bit of a rock left and I was still in my clothes know what I mean I just hadn't gone home hadn't gone you know I'd just been there we'd been talking and doing crack all night you know and we were really pissed 'cos of all the vodka and stuff like that and I got to work and suddenly I had to be straight ... '

To become intoxicated is to be absorbed in the present and yet to become too intoxicated is to forfeit the present at an experiential level. Intoxication presents an insoluble dilemma by demanding an absolute commitment to the present while at the same time requiring that a degree of self-presence is somehow retained if the present is to be witnessed.

If intoxication can shade into oblivion through a forgetting that is too complete, it is equally vulnerable to a remembering that makes absorption in the present impossible. Joanna provided an account of her changing experiences with LSD, which again highlights the importance of forgetting in the present to the experience of intoxication:

> 'I suddenly realized that I was tripping and that it had had its effect but some part of my mind had been able to resist it and one of the things that I've always loved most about acid is that it seems to completely break down the barriers between yourself and everything else so you just become part of your environment which of course can be a bit scary if it's not a good environment ... becoming part of everything else is one of the things I absolutely love about acid and it takes you out of yourself because everything is so beautiful or so scary or you know so engaging and so different that you're just not even aware of yourself any more so it's your kind of the illusion of self disappears for a while ... I realized that I'd got to the point where that didn't happen anymore that like somehow my mind could keep onto my everyday conception of things.'

When the experience of initiating novel events in the lived present, which the French philosopher Jacques Derrida describes as the greatest satisfaction humans can know, succumbs to familiarity, all possibility of transcendence and renewal through contact with the unanticipated is lost.[10] As a consequence, the mundane and routine can assert itself in the very midst of intoxication, as Tony acknowledged in this passage:

> 'certainly in recent years because you know with drugs like cocaine there have been instances where I felt the need not to sit around and talk bollocks until five in the morning and repeat myself over and over again with people who were doing exactly the same thing.'

In this instance, using cocaine does not succeed in propelling Tony beyond the familiar into a present that is experienced as unique. Instead, the events Tony participates in remain firmly within a linear series of identifiably similar episodes giving a sense of meaningless repetition rather than renewal, of 'doing exactly the same thing'. The tragedy of this state of disenchantment, which is commonly labelled as addiction when it is prolonged, is not, perhaps, that individuals become intoxicated too much or too often but that they no longer become truly intoxicated at all.

Intoxication and activity

The commitment to an evanescent reality that is indispensable for intoxication is typically manifested at a behavioural level in a passive or undirected demeanour or by engagement in activities that have an affinity with the present. These types of activity which are characteristic of intoxication will now be considered.

A recurrent feature that characterized people's accounts of their experiences of intoxication is the lack of any stated objective beyond becoming intoxicated. Intoxication appears as an end in itself, an aim without a purpose that contains its own meaning in the present rather than finding it in the future or deriving it from the past. First Tony and then Karen gave succinct expression to the self-contained nature of intoxicated states in these short excerpts where they recall some experiences with alcohol and cannabis:

> 'just drinking to get drunk that was the whole aim of it really … '

> 'you'd have your dub reggae going and everybody just got caned … '

When the present no longer serves the future, purpose and direction fall away and the present itself becomes the primary focus as something that is witnessed from moment to moment in its passing. This is an 'infinite' mode of engagement in which behaviours are renewed in order to sustain the moment rather than to attain a specified end that lies beyond the moment.[11] In the following excerpts first Geoff and then Robert describe what they would typically be 'doing' while becoming intoxicated:

> 'sitting around talking and smoking spliffs … '

> 'wandering around smoking dope stopping off here and there … '

What these activities have in common is that they can be taken up or left off without consequences since they have no intended outcome. These affronts to the idea of time as a resource that should be spent usefully and productively recur throughout the interviews. The example of some people's behaviour at music festivals and rave events, which a number of individuals identified as ideal venues for intoxication, is instructive in this respect. While the musicians and DJs perform at specified times, in accordance with a published schedule, there is no requirement, or even expectation, that those who attend will actually see these performances, which are deemed to be optional or even irrelevant to participation in the rave or festival as an event, as this report by Geoff makes clear:

> 'Yeah I mean we just got in there got some acid straight away kind of spontaneously and then just let everything flow from there rather than having the kind of [festival] we didn't take tents it wasn't the kind of [festival] where you go there and think oh let's pitch our tent here what bands are on at what time it's just a do acid and be completely care free about it and whatever happens will happen.'

Whatever the level of spontaneity involved, a willingness to accept, or at least to be open to, the unexpected possibilities that intoxication brings seems to entail a certain generosity with time. Time has to be given without any certainty about what will happen, or, in many cases, even how long it will take to happen. Although it is always a matter of degree, this relatively open-ended commitment of time contrasts with the circumscribed allocations of time typical of most leisure and social activities in modernity. Intoxication stands opposed to activities such as sport that usually occur within a predictable time frame where the important thing is that the game is concluded when the time that has been allocated to it has elapsed.

Although individuals clearly participate in the initiation, and prolongation, of intoxication, the *state* of intoxication has the quality of an event that is happening *to* them rather than the quality of an activity that is being undertaken *by* them. It is this eventful quality of intoxication as something that happens *to* people rather than being something that they *do* that principally distinguishes it from everyday activities. The relationship to these eventful happenings is not that of actors who are *doing* something but that of participants *in* something, something that is not just happening 'out there' but also 'in here', and happening now. Intoxication therefore does not appear to require an attitude that is more than minimally purposeful for its realization. All that is required is the desire to sustain the moment.

Intoxication and non-linear time

There are certain elements of existence that are open to subjugation by the clock and some that enjoy a degree of immunity from this fate. Although it would be possible, for example, to sleep for shorter periods in order to allow more time for work there can be no question of sleeping *faster* to achieve the same objective. Other aspects of life and culture also occur at their own pace and in their own time, in the same way that the body stubbornly rests at a certain rate thereby defying the impositions of the clock and the ambitions of the worker. Notable in the category of events that have their own distinct temporality are music, laughter, dance and the erotic. It would simply not be meaningful to hurry to the end of a piece of music, or to dance or laugh more quickly, in order to save time. If this were attempted, at least in the case of music and dance, they would be so fundamentally altered that it would no longer be the same piece of music or dance even though it would still be composed of the same sequence of notes or steps. In other words, the meaning of these events cannot be derived from their linear form as a series that occurs in a particular order.[12] This contrasts with aspects of existence that can be accelerated or slowed without losing their identity, such as the pace of a machine or an electronic signal. The reason that music, laughter, dance and erotic events cannot be hurried or slowed if they are to retain their particular meaning is because they exist only as an evanescent reality in a luxurious present. These events unfold in the present and, being complete in themselves, are not dependent for their meaning on the past or the future; they are grasped, like metaphors, in their totality at each moment.[13] When we hear a song or a symphony, even for the first time, we do not hear it as a series of discrete notes we hear music; each note implies and makes present a definite past and a definite future that coalesce time as the music unfolds. As a consequence, these events can neither be anticipated nor recalled in the uniqueness of their occurrence, existing as they do only in the present. It is for this reason that Levi-Strauss has described music as one of the 'machines for the suppression of time'.[14]

Intoxication also enjoys an immunity to the clock similar to that shown by music, laughter, dance and eroticism because it too exists only in the moment of its occurrence and requires no projection into the future or retention of the past for its full meaning as a lived event to be realized at any particular moment. The temporal meaning of intoxication is grounded ultimately in the body's mortality, shared with other bodies, and in its particularity as it interacts with elements of the world. Each such interaction produces a distinct reality that has its own specific temporality, such that the experience of time when using one intoxicating substance is incommensurate with the experience of time when using another. In other words, the body exists and decays in time, as do other bodies, as well as producing a subjective temporal reality that is its own. The experience of intoxication allows the objective temporal location of the body and the subjective perception of time that intoxication gives rise to, to be experienced as a single temporal event. This singular temporality is resistant to both measurement and intervention. In relation to this embodied temporality clock time can be invoked only as a heuristic device to communicate changes in the viscosity and apparent duration of time that are wrought by intoxication. In the following excerpts Robert and then Sally attempt to translate the embodied temporality of intoxication into the universal language of the clock, and to reconcile the two. The first quote from Robert recalls an experience with heroin while those that follow refer respectively to Sally's experiments with magic mushrooms and LSD:

> 'maybe a couple of hours I suppose maybe a few hours but it might have all been in the space of an hour I don't know ... '
>
> 'we walked home which seemed to take hours and hours and it was only like a ten minute walk from the park ... '
>
> 'it might have only been a couple of minutes but to me it was like about two hours ... '

On occasion, the discrepancy between these different temporalities becomes the object of direct perception, as in the following passage from Michael's interview where he describes an experience with magic mushrooms:

> 'I had the feeling that time had slowed right down and that everything was moving really really really slowly but then other people would go past at what seemed like an accelerated rate that I knew was a normal rate ... so I was able to differentiate between the two and not feel at all awkward about it.'

While the viscosity of time has dramatically increased for Michael, he remains able to distinguish between the particular temporality of the body he is experiencing and the 'normal' time inhabited by others.

We continually measure our existence and activities in relation to a linear conception of time that subjects experience to the despotism of the clock, but time is also measured by embodied experiences, both in the lived present and across the life course. As José Gil has observed:

> the body plays a role of absolute measurement, of an indivisible unit of measurement. In order for this to be possible, it has to carry in itself a self-measuring capacity ... [t]hanks to this property the surveyor-body integrates into itself the 'meaning' of space without having to relate it to another standard.[15]

Since space is simply time in a different guise the 'surveyor-body' is also, by definition, a 'chronographic body' that integrates into itself the meaning of time. According to Heidegger it is this embodied temporality that corresponds to the real rather than the 'objective' temporality of the clock.[16]

While the intoxicated body may be ill-suited to the temporal demands of everyday life in modern societies it does, at times, display an extraordinary affinity with those other temporal rhythms that lie beyond the reach of linear time, such as music and dance. Many of the participants noted this synergetic relationship between intoxication and aspects of existence that have an evanescent reality. Steven, an amateur musician, mused at length on the relationship between intoxication and playing an instrument, finally concluding that it could be both disastrous and, on occasion, extraordinarily beneficial:

> 'it's lovely to play an instrument with coke [cocaine] … everything that I'd ever learnt flowed freely … '

Geoff and Roger also pointed to an affinity between the rhythms of music and certain intoxicated states such as those associated with the use of the drug ecstasy:

> 'the music was going through you you could feel the bass and the rhythm and so you were dancing you know really without even thinking about it and if you thought about stopping dancing your leg would be tapping …'
>
> 'music as well obviously when you've taken some chemicals the music is also highlighted and you tend to hear your own tunes within the tune … '

Finally, in this excerpt, Karen recalls her experiences 'top shelving it', that is, drinking alcoholic spirits and the sense of physical liberation and attunement to music it produced:

> 'absolutely dancing singing spinning about … '

This frequently mentioned association between music, dance and intoxication would not perhaps be so striking if it were not for the almost complete absence of any references in the interview material to activities that have a distinctly linear form, such as writing. Only two examples appear in the transcripts of attempts to write while intoxicated and these produced only nonsense; appropriately perhaps leaving no tangible trace of the evanescent experiences they were intended to record. In the following excerpt George recalls a fruitless attempt to leave a note for someone after taking LSD:

> 'We'd written it about four or five times and argued about it … but the next day it made absolutely no sense at all.'

Sharing the present

We are forever debarred from a self-conscious experience of 'the vivid present of our Self', since to be conscious of our self is to experience it always already in the 'past tense'. However, this is not true of our experience of other people. We can experience each other in a 'vivid simultaneity' in which our living self is mirrored in the presence of the other.[17] To experience this 'vivid simultaneity', in which 'consociates are mutually involved in one another's biography; [and] are growing older together', is one of the principle motivations for becoming intoxicated to emerge from the interviews. The French philosopher Maurice Blanchot, in a meditation on the conditions necessary for community, stresses the importance of a common mortality for authentic human communication:

> the basis of communication is not necessarily speech, or even the silence that is its foundation and punctuation, but the exposure to death, no longer my own exposure, but someone else's, whose living and closest presence is already the eternal and unbearable absence.[18]

Almost without exception, the people I interviewed volunteered narratives highlighting how significant time shared with others in a similar state of intoxication had been to them. Tony, looking back on his experiences with a range of different substances and the friendships he had made, pointed specifically to this sense of being synchronized with others in the lived present of intoxication as important:

> 'we were all kind of experiencing the same thing and you do find that you get that sort of link with people in some kind of strange ethereal way when you're doing sort of the same drugs together … '

In the same way that the meaning of music, dance, laughter or erotic events can be grasped in their totality at each moment, so too it seems the meaning of the other can be grasped in the shared present of intoxication. This is quite different from the process of learning about another person by becoming acquainted with their biography and habits over time, that is, in a linear fashion. The 'vivid simultaneity' Schutz refers to implies a different order of knowledge that has the character of a revelation, a carnal knowing as opposed to a cognitive knowing.[19]

Sharing intoxicated states, which is to say sharing the present together, was deemed to be valuable not just in establishing contact and shared intimacy at the time it occurred, but also as a basis for enduring relationships of mutual acknowledgement, as in this passage from David's transcript:

> 'seems like every serious relationship I've ever had has been based around drugs for the start of it, any time you try something else it just only lasts five minutes it's like you've got a bonding … '

For many of the participants it had also played a central part in the formation of long-term commitments. One of the people I interviewed, Karen, described the day she met her future husband and the events that led up to his proposal of marriage:

> 'bought a bottle of Jack Daniels and we went off garden hopping with this bottle of JD and got absolutely hammered terrifying experiences over people's gardens dogs chasing us security lights going on but it was hilarious and it started raining and it was just a mad day but we were just laughing and laughing and laughing … '

Another participant, Peter, also identified the shared present of intoxication as the beginning of a lasting relationship:

> 'the first time I ever seen him we were sharing a bottle of amyl nitrate and a bottle of Blue Label Vodka and we both woke up green in the morning and we seemed to have bonded for the next 15 or 20 years actually … '

However, while physical co-presence is clearly necessary in order to share the present and encounter others during intoxication, it is not in itself sufficient. An element of luck and a degree of coordination also seem to play a part, as Karen's testimony makes clear:

> 'it's not very good finding somebody that's really pissed when you're sober and vice versa I'm sure … gone there together brilliant. When you're both really really pissed brilliant for you two. I know what it looks like from the outside … '

Despite Karen's optimism there are no guarantees that 'going there together' will be 'brilliant' simply because, as Tony remarked at one point in his interview, 'you can try and control it but ultimately it isn't really within your power'. When the conditions are not propitious, being with others in a state of intoxication can obviate rather than facilitate communication, as this excerpt, in which Edward describes his feelings after taking LSD when he was younger, suggests:

> 'just sat around with a load of mates acquaintances in a room and taking this stuff and then sort of suddenly looking around at everybody and they didn't really look like the people that I knew they looked like them but they didn't seem the same any more I didn't like the look of them … '

As fragile, transient and unpredictable as moments of mutual attunement in the lived present of intoxication may be, they appear to have a special significance for those who experience them. The sense that such moments are to be treasured may derive in part at least from the fact that they can only be *received* and never deliberately made to happen, endowing them with a quality that approaches the sacred. The reward for accepting these uncertain encounters seems to be found in an experience of mutual acknowledgement that comes from sharing the present with others, as another passage, also taken from the interview with Edward, indicates:

> 'probably one of the stronger reasons why I continue to indulge would be the one of companionship … the situation when a group of people, being people that you know very well or a loose group of people that you've just met in whatever situation, but realizing you've got this sort of some kind of common, can't think what the word would be, acceptance, you know, of the moment. It doesn't need to be any sort of grand idea it's just sort of this acceptance of the moment and for that to be just what it is whether it's made into seeming like something grander or just a very

simple situation of a few people hanging out certainly some of my most inspiring times have been in those situations … '

Embodying the past

The body allows the present to be experienced in its plenitude through the initiation of novel and unintended events during intoxication. However, at the same time as the body opens onto an unknown and unknowable future it also acts as a repository for the past and in doing so shapes our future experiences of time. By a curious paradox it is the changes wrought by time in the body that, in part at least, seem to diminish the desire for temporal change through intoxication. As time passes the novel events of intoxication gradually succumb to familiarity, and in becoming better known inevitably grow less enticing. At the same time the energies and desires required to meet the intensities of the lived present that intoxication opens onto gradually decline, giving the more predictable elements of existence a new attraction. Combined with the steady accumulation of responsibilities and commitments that 'fill up' time in contemporary society, these changes wrought by time itself mean that opportunities for encountering unanticipated events in the lived present through intoxication are likely to lessen with age. These changes could of course be attributed to normative expectations concerning age appropriate behaviour at different stages in the life course, but it seems clear that the sedimenting of temporal experience in the body also plays a crucial part.[20] It is those with the most energy and for whom time is most apparently abundant, the young, who are, it seems, most willing to forget the future, at least for a time, and plunge into the lived present of intoxication. As the replenishment of energy through rest and nutrition is overtaken by its diminution through the ageing process, and time comes to seem more meagre, people perhaps grow less generous with their time and more wary of gratuitous expenditures, as these thoughts from first David and then Joanna would seem to confirm:

> 'I dunno I just don't want to stay up all night doing that any more there's just not the crowd I'm not as young as I was I don't think I could handle the headache in the morning things like that I think I've done my term for LSD I think I've seen everything I could fucking see on LSD no I turn that one down know what I mean.'

> 'I've learnt enough from experience that I say no in that situation even though when I was much younger I'd have said yes and I did have really great times from saying yes when I was younger even though obviously we did regret it sometimes but I was in a different situation then I hadn't done the drugs to the point where I was actually quite bored with them and I didn't have lots of other things in my life … it was different circumstances then and I had a lot more energy I think that's if you come down to it an awful lot of the reason was to do with having more energy

> when you're younger and you can just cope with come down and stuff like that much better.'

This temporal trajectory is evident in almost all the interviews, with the only exceptions being those who are, for the time being at least, condemned to the disenchantment produced by the habitual use of intoxicant drugs. However, for most of the people I interviewed encounters with the unknown through intoxication remain a significant, if generally less frequent, occurrence. The sense of renewal that the experience of intoxication brings comes to operate as much through the evocation of past events and the shared intimacies that accompanied these as it does by confronting the intensities of the present. At this point intoxication takes on an additional symbolic significance by demarcating moments that are exempted from other cares and devoted to savouring the present, as in these quiet moments described by first Karen and then Michael:

> 'I associate it with relaxation so you know finished a shift sort of thing I won't smoke pot if I have to work that's just pointless.'

> 'it's one of those times of day round about tea time so I'll have a spliff and I thought well I did that thing where I thought well shall I not have one … and I thought no I'll just have a spliff so I rolled a spliff while my potatoes were cooking and read the paper kind of very skimily read the paper … and I think probably had I not spent the day with R shopping then I probably wouldn't have had a spliff but it just seemed almost like a holiday.'

Conclusion

Time in modernity has often been characterized as an uninterrupted linear flow that points exclusively in the direction of a singular death, and as being alienated from both bodily experience and the natural rhythms of life. By contrast, the experience of time in traditional societies has been viewed as cyclical in form, attuned to the rhythms of nature and the cosmos and marked by an alternation between the profane concerns of everyday life and sacred periods of heightened intensity focused on the collective and the body. The analysis presented above, of individuals' accounts of their experiences of intoxication, raises doubts about these discrete temporal demarcations. When considered from a phenomenological perspective, the body can be understood as a source and measure of temporal experience in all eras and under all forms of social organization. One of the ways in which this embodied temporality manifests itself at an experiential level is through embodied events such as intoxication. Intoxication restores temporal experience to the body and reconnects it with the sacred and the natural rhythms of existence, both through an experience of becoming in the lived present and by sedimenting a particular past. However, this embodied temporality has been displaced from the centre to the periphery of social existence in the conditions of modernity. The temporality of the body is no longer bound up with wider social and natural patterns of recurrence and must find expression in those interludes when the demands of the clock are in temporary abeyance.

Having considered when intoxication occurs and explored its wider temporal significance the next two chapters will turn to the related question of defining where intoxication occurs in contemporary society. The social location of intoxication will be explored by examining the question of community and formation of liminal communities, first at a theoretical level in the next chapter and then through the analysis of interview material in Chapter 7.

6 Theorizing community

The phenomenon of voluntary intoxication points to the body as a continuing source of meaning and social change in contemporary society. Chapters 2 and 3 examined the sacrificial economy that underpins the experience of intoxication, and then the temporal dimensions of the experience were considered in chapters 4 and 5. In this and the following chapter attention will turn to the social location in which intoxication as an embodied event occurs. It will be argued that intoxication is associated with the formation of liminal communities.

The patterns of interaction and connection revealed in the interview material collected for this book presented a significant interpretive challenge. Both within and between individuals' accounts of their experiences of intoxication there appear wide variations in the kinds of relationships reported. These range from instances involving blood relatives or leading to the formation of long-term commitments to the most fleeting, but still significant, contacts with total strangers. While some people reported membership of relatively stable social groupings within which they became intoxicated these were rarely either closed or exclusive and did not appear to be essential to the experience. At certain times individuals might pursue intoxication alone only to join large crowds, many of whom were intent on the same aim, at other moments.

These patterns of interaction and connection, by cutting across boundaries of scale, duration and longevity, at first seem to defy ready categorization. However, one concept presents itself as a possible framework for comprehending these diverse findings – the notion of community. To be fitted to this task, the concept of community would clearly have to be defined differently from its established usages. These have tended to define community by looking to elements such as common identities or beliefs, involvement in institutions, dense and enduring social ties or stable locations.[1] This chapter will consider whether a definition of community that does not rely on these staple features could be viable. If it is, then this will have the twin merits of accounting for the patterns of association found in the interview material and, in doing so, of rehabilitating a concept whose usefulness, in any formulation, has frequently been called into question.[2]

Defining the limits of the community concept

There are few concepts in sociological theorizing that have proved to be as enduring, or as elusive, as the idea of community. While the importance of community as an explicit object of theoretical concern and empirical investigation may have declined in recent years, the issues it raises remain as pressing and as intractable as they ever were.[3] To ask what makes community possible is to confront the fundamental sociological problem of understanding how humans can come together in a condition of mutual acknowledgement. At a time when 'banal associations' that promise to dispense with the need for such mutual recognition appear to be in the ascendancy the urgency of addressing this problem has never been greater.[4] In addition, an analysis of the conditions that foster mutual recognition must be a prime concern since many of the conflicts and inequalities that concern society, including those of race, class and gender, can be understood as emanating from a failure to recognize and acknowledge others as alike. However, the answers that have been given to the question: 'what makes community possible?' are as diverse as they are incompatible. As long ago as 1955, in a review of 94 separate definitions of community, Hillery concluded that 'beyond the concept that people are involved in community there is no complete agreement as to the nature of community'.[5]

At one extreme the idea of community is only conceivable as the product of particular social, cultural and material conditions. The German sociologist Ferdinand Tonnies's distinction between the *gemeinschaft* and *gesellschaft* form of society, which proposes that different types of social organization produce radically different moral and motivational outlooks, provides the classic formulation of this position.[6] Lying at the opposite extreme is the view that people come together *despite* the particular social, cultural and material arrangements which they live under by discovering a common humanity or identity that transcends their social location. The French sociologist Michel Maffesoli's concept of the 'masses' or the 'people', who are endowed with an inherent capacity for sociality and solidarity, marks the limit of this position.[7] While Tonnies's approach clearly specifies a set of prerequisites for community it does so at the cost of excluding other processes by which people might come together to form non-instrumental connections. Maffesoli, by contrast, asserts that the conditions necessary for community are always present in social life but fails to delineate their operation adequately. There is a need to explore whether it is feasible to theorize the possibility of community without resorting either to the fixity of 'blood and soil' proposed by Tonnies, or to the inclusive, but vague, community of everyone, suggested by Maffessoli.

Looking to the conditions of human embodiment as a crucial locus for the emergence of community may provide a means of theorizing the conditions of community in a way that allows for some specificity in defining the mechanisms of its formation, while avoiding the foreclosure characteristic of Tonnies's work. There are good reasons for believing that a focus on the body can yield insights into the nature and genesis of community. As the American cross-cultural psychiatrist Laurence Kirmayer perceptively remarked in relation to growth of interest in the body in sociology, 'the turn toward the body represents a longing for community, for bodily connection and participation in a habitable world of substance and feeling'.[8] The task ahead is to establish whether this longing for community can be fulfilled by the body's possibilities, and to say what kind of community these possibilities permit. This will require the adoption of a phenomenological approach to the topic that looks to the experience of bodily interaction as a vital basis of community formation. However, before this task can begin, it is necessary to consider, in greater detail, some of the affordances and limitations of existing conceptions of community.

Theorizing the relationship between structure and community

The purpose of the following discussion will be to establish a context for a more embodied conception of community in contemporary society. It will focus in particular on the way the relationship between community and social structures has been construed by different theorists. An assessment of the strengths and limitations of these different paradigms of community will bring into relief the possible benefits of a more embodied conception of community. This brief survey will begin by looking at Tonnies's distinction between the *gemeinschaft* and *gesellschaft* form of society which proposes that community and social structures can in certain circumstances form a single harmonious whole. Tonnies's view of the relationship between community and social structure will then be contrasted with Maffesoli's vision of community, which sees community as existing in opposition to social structures and as having the potential to overflow or subvert them. Having looked at theories that see community as necessarily either integrated into social structures or as transcendent of these structures I will turn to approaches, such as that developed by the sociologist Brint, that define community by its place *within* social structures. Finally, theories such as those proposed by Victor Turner and the Russian literary critic and semiotician Mikhail Bakhtin, which see community as occurring *between* social structures and as existing in a dialectical relationship to these structures, will be examined.

The total community: people and structure as one

Due, in part at least, to the influence of Tonnies's seminal text on the subject, *Community and Association (Gemeinschaft und gesellschaft)* (1955 [1887]), the idea of community has come to stand for everything good that has been lost by society in the process of social change and modernization and so for everything good that society could and should aspire to in the future.[9] At once profoundly optimistic and profoundly pessimistic Tonnies's model of community offers an Elysian vision of organic human interconnectedness while at the same time lamenting its inevitable passage at the hands of evolutionary social change. In this version of community all divisions are transcended through spatial and temporal continuity and a deep sense of belonging. Individuals are integrated into a social, material and spiritual environment that is so all-encompassing in its scope that it excludes alternatives and so precludes conflict.

Defining the *gemeinschaft* form of society

The *gemeinschaft* form of society, as Brint has noted, is defined by Tonnies through the elaboration of a long series of static ideal types that are deemed to characterize this type of social organization.[10] All the features that would normally be associated with small-scale settlements and a predominantly rural economy are present in the list of *gemeinschaft* characteristics: agricultural production, religious affiliation, the importance of customs and folkways, a connection to soil and place, and stable social relations. However, this model of community life does far more than simply describe these elements as discrete entities whose aggregation equals community. It suggests that they are mutually constitutive and that they serve to unite the moral and material aspects of existence into a single seamless whole. As a result, the *gemeinschaft* form of society, it is believed, gives rise to a particular set of motivational and behavioural characteristics that are termed by Tonnies 'natural will'. Central to the exercise of this form of will is a spontaneous and disinterested desire to act in ways that accord with the needs and aims of the community. The unfettered creativity this implies is founded on habit, conscience and reason operating in an environment where everything from psyche to soil exists in a state of harmonious interconnection. There is, then, a perfect fit at all times between action and environment in the *gemeinschaft,* with all activities unselfconsciously serving the common good.

This attunement to shared needs and aims does not imply that the individuals within the community exist in a state of equality in relation to one another. The hierarchical structure of the patriarchal household provides the basic unit of social organization and a pattern for the structure of the wider community. However, because the *gemeinschaft* is understood as an indivisible unit that functions in concert, the differentials of status and power that this hierarchical organization entails do not produce any difficulties or tensions. Indeed, those at the bottom of the hierarchy are assumed to be entirely content with their situation, and freely choose it, while those at the top do not exploit their position but instead act as protectors and guides to those below.

The enormous strength of Tonnies's conception lies in its appreciation of the way different aspects of social existence, from the material to the moral, can be intimately bound up and mutually constitutive. This valuable insight is extended in his analysis of the *gesellschaft* form of society which, although it marks the demise of community, is also understood as a coherent whole.

Defining the *gesellschaft* form of society

Broadly speaking, the basic characteristics of the *gesellschaft* form of society are also the defining features of modernity (urbanism, trade, rationality, the contract, science and the state). Again, however, Tonnies is not so much interested in listing the features of this kind of society as in describing the way of life which the interaction of its diverse elements fosters. He offers an equally comprehensive series of ideal types that are paired with, and opposed to, those given for the kind of village and small town life which preceded modernity. Each aspect of the *gemeinschaft* is replaced by a corresponding feature in the *gesellschaft*, with customs, for example, giving way to contractual arrangements as a basis for action.

However, these new elements do not cohere into a new and different form of community. Instead of community there is fragmentation, as the connections between different levels of existence and parts of society are severed in a newly rationalized social order. This gives rise to a distinctly modern type of motivation and moral outlook, designated by Tonnies as 'rational will', in contrast to the 'natural will' that preceded it. In the exercise of rational will actions are governed by ambition, instrumentality, consciousness and a thirst for power. A harmonious relationship between mind and body, individual and group is replaced by an entirely different set of imperatives. The body serves the rational purposes of the mind, and the group is atomized into competing units which can only prosper at each other's expense. This new moral and motivational framework, which reflects economic and cultural changes in society, is dominated by individual ambitions rather than collective needs. The rural community, governed as it was by a slow accretion of customs passed down from generation to generation, is transformed into an urban environment that is as anonymous as its rules are arbitrary.

By suggesting that there is a coherent relationship between material and cultural conditions and individual dispositions this pessimistic vision of modernity has found many echoes in sociological thinking. Examples of work indebted to this perspective include Georg Simmel's classic statement on the psychic consequences of life in the metropolis,[11] Wirth's account of social existence the city,[12] in which the main features of the urban–rural dichotomy are reprised and Mellor and Shilling's analysis of the effects of secularization on bodily experience in the transition to modernity.[13]

The view that contemporary society exists in a kind of fallen state in relation to community now that 'shared values, norms, and ideas are no longer binding, [and] culturally reproduced social integration has dissolved' has led some to conclude that the very basis of human interaction and interconnection has been fundamentally altered in the conditions of modernity.[14] In particular, it is argued that the significance of language and rational communication has been greatly heightened by the decline of established ties. Giddens, for example, has suggested that common aims and activities in the future will find expression only in shared projects contracted at the cognitive level with cooperation being maintained only for as long as it is convenient to all parties.[15] Even the most intimate dyadic relationships will, it is suggested, take on the character of a common enterprise that is only sustained by a continuous exchange of words. These new cognitive and confessional forms of interaction are understood by Giddens as providing new freedoms and opportunities that compensate for the loss of older forms of interconnection. The Polish sociologist Zygmunt Bauman's conclusions about the prospects for community in the future resonate with this new emphasis on the cognitive level. Although he is far less sanguine than Giddens about these perceived changes, for Bauman any possibility of community in the new conditions produced by modernity can only rest on a painstakingly negotiated compromise between competing interests and identities that can never be more than provisional in its outcomes.[16] While there is some disagreement, then, about whether the changes originally identified by Tonnies represent a loss or an opportunity, the idea that organic human interconnectedness is in terminal decline has received wide endorsement.

The limits of Tonnies's model of community

The enormous value of Tonnies's basic premise, that there is a strong interaction between different levels of social existence, whether in a rural or urban setting, is beyond question. However, there is a need to distinguish between this contribution and the particular claims that are made, both about life in small-scale traditional settlements and about the effects of the transition to modernity.

The main difficulty with Tonnies's conception is that it establishes a traditional way of life in small-scale settlements as a normative ideal and so, effectively, defines all other forms of social organization as involving a departure from, and diminution of, a fully human existence. It links this assumption to a fixed teleology which ensures that the positive qualities associated with the *gemeinschaft* way of life are consigned to the past or, at best, views their continuing presence as no more than a feeble residue of that which existed before. This is the great strength of Tonnies's model – that it understands society, whether in its *gemeinschaft* or *gesellschaft* incarnations, as an integrated whole. But from a different perspective this is also its greatest weakness. While Tonnies claims the position of a detached observer and analyst of change, throughout his work there is a palpable sense that all features linked to the *gemeinschaft* are to be venerated, and all those that are typical of the *gesellschaft* are to be deplored. This is so partly because the respective sets of characteristics attributed to the *gesellschaft* and *gemeinschaft* are seen as elements in an integrated totality. They cannot, therefore, be readily unbundled and are presumed to be mutually exclusive. To favour any aspect of the one is, as a result, to condemn every aspect of the other. Consequently, it is very difficult to associate any feature of the *gesellschaft* (e.g. urbanism) with any trait (e.g. faith) that is understood as being typical of rural or small-scale settlements.[17] Community ties are therefore understood largely in terms of their presence or absence rather than as a variable and contingent aspect of social existence. There is, for example, only a limited differentiation in terms of intensity between different kinds of ties, with those of blood always assumed to be stronger, and no account of different patterns of ties due to the influence of factors such as class, gender or stage in the life course. The ties that bind master and servant are assumed to be qualitatively identical with those that bind social equals or even family members since all are subsumed within the *gemeinschaft.*

The *gemeinschaft/gesellschaft* dichotomy, which suggests that different forms of social organization reliably produce radically different motivations and moral perspectives, has been subjected to significant criticism. The very idea that humans are even adapted to close and continuous involvement in small groups has been challenged. In an ambitious attempt to locate the origins of human sociality Alexandra Maryanski, an American sociologist, has conducted a meta-analysis of primate studies.[18] Her conclusions are that our nearest ancestors exhibited a pattern of mainly loose ties, with a limited number of more intensive involvements that varied over time due to factors such as stage in the life course and place in the group being present. These findings have led her to dismiss models of community of the kind proposed by Tonnies as romantic sociological myths. More importantly, empirical studies have found little evidence in human social groups of the 'virtues' ascribed to small scale traditional settlements. There is little to suggest that this kind of agrarian society is, in practice, characterized by high levels of altruistic behaviour and strong and enduring solidary ties. The familiar effects of power, inequality and differentiation are as likely to be evident as are those of integration and bonding at a community level. As Brint puts it, 'studies of communities of place have, by and large, found more Babbitry than fraternity'.[19] Conversely, the 'vices' expected of urbanism have not materialized on anything like the scale imagined, with *gemeinschaft* like connections proving to be remarkably resilient and adaptable in new conditions. The sociologist Fischer, for example has noted that ethnic and religious cultures can be strengthened as well as weakened by urbanism and that these processes do not correlate in any straightforward way with factors such as the size, density or mobility of urban populations.[20]

In seeking to comprehend society as a single unified whole, Tonnies's conception, perhaps inevitably, assumes a greater coherence between different levels of analysis than it is able to convincingly demonstrate. If these limitations in Tonnies's model are acknowledged this may raise wider concerns about the ambitions of all perspectives that seek to generalize about particular forms of social organization and their supposed consequences for human interaction. Having suggested that Tonnies's totalizing ambitions produce a vision of both the *gemeinschaft* and *gesellschaft* form of society that is overly rigid in its application and reliant on a number of unwarranted assumptions, it may be helpful to consider the altogether more fluid conception of community offered by Michel Maffesoli. For Maffesoli community does not exist in harmony with social structures, as in Tonnies's account, but instead exists beyond and in opposition to such structures.

The community of everyone or everyone in communities

For Maffesoli the conditions of late modernity provide an answer to the call made by Nietzsche for the emergence of a new aesthetic sensibility in response to the malaise of cultural exhaustion besetting western society.[21] Rather than being founded on established and enduring features, as in Tonnies's conception, community from this perspective is predicated on the disintegration, or at least the discrediting, of existing social structures. Maffesoli claims that as belief in the fundamental tenets and institutions of modernity recede, forces promoting spontaneous congregation and the re-enchantment of the world regain the ascendancy. This late flowering of community spirit is founded on the *puissance* of 'the people' which, it is suggested, has always opposed the disciplinary aspirations of *pouvoir* and only awaited its chance to emerge into the light.

Where Tonnies sees community as deriving from a highly specific set of material circumstances centred on place, blood and means of production, Maffesoli looks to the zeitgeist of contemporary society to explain community formation. Maffesoli acknowledges that the material apparatus of modernity is still fully operational, but claims that it has been divested of much of its power to constitute social relations. Rather than endorsing pessimistic assessments of modernity that see everywhere a retreat from the social, defined through the concepts of alienation or narcissism,[22] this account discovers the emergence of an 'empathetic sociality' amid the 'hollowed out' forms of modernity.[23]

An irrepressible human desire to establish meaningful contact with others finds expression wherever proximity is established. It is not even required that this proximity should involve physical co-presence provided it delineates a shared symbolic territory. Wherever there is a coming together, in any form that defies the dominant productivist ethos, a contribution is made to the ambience of community that pervades society. This demotheistic perspective elevates even the most apparently banal encounters, such as having a cup of tea with someone at a fast food restaurant, into sacred events. From this standpoint, community requires neither a material basis, specific location nor any degree of permanence to be recognized, although it certainly does not exclude these features. Community can be manifested in virtually any situation and forms an 'underground centrality'[24] that operates within society while displaying 'extraordinary resistance to the multiform impositions which constitute societal living'.[25] This spirit of community does not directly confront these impositions but rather avoids and neutralizes their effects through rouse, subversion or by simply ignoring them. For example, the trappings of consumer culture are endowed with new meanings by becoming the object of shared understandings and ironic investments. Fashion, the mall, sports events and media gossip are all potential fuel for community formation once they have been appropriated in this way. Even moral indifference and political quiescence can be interpreted as signs of group solidarity and of a healthy contempt for the ambitions of a bourgeois social order.

Although this celebration of everyday life occasionally comes close to endorsing an absolute moral relativism it does have the great merit that it understands human groups as potentially self-organizing and self-defining. This contrasts with Tonnies's more deterministic perspective which views participation in the *gemeinschaft* as freely chosen while providing ample demonstrations that the 'choice' is actually something more like a destiny given in the total conditions of existence. Rather than viewing community as overdetermined from above, in Maffesoli's account it constantly erupts from below.

Some implications of Maffesoli's conception of community

Although Maffesoli evinces a great impatience with the grand narrative pretensions of established sociological theory, clear echoes of some of these narratives can still be heard in his work.[26] In particular, a desire to continue the Durkheimian project of uncovering the archaic and unchanging forms that underpin society is evident throughout. Where Tonnies sees only change in the transition to modernity, Maffesoli focuses on persistence and recurrence, finding ancient practices and meanings resurfacing in new guises wherever he turns. These essentializing and naturalizing tendencies perhaps sit a little uneasily with his post-modern commitment to situated and relativized meanings. Nevertheless, Maffesoli's perspective provides an invaluable corrective to the linear view of change proposed by Tonnies.

Maffesoli does not, however, identify the constraints on and limits to community formation in a modern setting. If community formation is solely viewed as an immanent property of human interaction then any sense of historical specificity is sacrificed. Additionally, by defining community in such vague and ethereal terms with appeals to the *puissance*, organicity and empathetic capacities of the masses the concept becomes so all-encompassing in its scope that it risks defining nothing in particular. Thus, if Tonnies sets the bar for what can count as community too high to account for the interview material gathered for this book, excluding everything but an imagined past, this version of the concept of community perhaps sets it too low, rendering it indistinguishable at times from any other kind of interaction in a modern society. It does not explain in any detail how individuals come to know each other in their human particularity, and to form groups that transcend the 'seriality' of a mass society in which we live beside one another but not with one another.[27] The question remains whether it is possible to define community in such a way that account is taken of the particular conditions prevalent in modernity without viewing them as absolutely overdetermining.

A different approach to conceptualizing community

A different approach to the topic of community may be needed in order to move beyond conceptions that find community everywhere or nowhere in contemporary society. Rather than attempting to specify what community should be or what community is, it may be more fruitful to begin by specifying the conditions of its possibility and identifying the limits to its development in the context of contemporary society. The nature of human embodiment and the organization of society together provide opportunities for and constraints on community which are complex and sometimes contradictory. To theorize community in this way will entail a radical shift in perspective. Instead of viewing community as a static object that is fully present at all times, as in Tonnies's model, or as an immanent property of social existence that is all-pervasive, as in Maffesoli's account, it may be more productive to examine the experience of community in a particular concrete context. In other words, this approach will move from the specific instance to more general conclusions, rather than assuming that general conclusions can be applied equally to all specific instances. In order to begin tracing the interactions between body and society that can give rise to the experience of community, it will be necessary to separate out the different elements that have been conflated in the idea of community and which have led to its being understood as either society in its totality or as totally transcendent of society. To begin unbundling the community concept the next section will turn to an approach that understands community as occurring *within* the structures of society.

Unbundling the community concept: community within social structures

In an attempt to salvage the community concept Brint has proposed a more modest and serviceable set of criteria for defining this form of sociality than those provided by the accounts considered above.[28] He has developed a structural typology of community forms based on a set of variables such as rate of interaction, context of interaction, motivation, location, level of face-to-face contact and so on. However, each of these types of community structure has a common foundation in that each is composed of individuals who have a disinterested interest in engaging with others that they perceive to be alike:

> who share common activities and/or beliefs and who are bound together *principally* by relations of affect, loyalty, common values, and or personal concern (i.e., interest in the personalities and life events of one another).[29]

This essential requirement for community, that it is primarily based on 'relations of affect, loyalty, common values, and or personal concern' is seen to produce different outcomes depending on the type of community structure which it underpins. This allows for a useful distinction to be made between what might be termed the moral basis of community and its specific manifestations. The implication of disaggregating the community concept in this way is that the 'virtues' that have often been associated with the idea of community may not be found together – indeed they may actually exist in an inverse relationship to one another. Tonnies assumes, for example, that inequalities of status and power can only be overcome through integration at all levels into a stable social group. In contrast, Brint's model implies the radically different conclusion that inequalities of status and power could only be entirely absent in a virtual community that had no face-to-face interaction at all and was entirely voluntary and without obligations. For example, the absolute freedom and equality enjoyed by the denizens of Internet chat rooms is predicated on the absence of mutual obligations rather than on their presence. As soon as such mutual obligations exist this freedom and equality is curtailed since the burden of obligation is bound to fall unevenly as it shifts from one party to another. Conversely, the mutual support and solidarity promised by Maffesoli as a by-product of community would be unlikely to materialize without the presence of the kind of structural constraints and enforced conformities that he defines as societal impositions. Maffesoli perhaps underestimates the extent to which the fulfilment of obligations that may be onerous or aversive depends on an element of coercion.[30] For example, even in the most cohesive tribal societies the sharing of resources with others typically rests on an assurance of reciprocity that is backed up by effective social sanctions.[31]

The idea that community does not need to be understood as either society in its totality or as operating totally outside of society is a valuable step forward. It allows for the existence of temporary, incomplete or open manifestations of community that nevertheless share a fundamental moral basis, and in this sense fully express the ideal of community. However, by assuming that community invariably occurs *within* the structures of society Brint inevitably construes these structural features as determining the possibilities of community. Although this model promises a far more flexible and graded approach to the topic than the all or nothing implied by Tonnies's account, it is an approach that is ultimately confined to describing what communities are from the *outside* rather than analysing how they are formed from the *inside*. In other words, it fails to fully engage with the experience of belonging and mutual acknowledgement that makes the desire for community such a compelling and enduring feature of social existence. In order to move to an experiential understanding of community the next section will look to theories that see community as a coming together *between* the structures of society. It will focus on the significance of this liminal space and on the role of bodily interaction as an indispensable locus of its creation.

Community between social structures: illusion or reality

In a subtle analysis of sociability, Georg Simmel identifies a suspension of hierarchical relations and a setting aside of the profane concerns of everyday life as a crucial basis for this type of interaction.[32] Liberated from the exigencies of purpose that characterize normal mundane activities, interaction is free to take on a pure play form. This play form of sociality expresses the essence of other types of interaction while transcending the limitations which each of these entails as a result of its pursuing some particular end.

> Sociability is spared the frictions with reality by its merely formal relations to it. Yet just because of this, it derives from reality, even to the mind of the more sensitive person, a significance and a symbolic playful richness of life that are the greater, the more perfect it is.[33]

For Simmel this setting aside of everyday distinctions and inequalities creates a social space that exists outside society yet expresses it in a perfected form. This type of interaction rests on a stylized form of behaviour that excludes all mention of social and personal realities in order to maintain an atmosphere of equality that ensures a continued mutual enjoyment of the interaction. However, since the objective inequalities remain long after the subjective pleasures of the sociability have ended it really alters nothing and exists in a realm of artifice; albeit one that derives its energy and animation from life itself. In his typology of crowd forms, the Hungarian writer Elias Canetti has also analysed situations where differences are set aside, and concurs in believing that they are illusory because they do not last:

> the moment when all who belong to the crowd get rid of their differences and *feel* equal … is based on an illusion; the people who suddenly *feel* equal have not really become equal; nor will they *feel* equal for ever.[34]

Others, though, have discerned a more profound and transformative meaning as potentially present in the kinds of encounter that occur in the interstices of society, and have also offered a positive material basis for their understanding. Victor Turner, for example, has elaborated a theory of dialectical opposition between moments of structure and anti-structure present in all forms of society, from the simplest to the most complex.[35] In its anti-structural, or liminal, phase, the 'generalized social bond that has ceased to be and has simultaneously yet to be fragmented into a multiplicity of structural ties' is recognized and celebrated.[36] This recognition and celebration of a common humanity manifested in unique and mortal individuals is enacted through embodied practices that are at once symbolic and material. Typically these practices involve a sharing of physical ordeals and an overturning or suspension of existing structures that allows individuals to get beyond 'the statuses, roles and offices'[37] of everyday life and to 'fully experience the being of the other'[38] in 'cognizant mutuality and in all concreteness'.[39] This encounter with the other is viewed as a 'transformative experience that goes to the root of each person's being and finds in that root something profoundly communal and shared' and is to be distinguished from the 'pleasurable and effortless comradeship that can arise between friends, co-workers, or professional colleagues any day'.[40] José Gil has analysed the workings of this kind of liminal encounter in the context of tribal societies. Here, rituals serve to unleash forces in the body that overflow available meanings and signification engendering renewal and communion:

> This is a process that favours the progressive irruption of the uncoded body, which, significantly, can only exist in a state of trance or possession. It is only on this surface of inscription rendered virgin, that new meaning can burst forth.[41]

These rituals do not operate at the level of symbolic representation but instead involve a heightening of reality in which the ritual is 'truer than life; it is more real because it brings into play more powerful presences, calls forth terrible forces, and stirs up powerful emotions'.[42] Rituals achieve this heightening of reality through a sensual immersion that overwhelms the stable and familiar meanings of everyday life that find expression in language:

> pushing the codes and languages, for which the body is emblem, to the point of extreme confusion – music, incantation, hallucinogens and drugs, dance and the whole atmosphere pervading the event join forces in obtaining this result.[43]

The role of the body is to 'designate realities' through the actions and gestures of the ritual.

Mikhail Bakhtin has found a similar dialectic at work to that identified by Turner in medieval and Renaissance society, where carnivals and feasts restore and renew human energies through laughter, excess and a gay relativizing of all truths. He sums up the effect of these festivities in the following way:

> People were, so to speak, reborn for new, purely human relations. These truly human relations were not only a fruit of imagination or abstract thought, they were experienced. The utopian ideal and the realistic merged in this carnival experience.[44]

For reasons of religious faith and political commitment, Turner focuses on the positive potential of this capacity for mutual recognition to renew social bonds. However, such experiences need not imply either consensus or a basis for cooperation. For Bataille sensual engagement of this kind restores a sense of continuity with the world and with others that is obscured by our bounded nature and by the demands of civilization.[45] The American sociologist Thomas Smith has also focused on the significance of mutual recognition rather than any results it might produce when he suggests that soldiers facing each other in a battle could discover a sense of shared humanity through their common embodied experiences that is absent in their relations with others from their 'own' side.[46] The possibility he points to, of a radical discontinuity between the values and identities that people adhere to and the values and identities of those they feel able to acknowledge as alike, suggests a basis for community in shared bodily experiences that may be deeper than and even contrary to allegiances based on belief. Rather than marking a suspension of reality then, as was the case in Simmel's account of sociability, sociality in these terms asserts life and reality against the abstract and arbitrary distinctions of society.

From this perspective, community is not something that is made but something that happens spontaneously between people under certain conditions and always exists in alternation with the structural imperatives required for society's perdurance. This 'communitas', as Turner calls it, is founded in the body and revealed in what the body can do beyond all rational purposes and individual intentions. The next section will examine the role that the embodied experience body has played in the formation of community in other societies before going on to consider whether it still plays this role in our own through such experiences as shared states of intoxication.

Embodying the community concept

The body has been understood as providing a means of entering an experiential space *between* the structures of society, whether these structures are articulated by the segmentary divisions of gender, age and clan in traditional societies or through a hierarchical organization of social classes in contemporary society. In this space, the elements of human existence that are common to all take precedence over those that divide each against the other. Countless generations of adapting to the same basic environment has endowed humans with what Mikhail Bakhtin terms an 'ancestral body'.[47] This body, which marks the culmination of an evolutionary process, permits a connection with all those who are present now by containing all those who have gone before.[48]

In the rites of passage practised in societies without a state, the body of those who are to be acknowledged as members of the group are subjected to a variety of ordeals and often permanently marked. The privations of hunger, thirst, and lack of sleep may be endured for many days and the flesh mutilated by piercing, scarification or tattoo. According to the anthropologist Pierre Clastres these rituals, which all without exception must go through, ensure that each individual understands that they are essentially the same as the others, no better and no worse:

> The mark on the body, on all bodies alike, declares: You will not have the desire for power, you will not have the desire for submission. And that non-separate law can only have for its inscription a space that is not separate: that space is the body itself.[49]

By these ordeals an equality of the flesh is experienced in the flesh and the memory of this equality is embodied through a gesture of marking in which the material and the symbolic are united.

In societies with a state the body has played a different but analogous role in re-establishing the experience of communitas against the manifold distinctions and hierarchies of social structure. For Bakhtin the experience of carnival in medieval and Renaissance society is a celebration of 'the degrading and renewing power of the mighty lower stratum' through the feasting, drinking, copulation, birth, defecation and, above all, the laughter of the 'grotesque' body.[50] The necessary but desiccating routines and disciplines of everyday life give way to utopian festivities that are open to all and predicated on a free expenditure of abundant resources. Again the material and symbolic are united in this overturning of official structures and a common humanity founded in the body is upheld. Images and activities that invert or disrupt the normal hierarchies, particularly those which place the head above the body, predominate. A person from the lowest station might find themselves proclaimed king for the day, while those at the top are likely to find themselves liberally doused in excrement; whether symbolically or literally hardly matters.[51] This whole inversion of existing hierarchies finds its most telling image in the somersaults of the acrobat which establish equivalence between the head and the lower stratum through their rapid alternation. Again this is more than merely symbolic, since the acrobat's body communicates directly with other bodies conveying a meaning that precedes any process of decoding. José Gil has described this 'experiential communication' in another context.[52] According to Gil:

> Mimes do not speak to a verbal intelligence; they aim directly at the body of the observer ... – [understanding of mime] relates to the material possibilities of the body in space, not only of course to its anatomy and physiology, but also to its desire.[53]

The body, then, has been understood as central to the experience of communitas in both archaic societies and in those with a developed state. This temporary overcoming of divisions is realized in the flesh and in the present through practices that are simultaneously material and symbolic, real and ideal. The different modulations of this process in different circumstances are given by Turner in the following passage:

> Just as in pre-literate society the social and individual development cycles are punctuated by more or less prolonged instants of ritually guarded and stimulated liminality, each with its potential core of communitas, so the phase structure of social life of complex societies is also punctuated, but without institutionalized provocations and safeguards, by innumerable instants of spontaneous communitas.[54]

However, the differences to be overcome in contemporary society are not so much those of segmentarity or hierarchy, which prevailed in previous eras, as those produced by the atomization and fragmentation of society which Tonnies and others have pointed to. While Turner has suggested that these new conditions may be particularly conducive to the emergence of instances of spontaneous communitas, most commentators have taken the opposite view.

The closed body of modernity

Modernity has been widely understood as antithetical to the needs that community, in whatever form, promises to meet. Central to this perceived incompatibility between community and modernity is the emergence of a cult of individualism that has as its central ambition the creation of separate autonomous subjects. This ambition finds corporeal expression in a bodily ideal that emphasizes a controlled comportment and a smooth, hard outer surface. Armoured in this way, the body denies rather than facilitates contact with others.[55] The closed surface of the body serves as both a clear boundary to the self[56] and, latterly, as a means of self-presentation.[57] These 'paradigms of a humanity marked by self-possession'[58] assume a self that looks out on a world that forever remains 'out there' and a body that is no more than an instrument of this self. As José Gil puts it '[t]his "object" – through which death comes to us – seems to lend itself, always with the same docility, to a range of objective procedures'.[59] This docility of the body to the projects of the self is exemplified by an upright and erect posture which symbolically and literally gives the head precedence over the body. The self and the body as surface achieve their most refined realization in the face, which – as unique as a national insurance number and as much a product of modernity – seems to both guarantee and express this new individualism.[60]

It need hardly be stated that individualism in these terms has nothing to do with the individual in their human particularity but refers rather to a division of labour that has extended into virtually every aspect of existence, creating an almost infinite number of social roles for humans to fulfil, and a correspondingly infinite number of bodies for them to create.[61] The reason that these roles and bodies can never coincide with actual individuals derives from the fact that, in the words of the American sociologist Christopher Lasch, they follow 'the capitalist principle that human beings are ultimately reducible to interchangeable objects'.[62] They do not, then, express that which is unique or irreplaceable and founded in our mortality, rather they conceal it. However, as the Italian political philosopher Georgio Agamben has remarked, the 'slight human body continues its precarious existence' behind the mask of the 'glorious body',[63] that is everywhere emulated and aspired to and which finds its most lurid and graphic depiction in advertising. In the next chapter the importance of this slight human body to the experience of community associated with intoxication will be explored.

Conclusion

This chapter has considered a range of theoretical approaches to the problem of community, focusing in particular on the way the relationship between community and social structures has been construed. It looked first to Tonnies's conception of community which posits an intimate relationship between structural features and ways of being in the *gemeinschaft*. While acknowledging Tonnies's contribution to the theoretical understanding of societal forms some important objections to specific claims that are made in his theory were noted. In particular, the validity of the rigid dichotomy separating features of the *gemeinschaft* from features of the *gesselschaft* was called into question. The implications of this dichotomy for community in the future were traced in the work Bauman and Giddens. Both concurred in stressing that a loss of traditional ties would make interaction at a cognitive level more important. Tonnies's model of community was then contrasted with that offered by Maffesoli, where community is understood as a spontaneous coming together outside the structures of society. Despite its lack of historical specificity and vagueness about the exact mechanisms of community formation, this model was seen to make an important contribution by stressing that human groups can be both self-organizing and self-defining. Next, Brint's disaggregation of the community concept through the development of a structural typology of community forms was considered. His approach promises a more nuanced definition of community by accounting for incomplete manifestations of community and acknowledging the existence of contradictory processes in their formation. However, the model does not engage with the *experience* of community and confines itself to describing community from the outside. This led to an assessment of theories such as those proposed by Mikhail Bakhtin and Victor Turner that understand community primarily in experiential terms and as existing in alternation with moments of structure.

Although beginning from entirely different premises it could be argued that the work of both Tonnies and Maffesoli is coloured by a shared romanticism about the possibilities for community. Where Tonnies mourns a vanished past Maffesoli welcomes its return and the gulf between pessimism and optimism that seems to separate their perspectives is bridged by a common nostalgia. It may be this romantic element that leads them both to see community in all or nothing terms rather than as a contingent and variable aspect of social existence. Giddens and Bauman also find themselves inadvertently united in endorsing an all or nothing view of community. By arguing for a fundamental change in the basis of human interaction since our expulsion from the supposed Eden of traditional ties they end in basic agreement, despite their very real differences. To overcome the limitations of these kinds of all or nothing perspectives on community and to avoid the value-laden assumptions that often underpin them Brint shifted ground to a minimal definition of community that focuses on structural variations. As successful as this approach is in its own terms it is unable to make qualitative distinctions between different ways of being with others or suggest how these differences might arise. Since it could be argued that the ability to make such distinctions is essential to an understanding of why humans desire community in the first place it was necessary to turn to theories that see community in experiential terms. These diverged in their assessments of the reality that should be accorded to the temporary experiences of belonging they analysed. In some formulations, such as those proposed by Simmel and Canetti, these moments of mutual recognition and equality are ultimately illusory. However, for others, such as Turner and Bakhtin, these experiences mark a return to reality in which the arbitrary divisions of society are overcome. It seems likely that the approaches of Turner and Bakhtin will have most to offer when it comes to comprehending the experience of community that intoxication can give rise to in contemporary society. In particular, their focus on the body as a site where the symbolic and material aspects of existence are united may be useful in interpreting the interviews. To establish whether this is the case, the next chapter will be devoted to a detailed analysis of people's accounts of their experiences of intoxication. By focusing on the role of the body in community formation, the analysis begins with the assumption that community is a contingent and variable aspect of social existence rather than a set of fixed relationships or vague potentialities.

7 Intoxication liminality and community formation

In the last chapter, a range of theoretical approaches to the problem of community were considered. The models of community proposed by Tonnies and Maffesoli were compared and contrasted and their potential usefulness in accounting for the material gathered for this book was assessed. It was suggested that by relating the existence of community to a historically determinate set of social and material circumstances Tonnies's model was too restricted in its application to account for manifestations of community such as those associated with intoxication in contemporary society. Conversely, Maffesoli's vision of community was judged to be too vague and all-inclusive to specify either the mechanisms of community formation or the limits to community that are exerted by particular social settings. However, Maffesoli's theory was seen to contain the valuable insight that human groups have a capacity for self-organization and self-definition. The discussion then moved on to theories such as those put forward by Giddens and Bauman that see a decisive shift towards more reflexive and conditional modes of community formation in the conditions of modernity. These models were also found to be of limited usefulness in the present context by understanding processes of community formation as occurring largely at a cognitive level and as resting on a negotiated settlement between competing interests and identities. Brint's theory, which focused on the structural properties of community formations while acknowledging a common moral basis for community, was then appraised. While this model was seen to perform the valuable task of disaggregating the community concept, by failing to engage with the experiential dimensions of community, it offered only a minimal definition of this type of sociality based on structural characteristics. Finally, approaches such as those proposed by Victor Turner and Mikhail Bakhtin that develop an experiential definition of community in which the role of the embodied experience is foregrounded were considered. The potential usefulness of these theories in accounting for the manifestations of community associated with intoxication was highlighted. Consequently, the principal focus of this chapter will be on utilizing those theories that understand community in experiential terms, with other models being referred to where they can help provide a context for the analysis.

To theorize the experience of community associated with intoxication in contemporary society adequately will mean specifying both the ways in which it can be understood as resembling other forms of community, such as those described by Turner or Bakhtin, and also the ways in which it differs from these. For example, it might be argued that the rituals of intoxication found in contemporary society have a similar meaning to rituals found in other contexts or periods, but that their occurrence in a modern setting means that they are also different from these in important respects. The aim is to analyse the interviews in a way that attends to the particularity of these concrete instances of community rather than assuming their identity with other processes of community formation in other settings. By doing this it is hoped that some tentative conclusions can be reached about the wider possibilities for community in contemporary society.

The analysis will look first at the rituals that often precede intoxication. Having suggested the possible meaning these rituals may have, attention will then be focused on the role the body plays in the experience of community associated with intoxication in contemporary society. Finally, the kind of community that intoxication in contemporary society permits will be analysed. The results of the analysis will then be used as the basis for a discussion of community that moves beyond the immediate concerns of this book.

Rituals of intoxication

It would be overstating the case to suggest that those in our society who become intoxicated are consciously engaged in a subversion of the individuated, rationally guided self of modernity and of the closed body that expresses its ambitions. Nevertheless, this is a frequent effect of their behaviour and can be interpreted as the very meaning of their actions. Although intoxication in contemporary society often lacks the pageantry and ceremony associated with the creation of liminal encounters in earlier periods or other cultures, the ad hoc rituals of intoxication can be viewed as leading into a similar experiential space. This space, which is at once real and ideal, symbolic and material, is realized in the intoxicated body as it opens to the world and to others. However, an experience of 'communitas', as this term is defined by Turner, is never guaranteed since the forces released by intoxication in the body, once the grip of rational control has been relaxed, do not *create* communitas so much as provide a liminal context in which it can, under propitious conditions, sometimes be realized. The rituals of intoxication can be understood as an attempt to manage the release of these forces in a coordinated way so that people can come together in the liminal space they help to open up.

From the custom of buying rounds at the pub, or passing the joint around, to the exquisite intimacies of sharing needles among intravenous drug users, the rituals of intoxication both assume and ensure equality. By insisting that all present partake in roughly the same measure, they guarantee that no one is excluded, or exempted, from participation. The real importance of these rituals, it could be argued, does not lie in the merely formal equality of identical shares they enforce but in the demand they make that this symbolic equality is realized and acknowledged in the body at an experiential level. While in practice these rituals may not always be strictly observed their very existence points to both a desire for equality and an intuition that it can be realized in the sharing of intoxicated states with others. Though it is neither necessary nor likely that those who take part in these rituals will view them in this light, at a conscious level, it is certainly possible that they will be, as José Gil puts it, 'unconsciously conscious' that they have this underlying significance.[1]

A great variety of these rituals were reported by the people I interviewed, of which just a few examples are provided below. In the first passage, Roger recalls a birthday celebration and the unusual cake that was shared by the guests:

> 'we made a cake with there was about a thousand [magic]mushrooms in there and a bottle of brandy and an ounce of grass [herbal cannabis] we baked him this cake and here was about I dunno must be a good twelve or fourteen of us and we all had a bit of this cake only quite a small bit but it was unbelievably strong and I remember we all went to this we all went to this pub it was firework night that was it and we were all sat in this pub and all of our I remember looking round and all of our faces they were all contorted and I've never seen anything so weird in my life but everyone's face was just not right it was that strong God knows what we must've looked like but there was a whole table full of us with contorted faces and I don't really remember much after that really it was quite a funny night anyway and we were just laughing all the time.'

Eating typically marks a point of separation from others. It separates in a very literal sense because, as Simmel insists, 'what the individual eats, no one else can eat under any circumstance'.[2] But eating also separates in another more subtle way in that it is always preceded by a moment of distribution that is inherently divisive. The problem of the surplus and its distribution has been with us since the first occasion on which an animal was able to take a prey larger than it could consume at a single sitting.[3] For Canetti the isolation of eating and the problem of the surplus are insurmountable:

> The isolation which eating entails is one of the roots of that terrifying growth called power … Whenever men went hunting together the sequel was distribution. As a pack they had been united, but when it came to the distribution of the prey they had to divide.[4]

Eating rituals that are predicated on equality and promise entry into a common state can be read as attempts at overcoming the isolation of eating and the divisive implications of the moment of distribution that precedes it. The cultural theorist Pasi Falk has suggested that communal eating in tribal societies can serve to integrate those who partake when the eating is structured by the reciprocal principle 'to eat and be eaten by'.[5] By making the food part of themselves those who eat are in turn made part of the community. According to Falk this is how 'the bridge between an open body, a group-self and a society as an "inside" is built'.[6] The Christian sacrament of communion enacts this desire for reciprocal incorporation at a symbolic level. It promises to restore a primordial unity through the ingestion of bread and wine that have been magically transformed into the flesh and blood of a single body. By taking this body into their body the communicants are in turn taken into the body of the church and become part of its indivisible community.

It could be argued that in sharing the cake with his fellow celebrants Roger entered with them into a common and equal state, symbolized in the equal portions and realized in the body. This is indicated in his account by the constant use of the collective pronoun 'we' but even more tellingly when he says that 'our faces all of them were contorted' rather than saying, for example *'their* faces *looked* contorted to *me'*. The knowledge that all of their faces *were* equally contorted to all who were present is implied in the choice of words and indicates a reciprocal sensual reality. The difference between the two possible formulations is the difference between an 'inside' that is collectively experienced and an individuated self looking from a position 'outside'. This 'inside' demarcates a community whose boundary is also given in the passage when Roger says 'God knows what we must've looked like'. Evidently, from the 'inside' where everyone has a contorted face it is difficult to conceive of looking on this scene from the 'outside' and imagining what you would see. That they were laughing 'all the time' also suggests a reciprocal sensual engagement whose significance we will be analysing in more detail later on.

In a passage from Amanda's interview this distinction between an 'inside' of shared experience and an 'outside' that is observed is played out with even greater clarity as she shifts between these two perspectives in recounting her story:

> 'the first time we all did [magic] mushrooms in a big sort of way I can't remember how many but we had a big saucepan full yeah we were making tea and it was such a good sort of trip everybody was imagining well you imagine these mushrooms are all crawling out of the saucepan and we'd all drunk the tea and it was brilliant everyone was feeling really just it's your senses isn't it everything becomes clear it's like oh yeah now you can see things from a different sort of parallel.'

Realizing that the interviewer occupies the position of observer rather than participant and may not understand the collective nature of the experience Amanda corrects herself when she speaks in the voice of the group and takes personal ownership of the events she is describing: '*everybody* was imagining well *you* imagine', '*everyone* was feeling really just it's *your* senses'. In noticing this slippage in perspective and correcting it a boundary is again drawn between those who had 'all drunk the tea' and those on the outside who are observing this fleeting community of the senses through her account of it.

Other rituals reported by the participants also displayed the same reciprocal structure in even simpler forms, as in these excerpts from the interview with George describing first a night out clubbing and, in the second passage, a night at the pub with friends:

> 'we were just breaking pills [ecstasy tablets] in half and tapping each other on the shoulder and throwing one down the throat a lot of dancing was going on.'

There were no practical reasons for adopting this arrangement of 'tapping each other on the shoulder and throwing one down the throat' rather than simply taking their own ecstasy tablets. Indeed, as George later explained, by increasing the likelihood that members of the security staff at the club would detect this prohibited activity it entailed some additional and, from a purely practical point of view, unnecessary risks. The most plausible explanation for this practice is that sharing the tablets is symbolic of sharing the intoxicated state they engender. Here, dancing with others rather than contorted faces or crawling mushrooms provides the shorthand for a reciprocal sensual engagement. In this excerpt, again from George's interview, the same structure and motifs appear:

> 'during the evening we were all buying drinks for each other which was quite pleasant in a nice social atmosphere and all allowed our barriers to drop together with the help of the evil alcohol.'

The symbolic reciprocity of 'all buying drinks for each other' becomes the actual reciprocity of affective engagement in the group when 'all allowed our barriers to drop together'.

Immersion and autonomy

Taking the same intoxicating substances with others, whatever they may be, is to give symbolic and literal assent to entering a common state with them by sacrificing the competent and bounded body of everyday existence. This common state expresses a desire that is neither individual nor democratic but derives from the group and its interactions. In a culture that valorizes individual autonomy, this kind of surrender to the forces of group interaction can be both threatening and alluring. It was Tony who was perhaps most articulate in expressing this ambivalence as he looked back on an earlier period in his life:

'it was never so much about what I was you know individually I was getting from the drugs that I was doing but it was more about what I was experiencing as part of a group full of people who were all experiencing something that was slightly different from the norm you know so I think you know there were times when you know I was out at parties and things like that and I'd actually think well personally I'm not really that happy being this off my head you know I'd like to come down now a little bit or I'd like to you know because I'd like a little bit more control ... and you know in some ways I wished I wished that at certain times I hadn't gone quite so far you know but still you know I enjoyed being there because all of these people were there around me.'

The tension between the desire for control and autonomy and the desire to be 'part of a group full of people who were *all* experiencing something' together remains unresolved but the surrender of autonomy is accepted in this case as the necessary cost of participation. In contemporary society, surrender to collective experience is in general entirely voluntary and typically constructed as hedonistic enjoyment. However, in practice the real existential consequences of surrendering in this way to group forces may be disturbing and unacceptable to many. Having become accustomed to the feelings of safety and control that individual autonomy in contemporary society brings us, the potential benefits of relinquishing some of this control may be difficult to grasp. By contrast, participation in rituals of inclusion in a tribal setting, such as initiation rites, has the character of an entrenched custom that all must follow and a meaning that would be well understood.[7] Consequently, in a modern context the very rituals that express an inclusive desire can also be implicated in processes of exclusion. When surrender to the dynamics of the group becomes too threatening participation can be experienced as oppressive rather than as leading into the experience of communitas described by Turner. When this occurs withdrawal from the group ensues, as in these excerpts from first Edward's and then Joanna's interviews:

'just sat around with a load of mates acquaintances in a room and taking this stuff and then sort of suddenly looking around at everybody and they didn't really look like the people that I knew they looked like them but they didn't seem the same any more I didn't like the look of them ... on that occasion anyway I just sort of made some excuse and sort of disappeared like sort of wake up in the morning everything is alright.'

'here I was in this really warm situation with my friends us all like sharing drugs I mean it was incredibly generous of them to give me the coke [cocaine] in the first place that's the other thing I always feel really churlish turning it down and yet I felt completely cold and distant so anyway I was sort of sitting there sort of not enjoying it and everything and then people started passing round spliffs and somebody just pointed out to me before I smoked the spliff that it had coke in it because at that

> point I had just turned down a second line of coke and the trouble was that because I was off my head by this time I turned it down practically with fingers crossed "are you the devil?" offering me this stuff and then I felt even worse for being so ungrateful you know to act like people were like trying to do my head in by generously giving me another line of coke which everybody else was really into so in the end I insisted on leaving.'

While the dilemma between immersion and autonomy that is evident in these excerpts may be heightened in contemporary society with its emphasis on individual autonomy it is not perhaps unique to it. In the following passage, from their epic meditation on the body *A Thousand Plateaus*, Deleuze and Guatarri recount the dream of a patient under analysis. The dilemma between immersion and autonomy is expressed here in an archetypal form in which the forces of repulsion and attraction are intrinsic to social existence itself. If it is true that these forces are intrinsic to social existence this may in part explain the constant alternation between moments of structure and anti-structure, communitas and separation that Turner has identified as a fundamental regularity underpinning all social formations:

> *I am on the edge of the crowd, at the periphery; but I belong to it, I am attached to it by one of my extremities, a hand or a foot.* I know that the periphery is the only place I can be, that I would die if I let myself be drawn into the centre of the fray, but just as certainly if I let go of the crowd. This is not an easy position to stay in, it is even very difficult to hold, for these beings are in constant motion and their movements are unpredictable and follow no rhythm.[8]

However, for most of the people I interviewed the moment when their differences became lost in the group, which Canetti has evocatively described as the moment of '*discharge* … when all who belong to the crowd get rid of their differences and feel equal'[9] was, in general, an unambiguously joyous sensation. The significance of these communal states will be considered further but first it is necessary to look in a little more detail at what intoxication entails in the context of the individuated modern body, and how it can open the way to an experience of communitas.

Relinquishing the rational body

The liminal experience of communitas that this chapter is concerned with is predicated on the boundaries of the closed modern body being breached. It is consequently important to analyse what this breaching of bodily boundaries means in the context of intoxication. The last chapter included a brief portrait of this closed modern body; in this section the role of intoxication in opening the closed body will be examined.

When asked whether the unusual behaviour of those he had been with while taking the drug ketamine had been frightening or disturbing, Tony speculated on the meaning of the kind of behaviour he had witnessed and participated in, and about the states that precipitate it, in the following way:

> 'No because I was kind of under the influence of it as well it wasn't scary no it was kind of hilarious I remember laughing at the whole ridiculousness of the situation … it suddenly hits you but it hits you in a way that you'll find yourself doing something without even realizing that you're doing it and then you'll suddenly catch yourself like you're looking at yourself from outside almost like an out of body experience and you'll see yourself literally trying to climb up the wall or falling around on the floor and you'll suddenly catch yourself and I remember just one instant of sitting in my mate's lounge and just having maybe ten seconds of kind of clarity of awareness and looking at all of the people around me crawling around … and it was kind of bizarre specifically because with everything else that we do in life we're trying to sort of build up something that is rational and understandable and yet we can actually get into states where we can function and behave without any of that without any of that rationality without it even being present in your mind you know these substances can remove it and what comes out is almost like dreaming do you know what I mean you're doing things that your subconscious mind is doing without having to actually think about it.'

While this degree of introspection about the nature of intoxication was highly atypical of the responses obtained in the interviews it does convey a sense of wonder at what bodies can do beyond the capabilities that are developed by rationally guided activity. While many of the participants reported equally extraordinary changes in behaviour and perception in general the significance of these events remained unanalysed by them. For most, the sense that the normal rational self has been overwhelmed or undermined by the body's responses to a situation was communicated more succinctly, as in the following short excerpts:

'we were completely off our heads' (Geoff)

'you're all off your face' (David)

'everybody was off their heads' (Karen)

'we were that fucking off our heads he just stabbed me up like a pin cushion' (Robert)

'you're just off your head' (David)

'we used to just drink to get seriously off our nuts' (Simon).

Intoxicants appear to be defined as much by a negative, the condition they transcend or subvert, the rational self in full control of a closed and individuated body, as they are by a positive, the particular state they induce. While distinctions are made between this or that substance and its effects an equally important distinction is that which is made between being 'off your head' or not. A number of the participants noted wryly that their worst drug experiences were with drugs that did not work, indicating that substances can be judged by their effectiveness in inducing the sensation of being 'off your head', as well as being differentiated by their specific characteristics. Despite the very variable effects that different substances can have at a psycho-physiological level they appear to share a generic quality at an experiential level. This suggestion would seem to be confirmed by Pearson's study of heroin users in the North East of England where he found that while the names that designate particular drugs are numerous and subject to continual change and innovation the states that these various substances produce tend to be given designations that are minimal and interchangeable. For example, no distinction is made between being under the influence of cannabis or under the influence of heroin, with both states being rendered simply by the term 'stoned'.[10] An alternative explanation for this lack of differentiation between the states induced by different substances could simply lie in the ineffable nature of these experiences.

If intoxication is about throwing off the limits of the rational self of everyday life and the bodily comportment that expresses it, conveyed in the idea of getting 'out of your head', or 'off your face', it is also, and equally, about experiencing what Margrit Shildrick has termed a 'corporeal irruption'.[11] The interview transcripts are replete with expressions that convey a sense of bodily violation in which clear boundaries, particularly those that separate the head from the body, are lost; these are just a few examples:

'we were all quite wankered' (Philip)

'just still absolutely fucked' (Robert)

'we got ripped' (Simon)

'we were bladdered' (Karen)

'you're really fucked up you know' (Simon)

'we were completely fucked really' (George)

'pissed as a cunt you know couldn't walk' (Simon)

'my head was like screwed absolutely battered' (Karen).

It is an intriguing question to what extent this use of images which convey the sense that the head has been supplanted by the 'mighty lower stratum' marks the continuation of an uninterrupted linguistic tradition that stretches back to the Rabelaisian world described by Bakhtin, and to what extent it is invented anew in each generation. Whichever is the case these usages speak eloquently of a visceral engagement that challenges the normative ideal of continuous rational control.

Language and the language of the body

In a society which has come to be dominated by the spectacle, and by a use of language that often reduces it to the literal meaning of words,[12] these metaphors of physical violation speak of an event that invites comprehension in the body as much as in the mind. Intoxication gives rise to a use of linguistic idioms with a visceral referent that is likely to remain enigmatic to those who have no significant experience of these states. In this sense it inverts the procedures of modernity (which this book participates in) of distilling embodied experience into words and objectifying it. It is clear from the interviews that people knew precisely what they meant when they described themselves as having been 'screwed', 'fucked' or 'off their face', and that they assumed that these terms would be readily intelligible to anyone who knew what they were referring to without further elaboration. Recalling his recent attendance at an outdoor concert David summed up his experience of being 'faced off alcohol' and 'minging out off the pills' [ecstasy tablets] as being 'Scotted'. In the course of the interview with David it emerged that this was a reference to the cult television series *Star Trek*. This science fiction drama features a 'transporter' device that can de-materialize the human body before relocating it to another place and re-materializing it there. The transporter is operated by a character named Mr Scott whose services are summoned with the words 'beam me up Scotty'. As evocative as this image of bodily transformation is, its full meaning is likely to be reserved for those who have also been 'beamed up':

> 'Yeah yeah lovely summers day sitting in the cheap seats just being Scotted minging out off the pills and that just faced off alcohol.'

When experience constitutes language rather than language constituting experience, and the words have little or no meaning beyond the body, communication *with* words becomes communication *between* bodies. This embodied use of language may allow for a shared evocation of intoxicated states and an extension of the corporeal communication discussed above beyond the immediate situation of shared intoxication. However, the intoxicated body does not have to await a linguistic expression of subjective states in order to be communicative.

It has been suggested that language only emerged when the direct communication of the body began to falter as the size of primate groups increased,[13] and that the use of language does not promote communication so much as signal its failure.[14] If this premise is accepted then moments when words become superfluous between people perhaps mark a return to a more embodied form of communication that does not require continuous translation into words. For the sociologist Ian Burkitt such communication has already passed out of existence:

> language is the primary means through which the self finds expression with the demise of the grotesque body ... the subject becomes an author in discourse and the body sinks beneath the discursivity of the subject.[15]

The evidence of these interviews, however, suggests that the grotesque body remains communicative in contemporary society, at least within the realm of intoxication. The importance of language as a medium of communication seems to be greatly diminished in these situations of shared intoxication. These passages from the interviews with first Tony and then Roger would seem to confirm this point:

> 'it was good because we were all kind of experiencing the same thing and you do find that you get that sort of link with people in some kind of strange ethereal way when you're doing sort of the same drugs together and stuff like that you appreciate similar things.'

> 'why do I like doing them is because I feel a lot more tuned in to people and the environment like I always seem to know what people want to hear and what they are going to say before they've even said it I just seem to be on a different level much more in tune to people really I'm quite a shy person quite nervous shy you could say but I do tend to lose that and my real self comes out more at the end of the day and that is probably why I do it plus it keeps you awake (laughs) so the party doesn't end ... so quite often you know saying nothing is very acceptable because you're you know other people that you're with don't need to well they know what you're saying already.'

In the shared space of intoxication the *exchange* of words, which act like a currency with meanings that can be spent anywhere, gives way to a *reciprocity* of the senses that is intelligible only in the immediacy of the situation. Bodily communication during intoxication can be manifested as an absence of the need for words; it can also take the form of active corporeal expression, as the next section will suggest.

Inhabiting the playful body: intoxicating laughter

The liminal space that intoxication opens up is realized in the body through a loosening of rationally organized corporeal competences and the simultaneous adoption and acceptance of a more playful way of inhabiting the body. Instead of a body with a singular meaning that can be reduced to its rationally intelligible functional possibilities, the intoxicated body takes on an amorphous shape in which a functionally rational comportment plays a diminishing part as intoxication progresses. The potential attractions of inhabiting this playful body have been hinted at by Deleuze and Guattari in the following way:

> Is it really so sad and dangerous to be fed up with seeing with your eyes, breathing with your lungs, swallowing with your mouth, talking with your

> tongue, thinking with your brain, having an anus and a larynx, head and legs? Why not walk on your head, sing with your sinuses, see through your skin, breathe with your belly?[16]

Discovering this playful synaesthetic body and sharing it with others is exemplified in the interviews by the experience of intoxicating laughter that the participants described. In his analysis of the festivities surrounding medieval and Renaissance carnivals and feasts Bakhtin accords laughter a special place in the proceedings, viewing it not only as a uniquely human attribute but one that is uniquely affirmative of life and becoming, in opposition to the desire for permanence and structure. Laughter is connected, in this account, with bodily existence at its most carnal and with the celebration of the 'lower stratum': 'the medieval culture of laughter was the drama of bodily life (copulation, birth, growth, eating, drinking, defecation)'.[17] Always spontaneous and inherently democratic, since only equals may laugh together, it 'degrades and materializes' as it heralds renewal and rebirth.[18]

In the narratives of intoxication analysed below laughter also plays a crucial part and not just in the sense that 'having a laugh' is shorthand for the sensations of fun or release expected of intoxication. Laughter has a double significance in these narratives. First, because laughter often plays a vital part in the experience of intoxication itself it can tell us something about the nature of this experience. Second, because laughter had an integral place in the *recounting* of these experiences it reveals much about their meaning that might otherwise have remained obscure. The relationship between these two moments of laughter requires explication, but first they must be examined in their own right.

Many of the participants reported occasions when they had been convulsed by uncontrollable laughter at the height of intoxication, and it is important to think through the significance of this beyond the obvious conclusion that they were clearly having a good time and enjoying themselves. The excerpts below give a flavour of some of the events described, unencumbered by extraneous contextual details:

> 'I remember just falling all over his living room just absolutely hysterical out of control couldn't stop myself laughing he couldn't stop himself laughing it was ridiculous.' (Tony)
>
> 'every time we tried to open our mouths it came out as laughter.' (Roger)
>
> 'we might have been drinking you know but we'd definitely been smoking loads and probably just the fact that everyone who'd gone down there with me was just laughing their heads off.' (Steven)
>
> 'then about 20 minutes later we were all completely off our heads and we went into the tent just for somewhere to sit down and we were just like falling about on each other and laughing laughing like anything I don't know why but you know it just felt like we were in a really funny situation and it was just really good.' (Geoff)

> 'being in hysterics just walking through these woods not being able to stand up properly not being able to climb over trees that you'd normally bounce over without falling over.' (Robert)

> 'it was just one of them days it was just so fucking funny everyone was just laughing their faces off.' (Peter)

> 'going into hysterical laughing and it felt like I'd echoed the whole room with my laughter.' (Sally)

When this kind of laughter takes hold the unity of mind and body are experienced in an ecstatic paroxysm that exceeds any particular trigger event or specific idea, and it can become self-fuelling. It can also have an infectious quality as it is transmitted back and forth in an intense but wordless communication, as in this description given by Steven of an evening dominated by laughter and by fruitless attempts at resisting it:

> 'just spent most of the night just really trying to suppress our giggling 'cos you know we had just every time we looked at each other we were just cracking up … we were just giggling like school children and everything we said just seemed the funniest thing you know just everything seemed so funny.'

To share laughter without an object requires a body that is open to forces that are uncontrolled and unanticipated. This laughter is an expression of forces that have yet to be contained and domesticated by language and technique.[19] While not all of these forces are as benign as laughter, they each share its quality of revealing a world beyond the bounded purposes of the closed body and the rational self. Strong emotions, erotic desires and disease processes all irrupt in the body and make themselves known prior to any meanings that might be placed on them and so it is with laughter and the other forces released by intoxication in the body. The intoxicated body tends toward a sensual and open state and an expressiveness that is unmediated. The communication of laughter relies not on language but on a body whose surfaces are permeable and reversible, exemplified by the eye which sees as it is being seen and the skin which touches as it is being touched.[20]

Intoxication leads to encounters with a body that both exceed and fall short of the possibilities provided by the rational comportment of everyday life. Normal competencies are often compromised, while 'uses' beyond the exigencies of function are discovered. The body is revealed as fragile and materially constrained as well as being host to unimagined forces that open it to the world and to others. Both of these aspects entail at least a partial relinquishing of control and an acceptance of possibilities that can be unpleasant, delightful or, as often as not, some admixture of the two that defies ready categorization.

This quality of acceptance revealed itself in the interviews in the form of laughter. Even when the events they were describing had clearly been extremely aversive the people I interviewed displayed an ability to find humour in their stories which established equivalence between an extraordinarily disparate range of experiences and lent them a coherent meaning. It is evident from the interviews that the possibility of communitas is one of the principal attractions of intoxication for the participants. However, to obtain this communal state entails the acceptance of various risks and potential costs. The physical dangers associated with intoxication, both long and short term, are well known but there are also social consequences that need to be faced. While intoxication creates the potential for an 'inside' that is experienced with others, it simultaneously produces this 'inside' as an excluded 'outside' to a sober and competent society. Laughter provided the participants with both a means of sharing the anxieties generated by these difficulties and of converting negative events into positive experiences.

The importance for social standing (upright citizenship) of being able to perform competently in the 'interaction order' and the consequences of any failures in this arena have been well documented. Erving Goffman, the symbolic interactionist, for example, has produced a comprehensive taxonomy of situations where identity can be compromised and where stigma ensues from such failures.[21] Canetti has taken this even further by suggesting that an inability to maintain a competent demeanour and upright posture excites a predatory response in those who witness it that has an evolutionary basis: 'A human being who falls down reminds us of an animal we might have hunted and brought down ourselves.'[22] There is, he maintains:

> even amongst civilized people a faint feeling of contempt for anyone to whom this happens. They procure him the help he needs, but in doing so expel him from the society of the erect.[23]

A body that reacts in unexpected ways or is diminished in its normal competences has entirely negative connotations in everyday life. At best it is inconvenient, at worst it is socially or even primordially discrediting. It poses an unacceptable threat to the normative ideal of a 'clean and proper body' that is everywhere enforced.[24] However, in the space of intoxication accepting such a body is the acceptance of life itself against the fantasies of bodily perfection, continuous competence and unlimited survival that dominate our society. Rather than being a site where social or evolutionary imperatives are always enforced, the 'interaction order' of intoxication bears a closer resemblance to the face-to-face world of emotional and moral accounting that Shilling has described.[25] In this space, mutual acknowledgement is accomplished not only by following the rules that produce social order but also through a shared acceptance of moments when the competent social self of everyday life is compromised and the rules cannot be followed.

The intoxicated body asserts its corporeal presence in ways that limit the capacity for competent performance in the interaction order. In doing so, intoxication encourages acknowledgement of the 'precarious existence' of the 'frail human body' and the limits to our control over it. This acknowledgement applies to the body as such and not just to this or that particular body that is always already 'theirs' or 'ours'. In the space of intoxication, bodies succumb to common forces and a common bodily existence is experienced beyond the countless differentiations of everyday life. While the people I interviewed did, at times, attempt to maintain narratives of mastery and control that served to differentiate them from others, these were invariably undercut by the realities of the events they described. Accounts of others' experiences rapidly became interchangeable with accounts of their own, and the equivalence of the two was readily conceded. This excerpt from Robert's interview captures a moment of bodily attunement and the mutual recognition and acceptance required to share intoxicated states:

> 'we both tried running but we'd done that much valium and alcohol and morphine by that point running just wasn't the … option [laughs] so we did a few steps and were taking it in turns to sort of fall over.'

This sense that all are equally susceptible to the forces that intoxication releases in the body is sometimes obtained at the price of tragedy, as in this incident reported by Philip:

> 'you know I said what's it like and they said oh go and look at Dave see what he's like he had some last and he's still stoned went in and my mate shook him could just hear sick slopping about in his lungs he was dead.'

Despite the obviously aversive nature of some of their experiences the participants displayed a marked reluctance to define them negatively, preferring instead to embrace these 'failures' of bodily control and rational understanding as an inextricable part of becoming intoxicated. When asked to recall some of their worst experiences of intoxication the following excerpts show how some of the interviewees concluded their stories:

> 'that's my bad experience I suppose but I don't really class them as bad experiences they're just it was they're just happening ain't they.' (Peter)

> 'this was a bad one really it was a great one because we are gonna always be the best mates ever.' (Karen)

> 'I suppose in a way it's quite funny it's sort of a positive and negative drug experience I guess.' (Robert)

> 'the first time I did it I had it injected and it was too much and I remember just being face down unable to move on this guy's bed just thinking this is it you know but then I came round and it was lovely so that was terrifying for a moment but … ' (Karen)

> 'I've had loads of experiences where I've been passing out or throwing up or freaking out but I don't really take those seriously they're just kind of

> part and parcel of taking drugs and you know in a way the drugs wouldn't be good if you [laughs] didn't have that aspect so I don't count that really as bad.' (Joanna)

Of the many negative experiences that were recounted in the interviews with few exceptions it was only those that adversely affected relationships with others that were actually categorized as regrettable by the people I interviewed; and even here there was a tendency to balance these events against the positive experiences of being with others that intoxication had brought them, as in this excerpt from Karen's interview:

> 'I don't really regret anything I wish that I could stop when I know that I've had enough but I'll have to practise at that but yeah most of my drinking that my drinking has made me more friends you know than enemies I reckon I think it's a positive thing that I take too far on occasions but yeah the mates that I've made through drink are pretty special yeah.'

Inhabiting the playful body means both encountering unanticipated possibilities that may be joyous and renewing but also accepting the vulnerabilities of the flesh. By embracing this playful body the manifold distinctions that find expression in the habitus of everyday life are, temporarily at least, set aside and a common destiny revealed. This setting aside of distinctions in the body, which is at once symbolic and material, finds homologous expression in the patterns of interaction reported by the people I interviewed, as the next section explains.

'Rhizomic' interactions

If intoxication often begins with rituals that enact a desire for equality, this undifferentiated condition is reflected in a circulation of bodies that is typically open and unpredictable. The loss of strict determination in the intoxicated body is mirrored in the spaces this body occupies and in its trajectories. Paradigmatic of these intoxicated spaces are the venues most readily associated with intoxication: club, pub, festival and rave which all allow for a free circulation of bodies and for their spontaneous interaction. In this context pre-existing statuses and relationships are often less important than active participation. Deleuze and Guattari have defined social structures that are open and fluid by analogy with the rhizome, which can make new connections at any point and is equal in all its parts, lacking as it does a defined centre, top, bottom, beginning or end.[26] They contrast this with the 'arborescent' structures that tend to govern normal day-to-day interactions and have a clear hierarchy and points of connection that are effectively predetermined. The following excerpts from the interviews give a flavour of the open and sometimes chaotic patterns of contact and communication that can accompany intoxication:

> 'they were so off their heads he rang us back and went "oh we'll come round and pick you up in a car and take you somewhere" we thought we were going to be taken up P to this pub we've never been to but then when they got here we had a quick spliff and then they were so manic they couldn't even wait to smoke the spliff we had to take it with us and smoke it in the car and we were meant to be going to K's because the friend of our friend apparently needed to meet somebody there but we all forgot that was where we were meant to be going and the friend just stopped outside the G strangely enough 'cos I hadn't even mentioned that as somewhere we were going to meet the other person I hadn't arranged to meet the other person but I knew this other person was so we went to the G and sure enough our other friend showed up there and we sat outside at the front which is really nice so it was pretty nice 'cos it was like lots of different people some coming and going sitting at the front which is nice 'cos you can see everybody coming and going.' (Joanna)

> 'went for a big wander and didn't come back all night and spent the whole night sort of drinking with people and it was about dawn on the Saturday morning this guy had given me the acid … ' (Steven)

> 'I just remember lots and lots of times just doing E's [ecstasy tablets] going up to N's nightclub or various other rave type places and just having a great time with everyone being friendly and you know … people generally you'd always talk to lots of strangers meet lots of girls and just have a good time generally just be really chatty and friendly with people.' (Geoff)

> 'everybody is light-hearted everybody is drinking at the same pace you know and you're kind of going on this voyage together you know and it isn't organized it's just totally you know it's random anything could happen you could get you know you could bump into anybody have a drink with that person and you know most of my friends are drinkers so it could go in any direction.' (Karen)

> 'I don't know probably I think we just wandered round aimlessly pretty much.' (Geoff)

Even spaces that have no particular association with intoxication take on an indeterminate character as they are given over to spontaneous interaction and free circulation. This passage from Philip's interview shows the same forces at work in a different context:

> 'there's nearly always there tends to be a lot of people about, taking drugs is quite a sociable thing although rather than like the pub which is a social thing, because it's legal you all go to the pub, with drugs you tend to all go round to each other's houses.'

Freed of the defined purposes that normally govern action impulse, the desire to be with others who are perceived to be alike and the urge to maintain this festive and playful condition can take over, as the following excerpt from George's interview describing a typical night out makes clear:

> 'we had they do this drink called the M it was about four or five different shorts all in together turned out to be quite a sweet drink so we raced each other and had about four or five of those which is the most I've ever drunk of those so I was completely out of my face then we thought right let's get some drugs 'cos we're never going to last the whole evening out we needed some stimulation before we fell asleep or went berserk so we got a bag of cocaine each got about a gram and probably had about half of that and then we went to a club the D club probably consumed about four or five pills [ecstasy tablets] on the way had many lagers in a couple of pubs can't remember the exact details and then towards the end of the night we thought you know we better sort of get on our toes because we were completely fucked really so the club turned out ended up got stuck because we were so out of our faces chatting to people just chatted to loads of people then sat down on a bench built a spliff …'

It would be wrong to overstate the degree to which the forces of spontaneous congregation associated with intoxication actually lead to contacts that transgress normal social boundaries, since interaction will in practice largely be confined to those who are already close in social terms, but they do contain this possibility and certainly express this desire. However, even if conventional social boundaries are not crossed, it is clear from the interviews that the basis of interaction is often substantially altered from that which pertains in everyday life. Liberated from the normal burdens of purpose and calculation that subordinate the direct contact of the body to the mediated contact of language and rationality, interactions are governed largely by desire and impulse. This means that those present can feel they have come together for no other reason than that they wish to be with each other, opening the way to an experience of communitas in the shared state of intoxication. However, it also means that dispersal of these open and informal groups can occur with equal spontaneity, as in these excerpts from first Karen's and then Peter's transcripts which describe the end of an evening of celebration and the aftermath of a rave:

> 'there was loads of us and then everyone vanished but yeah I threw my guts up I haven't thrown up on alcohol for ages but that was a celebration that was me out to celebrate.'

> 'you close your eyes bang and when you wake up no cars in the car park you're the only one left.'

The very conditions that permit spontaneous interaction, then, also ensure that these interactions will be transitory. While they last a utopian desire is realized but it is one that can never endure.

Ephemeral utopias

If everyday life has always been constrained by care for the future that is occasionally relieved by moments of abandon, this archaic rhythm has taken on new dimensions in contemporary society. The processes of accumulation that have come to dominate day-to-day existence have found their apotheosis in a continuous injunction to preserve and increase bodily health.[27] In this context, individual survival has replaced salvation as the highest goal of existence and all gratuitous expenditures that seem to threaten this goal have taken on the aura of sin.[28] This has had the effect of transforming the riches of the body into a miser's store of treasure. In contrast to this hoarding of resources that are never experienced as sufficient, and in any case are always diminishing, intoxication is associated with images of utopian abundance and a free, even at times ruinous, expenditure of the body's resources. While no one can seriously believe that any regime of exercise, diet or medication can *guarantee* even one single extra day of life, it is widely believed, and possibly with some justification, that the right drugs consumed in sufficient quantities are likely to guarantee a shorter life. Since choosing a longer life is out of the question the only power we can realistically exercise over death is the negative one of accepting the possibility of a shorter one. In doing so, the pernicious illusion that death and decay can be indefinitely postponed if we just make a little more effort and avoid certain things is dispelled. It is perhaps this combination of empowerment and acceptance that lends intoxication the luxurious quality that has been alluded to by writers such as Baudrillard and Klein.[29] In any case, to embrace intoxication is to set aside the capital that has come to reside in the body and swap the parsimonious grind of accumulation for the pleasures of a free expenditure. This is not to say that the drugged body cannot itself become the object of investments that place a value on its attributes, as in those images of drug-ravaged bodies once sold as 'heroin chic' by unscrupulous advertisers, but that at the experiential level it resists these processes of investment and accumulation at the moment of intoxication. Intoxication can, when the circumstances are propitious, establish a utopian realm in which generous expenditure rather than careful husbandry predominates, and a sense of abundance is shared.

When asked to recall which drugs they had been using at the time of the incidents they were describing, several of the participants answered with replies that were not merely factual but instead were filled with images evoking a time of ease and plenty, as in these examples from the interviews:

> 'A trailer load of sulphate [amphetamine] still doing the odd bit of glue loads of cider at the time loads of acid loads of pot pot was different back then though wasn't it cannabis they had some culture to 'em now it's just skunk weed or really crap re-pressed hash isn't it you were getting pollens you were getting African weed you were getting Malawi weed and just loads of different stuff from Europe but liquid files of LSD we were

getting just took you away jelly trips wasn't there big barrelled micro dots there must have been at least thirty different kinds of sheet LSD to choose from at the time there was just abundance.' (David)

'Well you get paid fuckin' hell £32 a week for a 40-hour week fucking … give the old man a fiver and the rest of it was yours weed dope was like £3 an eighth pills were like 15p pints were 15p packet of fags I dunno 8 and a half p [laughs] and you had 25 quid just fuck off all week-end just pilled up just speed all the time all these little blues [amphetamine] and black bombers [amphetamine] loads and loads of little black bombers.' (Peter)

'he used to turn up with loads of crack all for free you know just like some nights we'd spend literally all night from when you know from when he arrived to like six, seven in the morning just smoking and as soon as the first rush went we'd be doing another one it was just endless.' (Simon)

'just went round the whole festival just getting every single pill [ecstasy] we could find and just half half half and did the whole lot in about an hour and just goose bumps everywhere just all over me and it just stopped raining and we were standing under this tree and the water was dripping and going down the back of our necks and it just sent you like electric shocks and it was just ahh … doing moon walks everywhere 'cos you just can't feel your legs properly can you and it's all uneven ground yeah just jelly legs and tingling like anything and just the smell of smoke and just really crazy music playing everywhere just I dunno just felt heavenly didn't it heavenly body.' (David)

While these 'heavenly bodies' of course have to return to earth, and often do so with a bump, for a brief period at least they allow a communion with others that, according to many of those I interviewed, is simply not available in the ordinary encounters of everyday life. Since this contact is predicated, in part at least, on a sense of utopian abundance that forgets the future, it is not perhaps surprising that calls for a careful and prudent use of intoxicant drugs, which always imagine intoxication as a form of sobriety, often go unheeded. There are two distinct ways of being that are evident in the interviews that obey different imperatives. The following passage from Roger's interview encapsulates this alternation between moments of expenditure and moments of conservation perfectly:

'I don't think your body will take it very well if you do it [use intoxicant drugs] every day and I tend to eat very well healthily during the week hardly eat anything at the week-ends so really my mission during the week is my other life … '

If much of life is necessarily taken up with an apportioning of resources that are perceived to be scarce, surrendering to intoxication demands at least a partial suspension of this discipline. While this inversion of priorities can clearly never establish a lasting utopia it would be wrong to infer that the ephemeral utopias it does allow are therefore in any way unreal. The idea that states that perdure are inherently more authentic than those that are ephemeral such as intoxication is dismissed by the sociologist Angus Bancroft in the following terms: 'Intoxication is the means for escaping one state, criticized as a false and deceptive "escape", as if impermanence equals unreality.'[30] As Mary Douglas has remarked, when attempting to categorize these forms of sociability:

> '[t]hey are not false worlds, but fragile ones, momentarily upheld and easily overturned. They are more precarious than worlds constructed upon a stable distribution of power and that is the only reason for putting them in a separate section.'[31]

It is now time to consider in more detail the nature of these transient utopias and their significance in contemporary society.

'Going there together'

In a society where the enduring social ties that Tonnies looked to as the basis of community are largely absent, intoxication opens a liminal space where intimate human contact and mutual acknowledgement can still flourish. The effects of accelerating rhythms of work and consumption and the pressures of globalization and increased mobility mean that if contact is to be established with others, beyond the instrumental relations of the market and the state, it needs to be established quickly or it may not be established at all. Added to these pressures, increasing amounts of our time are spent in the 'non-places' analysed by Auge as enforcing a sterile isolation from others, such as the mall, the airport terminal and the motorway service area.[32] From this perspective, rather than being the nemesis of community that it is widely supposed to be, intoxication may be one of the last bastions of authentic human interaction. It is the kind of contact intoxication permits, invariably described as qualitatively different from their normal day-to-day encounters, that is decisive in the accounts of almost all the people I interviewed for the book. In an everyday world in which the body is often reduced to mere surfaces, and the identity it expresses is subject to infinite and divisive differentiations, intoxication allows contact between 'ancestral bodies' that are at once unique and common to all.

It is the discovery of this body, or rather its irruption, that may account for the curious sensation of both losing identity and acquiring a more authentic identity that many of the people I interviewed reported. Often the same individual would claim that they were not themselves when intoxicated, meaning that they had behaved in unexpected ways, only to say a little later that intoxication let their real self come out, meaning perhaps that they had encountered something beyond the 'statuses, roles and offices' that constitute social identities and ensure that perceptions and behaviours remain predictable. This relativizing of the everyday self, and the element of unpredictability that such relativizing entails, raises issues of moral responsibility that many of the participants were forced to wrestle with. It also provides opportunities for trust, forgiveness and redemption that are often obviated by the controlled autonomy of the modern self. These examples from the interviews with first Amanda and then Steven serve to illustrate this aspect of intoxication in contemporary society:

> 'I was really frightened and I didn't know what was going to happen next you know and they were saying it's alright we're with you and they took me out and went for a walk round the parks outdoors they said it will probably be better and it was … '
>
> 'I've blacked out and not remembered well I've blacked out several times with alcohol and ended up being sort of carried places and physically removed from one building to another across several miles without knowing anything about it you know and that worries me that concerns me … you know luckily I've been with people who've looked after me but you know what I mean anything could happen couldn't it when you're in that condition you know.' [33]

Friendship also of course relies on a capacity for shame and forgiveness, and again the interviews provided many instances of both, including these examples from first Karen and then Michael:

> 'there's a lot of mornings when you think oh dear better keep my head down for a day or two and get embarrassed 'cos you drank too much and made a fool of yourself.'
>
> 'even the bloke that I hit years later came up to me in a pub and sort of stuck his hand out and started shaking my hand and I said I'm not sure who you are and he said you hit me once and I thought oh it's you.'

While the kind of ephemeral communities that intoxication permits are not the stable, worthy and productive entities that might be envisaged as sociological ideals, they are nevertheless highly valued by their temporary inhabitants, as these passages from the interviews with first Edward then Amanda and finally George makes clear:

> 'last week-end? Well just what I said just sort of hanging round the fire with a few mates just sort of chatting and … I had some ecstasy last week-end yeah just sort of hanging out by the fire the night went by just sort of collecting wood and done some food done some cooking shared that just shared a sort of outdoor space for the night yeah I just finally felt good because I felt comfortable and sort of a power that I don't seem to get in other places an empowerment.'

'we had this social circle 'cos you were able to be yourself more and everybody trusted each other and we had each other I would definitely say that the hash and mushrooms obviously when they are in season brought us all together yeah.'

'the majority of the people had gone and the sun was just coming up and we were just sitting there and there was a tune on by N called M and we're sitting there smoking these huge reefers each tripping our faces off it was quite a bonding moment then we drove home [laughs].'

The interview material makes it clear that these moments of intoxicated communitas are best understood as an end in themselves that requires no further validation or explanation, but it is equally clear that they can also play a part in the formation of longer-term commitments. These excerpts from the interviews with first Karen, then David and finally Tony convey their role in fostering lasting relationships:

'that's what's connected me with most of the people in this town and I've probably had a session with nearly everybody that I know you know I don't I think there's maybe only one that I haven't got pissed with out of nearly everybody I know yeah but I could have got pissed with him I got really stoned with him that's how I connected to him.'

'seems like every serious relationship I've ever had has been based around drugs for the start of it any time you try something else it just only lasts five minutes it's like you've got a bonding innit go and get off your face at the week-end.'

'well it was just the kind of bonding process that you felt with people do you know what I mean whether it was imagined or not it was something that you always remember the next day or you know the most important thing that we got out of that was you know that it kind of it opened us up to meeting so many new people and we always had new groups of people from different towns and cities that we'd met at parties drifting by to you know to kind of join in this sort of thing but it I think those were the times when we really established sort of true friends with each other and really throughout that whole experience of maybe five or six years it that was kind of it strengthened us all as a group and you know we lost people on the way and things like that but it kind of kept us together and I think that when we actually started to do less of the drugs it made us kind of drift apart in a way do you know what I mean I mean we found other directions you know.'

The paradox of communitas

Where Tonnies' model of community is steeped in nostalgia and Mafessoli's purveys a relentless optimism, the vision of community that has emerged here is one that is characterized by a certain degree of poignancy. Although the desire for community is in constant evidence in these accounts of intoxication, the possibilities for its realization are uncertain, ephemeral and often achieved only at considerable cost to the individuals involved. While this may in part be inherent to communitas since it belongs to a realm of becoming that resists institutionalization, this is not perhaps the whole story. The absolute divorce that seems to exist between these liminal periods and the projective activities of day-to-day existence is perhaps a peculiarly modern phenomenon. These liminal encounters do not so much serve to renew everyday activities, as they may have done in previous eras or other cultures, as to offer relief from them and the opportunity to participate in the 'habitable world of substance and feeling' that Kirmayer has discerned as central to the experience of community.[34] There is, then, a paradox at the heart of the experience of communitas as revealed in these interviews. When the sense of being attuned to others is at its height it seems to hold out the promise of a future of shared projects which in reality can never come to fruition, and which, if it did, would almost certainly destroy the very sensations of belonging which gave rise to it. This is the case because, as the social historian Calhoun explains, there is an inverse relationship between the experience of being with others and the possibility of doing with others:

> The more concerted the action which a group attempts ... the more elaborate must be its external or specialized regulatory mechanisms. Its communal nature will be proportionately sacrificed.[35]

To move towards projective activity is then to move away from the experience of community. However, even if being with others and doing with others are necessarily separate modes of existence they still exist in a relationship to each other and this relationship may have altered in the conditions of modernity. It may be that in other cultures or other periods the transition from moments of being together to moments of doing together was less stark and potentially alienating since the projects of these societies did not require the 'elaborate or specialized regulatory mechanisms' essential to the complex projects of modernity. This contradiction between the promise that being with others seems to hold out and the potential for doing things with others which it actually permits was summed up by one of the participants, Edward, in a passage that is worth quoting at some length:

> 'probably one of the stronger reasons why I continue to indulge would be the one of companionship a sort of a this sort of self-empowerment one the situation when a group of people being people that you know very well or a loose group of people that you've just met in whatever situation but realizing you've got this sort of some kind of common can't think what the word would be acceptance you know of the moment even it doesn't need to be any sort of grand idea it's just sort of this acceptance

of the moment and for that to be just what it is whether it's made into seeming like something grander or just a very simple situation of a few people hanging out certainly some of my most inspiring times have been in those situations some of the most self-empowering times have been in that situation where I've suddenly thought we could do anything … Yeah I suppose it is yeah it's sort of one of the funny one of the horrible things about them the drug culture thing you do tend to look at anybody who doesn't take drugs who's straight as kind of bland and not really too inspired by things and not this zest this zing for sort of life as such which although while I'm saying that I'm sort of thinking the opposite you know that often drug culture that's exactly what it does entail a lack of enthusiasm for things 'cos it's all kind it's quickly there and then it's gone you know well I've had particular moments when we have this kind of group situation whether it's been just a sort of conversation at the time that sort of bonding I got with a few people or whether it's been where the conversation led to some action so I can then look back on it later on and see what we've achieved that's probably some of the greatest times I've had like that and I don't get that so often when I'm with a sort of group of people who are not indulging … '

While the experience of communitas associated with intoxication is not absolutely inimical to projective activity, it is clearly not conducive to it. There is little to be expected from this kind of encounter that would fulfil a desire for progressive social change and this is perhaps why it has been of limited interest to the state or other institutions. Unable to find a useful purpose for it, they have tended instead to construe it as part of a problem that requires a solution. As Georgio Agamben has noted, community that eludes or refuses identity and cannot be put to use can sometimes provoke hostility:

> What the State cannot tolerate in any way, however, is that the singularities form a community without affirming an identity, that humans co-belong without any representable condition of belonging.[36]

The real significance of these liminal encounters should not perhaps be sought in any measurable results they might produce, since they are best understood as an end in themselves, but rather, as Bahktin believed, in what they reveal:

> [t]his truth was ephemeral; it was followed by the fears and oppressions of everyday life, but from those brief moments another unofficial truth emerged, truth about the world and man.[37]

Conclusion

This analysis has set out to uncover the intoxicated body's role in the creation of liminal spaces where an experience of community can sometimes be realized in contemporary society. By understanding community in experiential terms rather than as a fixed set of relationships or vaguely defined potentialities it has been possible to specify some definite material conditions centred on the body that permit, but do not guarantee, community formation in contemporary society. It has been shown that the desire for community and the realization of this desire remains a dynamic force in social existence, and that reports of the 'grotesque' body's demise may be premature. It has also been shown that some of the conditions that allow an experience of community to develop ensure that this experience is often short-lived, precarious and contingent. The picture of community that has emerged in this analysis makes it possible to endorse aspects of both Tonnies's and Maffesoli's accounts, outlined in the previous chapter. While there are certainly grounds for accepting elements of Tonnies's pessimistic conclusions about modernity the picture of the *gesellschaft* form of society he presents perhaps underestimates the human capacity for self-organization and self-definition that are emphasized by Maffesoli. One of the ways this capacity finds expression in contemporary society is through the utopian festivities of intoxication which promise both the pleasures of sociability and the possibility of communitas. While these ephemeral utopias can never be the basis for projective activities, since they take their very meaning from the subversion of all such institutionalized endeavours, they are nevertheless of great importance to those who participate in them. By allowing interaction beyond the 'statuses, roles and offices' of everyday life they provide an authentic contact with the world and with others in a late modern environment that is increasingly dominated by arbitrary symbolic meanings. This contact is grounded in a common 'ancestral body' and a shared experience of intoxication rather than being mediated through language.

8 Conclusion

In this final chapter I will begin by briefly recalling some of the key themes that have emerged during the course of this discussion of intoxicant drug use, before going on to consider the implications of these ideas for the ways in which drug use and drug users are viewed in contemporary society and what would be required for this to change. The conventional understanding we have in western societies of what it means to be healthy will be called into question and an alternative way of thinking about health and how we can best achieve this desired state will be suggested. Ideas about health are important in this context because the construction of intoxicant drug use as a social problem is grounded in the claim that it poses a threat to our health and well-being.[1] Having considered what we mean by health, and challenged some of the apparent certainties that underpin our beliefs about it, the book will end where it began, with the unresolved ambivalence we feel about intoxication in modern western societies. However, the aim is not only to explore the contours of this ambivalence but also to point to a potential way to resolve it.

Intoxication as a sacrificial gesture

To understand what we are doing when we become intoxicated we first had to explore the meaning of sobriety, and in particular the meaning of sobriety in a modern western society. Sobriety was theorized as an orientation to the world and to others that is typically rational, acquisitive and focused narrowly on means and ends, whether in the meeting of primordial needs or in the pursuit of our modern projective goals. This way of being was contrasted with the passive opening to experience that characterizes intoxication. However, it was noted that intoxication is not a state of being that is entirely separate from our everyday sober self but one that exists in a delicate and dynamic relationship with it. The upright, bounded purposeful body of modernity, which is engaged in rationally ordered activities, is not supplanted by the grotesque body of intoxication but rather subverted by it. This subversion is the result of a sacrificial gesture that temporarily sets aside the goods of the world as something useful to human purposes in favour of an experience of the world and the other that is touched by the sacred. This encounter with the sacred reveals the world to us as it exists prior to the manifold differentiations imposed by our primordial needs and by our rationally conceived projects. Having actively chosen to make this sacrifice, intoxication, as a state of being, is a gift we receive from the world rather than an activity we engage in, an event that happens to us which lies beyond our conscious volition. A free and generous expenditure of resources that could otherwise have been put to more productive use is the key that opens the door to this other way of being. Intoxication and the sacrifice that makes it possible can never be useful, since it exists only in the present and leaves no trace behind when it passes out of existence. However, the essential element of sacrifice is lost and the limit point of intoxication is reached when the useful is entirely forgotten, opening the way to oblivion, chaos and death. It is only when the useful is recalled at the same moment that it is entirely forgotten that the *impossible* state of intoxication comes into being and can be experienced as a transgressive event.

The possibility of sacrificing the rational body of everyday life in order to experience intoxication exists because that body is essentially an accomplishment that is acquired and maintained through social interaction. Everything that society has made us, and everything that we desire to become, finds expression in our body and in the way we present it to ourselves and to others and in the ways we make use of it. The way we speak, the way we walk, the things we like, how we dress, our fears and ambitions are all brought into being through a complex play of social forces that we actively participate in but can never control. Each of these attributes which we think of as expressions of our own individuality, but which actually result from our patterns of social interaction, has a specific social value making us more or less successful, more or less desirable. These markers of identity and distinction affirm who we are, to ourselves and to others, but also divide us one from another.[2] Walter Benjamin summed up our relationship to each other, in a modern society, when he compared the way our gaze passes over other people in a city street to the way we examine fruit in a market, finding some perfectly ripe and inviting, others spoiled and repulsive.[3] Gazing and gazed upon we place a value on others and are valued by them in our turn, helping to sustain the ordered social balance. Whatever the particular social value our own bodies may have we are nevertheless obliged to inhabit them and conform to the expectations society has of us, and to enforce our expectations on others as members of society. The burden of these expectations and the rigour with which they are enforced has increased dramatically as the complexity and rationalization of society has progressed, and has shifted from being a discipline that is external to us to being one that is often fully internalized.[4]

However, while the forces of a rationalized modern social order may traverse the body with ever increasing intensity, their influence is never absolute or final – as the feminist scholar Judith Butler,[5] for example, has persuasively argued. According to Butler, while the 'embodying of norms, is a compulsory practice, a forcible production' it can never be a final and definitive state of being.[6] The reason why norms of embodiment remain unstable and open to change and challenge is to be found in the imperfect and iterative process by which they are reproduced and maintained. For Butler the possibility always exists that in the gap between the imposition or adoption of any behavioural norm or bodily ideal and its realization through repeated enactment that same norm or ideal may be subject to processes of modification, appropriation or subversion. In other words, forces that constitute bodies in one form may be subject to modification or annulment by other forces that traverse the body constituting it in entirely different ways.[7] Intoxication represents one way in which the body can be subject to transformations that remake it in a new form that undermines the influence of existing normative constraints. Because the body is always vulnerable to radical change in this way, even the most compelling normative categories remain fragile. The body therefore is not only a repository of socially constituted norms, and a vehicle for our projects and ambitions, but also potentially a gateway to realms of experience that help us to recover a primordial relationship to the self, the world and the other. When we choose to become intoxicated we sacrifice our everyday self and set aside the competent body that expresses our identity and ambitions. This transformation through intoxication is manifested in the playful way we inhabit our bodies in this altered state, in contrast to the serious and deliberate habitus of normal life. This sacrifice of the competent body, as is the case with the embodying of norms itself, can never be complete or final but exists only in that *impossible* space between the embodying of norms and their absolute destruction. If our expenditure of resources is too heedless intoxication shades over into oblivion or the destruction of the competent body, but if our expenditure is too prudent the experience of intoxication remains within the realm of everyday life and its normative constraints.

Intoxication and temporality

Time in modern society exists independently of our corporeal experience as a standardized measurable objectified reality governed by the clock. Whereas in the past our experience of time was intimately linked to natural cycles, the wider rhythms of the cosmos and human durations of growth and decay, time has now become a universal tool for planning, organization and the effective monitoring and deployment of resources, including the resources of the individuated self and the bounded upright body that gives it expression.

When we sacrifice the rational body of everyday life through becoming intoxicated we transcend the impositions of the clock that order our everyday existence in order to inhabit the lived present in its passing, on the fleeting cusp of the future and the past. What we give up when we make this sacrifice is, ultimately, time itself. We live under a continuous injunction to make time useful by doing useful things in the time we have left to us but when we become intoxicated we resist this imperative in favour of a luxurious and wasteful expenditure of time in the present. This gesture of giving time to a state of being that is without use or purpose is inherently generous and sacrificial in nature because the time we give is irrecoverable and the use we could have made of it is lost forever. It is also generous because intoxication opens onto an unknown and unknowable future and the duration of its occurrence, at both a subjective and objective level, is often uncertain. Again, this sacrifice of time retains its transgressive character only on the condition that we retain a sense of time as something that could have been made use of, either to make provision for our future needs or to pursue our future-oriented projects. The time of intoxication is the *impossible* moment when this future that is sacrificed is at once forgotten and recalled.

By seeking intoxication we resist the impositions of the clock in a literal sense, by setting aside time for this experience that is outside the normal temporal constraints of day-to-day life. We also resist the objectified linear time of modernity in a more profound sense because the intoxicated body secretes its own subjective temporality that has nothing to do with the clock. Time can alter its viscosity dramatically while we are intoxicated, becoming so glutinous that it seems to have stopped altogether or flashing by in an instant leaving us wondering if we were even present at its passing. In this respect, intoxication has affinities with other elements of existence which are resistant to the alienating temporality of the clock and occur in their own time, such as music, laughter and dance.

As well as allowing us to inhabit a lived present and a temporality that emanates from the body rather than the clock, and which thus reconnects us with the rhythms of nature, intoxication also allows us to share this lived present with others. When we grow older together in the lived present of intoxication we recognize and acknowledge each other as unique and irreplaceable. This form of mutual understanding is grounded in the finitude of our bodies and the reversibility of the senses, the eye that sees as it is being seen, the hand that touches as it is being touched and has nothing to do with the rational knowledge that we will all die one day. These shared experiences of intoxication are sedimented in the body to form a personal history whose passing is recorded in the flesh rather than by the clock and which can provide the basis for an enduring form of mutual recognition. This deep form of mutual recognition goes beyond the normal interactions of everyday life where common interests or identities may be discovered and acknowledged.

The liminal communities of intoxication

Modern western societies are typically characterized by weak social ties, and the atomization and fragmentation of communities. In these conditions, there is often little scope for fulfilling the deep and enduring human desire to experience a sense of belonging with others that is characterized by a mutual acknowledgement of equality. Shared states of intoxication provide one means through which the isolating effects of contemporary society can sometimes be overcome, at least temporarily, and this sense of equality with others and mutual acknowledgement experienced.

When the competent rational body of everyday life is sacrificed, and the lived present is shared with others, a liminal space is opened up between the structures of society. In this temporary and fluid space, an encounter with the other can be experienced that is qualitatively different from the normal interactions of day-to-day existence in the modern world. A social transformation can occur that allows us to experience ourselves as one amongst equals. As Victor Turner has suggested, the basis for this sense of equality lies in the synchronization of corporeal experience that shared states of intoxication brings about. Through the shared ordeals and ecstasies of intoxication, a form of mutual acknowledgement can be experienced that does not depend on either pre-existing shared identities or on a rational reconciliation of competing positions. This loosening of structured and hierarchical relationships is reflected in the physical spaces that are associated with intoxication in contemporary society. These spaces typically allow for a free circulation of bodies and 'rhizomic' interactions, as opposed to the generally hierarchical and predictable interactions of everyday life. The most complete manifestations of this kind of rhizomic interaction can be found in the free festivals, acid house raves and squat parties that celebrate intoxication and communitas outside the corporately controlled spaces where sociable interactions normally occur such as clubs, pubs and commercial events.

These types of liminal community are inherently fleeting and unstable in contemporary society and therefore do not provide a basis for cementing enduring solidary ties or for the pursuit of shared projects. It is a cruel paradox that these moments of community realize so fully the desire for a sense of belonging with others without containing any means for this sense of belonging to be sustained. Although such experiences of communion are sometimes associated with the creation of longer-term commitments, their principle significance remains in the lived present and the 'finite world of meaning' they allow individuals to share.[8] If these moments of communion were to become the basis for common projects or an organized community they would lose their special quality as a space *between* the structures of society and instead would simply become one of these structures. This is not to say that there can be no relationship between the social spaces of everyday life and the liminal space of 'communitas'. In traditional societies this kind of liminal space was deliberately opened up as part of the regular rhythm of social existence and served to renew the social bonds of the group. By contrast, in contemporary society the opening up of liminal spaces of this kind is typically ad hoc, random and dissociated from wider social structures and patterns of interaction.

Intoxication, health and the place of drug users in contemporary society

In western societies there is a more or less unquestioned assumption that material reality is the only reality and that this reality is made known and put to use through rational observation and practical endeavour. This rational and materialistic world view is the basis on which western culture has been built and the foundation of modernity and its manifold projects. Experiences that are not reducible to rational intelligibility, such as intoxication, are therefore likely to be misunderstood and rejected as flights from reality that have little to contribute to either the well-being of the individual or the functioning of society. At best, intoxication is seen as a distraction from the real and serious business of society, and at worst as a threat to society's very existence. Despite the ubiquity of intoxicant drug use, and the great importance many users accord to their experiences, intoxication remains an excluded other that is denied a legitimate and socially sanctioned place in our society. In a culture dominated by rationality and materialism intoxication is almost always construed negatively and any serious recognition of its positive significance tends to be either silenced or dismissed. Because intoxicant drug use can be regarded as both unnecessary and without identifiable purpose, it is typically viewed, in a society devoted to a rational utilization of resources and the optimization of bodily performance and longevity, as an experience that is therefore without any real value or meaning. However, as I have argued, the value of intoxication as an experience can be seen to lie precisely in its stubborn resistance to being incorporated into the endless chains of production and consumption that make up everyday life in a modern society. It is this quality of not being useful that makes it possible for intoxication to open up a space in which the self, the world and the other can be encountered beyond the needs and investments of everyday life. Fundamental questions are raised by the consideration that something which is avowedly not useful, and may sometimes even be harmful in purely physical terms to those who experience it, may nevertheless have a positive value. The phenomenon of voluntary intoxication invites us not just to think about how the intoxicated body can be a source of meaning and social change, for example by creating a sense of belonging with others through shared states of intoxication, but to confront the even more basic problem of deciding what our bodies are *for* and who decides this.

Intoxication and the meaning of health

In this book I have argued that intoxication is often viewed as a threat to society because as a state of being it is at odds with the rational and materialistic assumptions that are foundational for western culture. This distrust of non-rational experience is most often and most forcefully expressed, in relation to intoxicant drug use, in the unqualified claim that it is likely to undermine the health and well-being of the individual and consequently of society as a whole, and therefore it should be minimized or outlawed altogether. Whatever the validity of this claim in relation to any particular substance or practice, its unquestioned adoption as a global generalization in defence of a rationalized social order is, ironically, itself a product of irrationality, fear and prejudice. Simply to state that intoxicant drugs should be avoided because they are a threat to health and well-being is the equivalent of saying that kitchen knives or cars are dangerous without enquiring into the circumstances in which they are being used. To take the most reviled drug of all, heroin, for example, there is no good evidence that its prolonged use shortens life or damages the organs of the body in any way, provided the supply is pure and administration is carried out in a hygienic way. If drug policies were really concerned with the preservation of health, rather than being a moral crusade against intoxication, the rational response to the problems of heroin use would be to supply clean drugs and equipment and educate people in their correct use. However, to do this would risk conceding that the very real dangers faced by heroin users in contemporary society derive almost entirely from their marginalized and stigmatized social situation, rather than from the drug itself or the state of intoxication it induces. This point, that it is the marginalized social situation of drug users that makes drugs dangerous rather than the drugs themselves is rarely if ever acknowledged in official discourses on the subject. As well as denying help to drug users who are deemed unworthy, drug policies related to health have also ensured that those who suffer from conditions such as multiple sclerosis, cancer, depression and post-traumatic stress disorder have been denied the medicinal and therapeutic benefits of substances such as cannabis and ecstasy simply because of their association with intoxication. Research into these and other compounds that might be of benefit to patients has been delayed for decades or banned outright as the result of an irrational prejudice which makes it impossible to countenance the idea that intoxicant drugs could be used for positive ends.

To understand why the preservation of health has come to provide the ultimate justification for denying intoxicant drug use a legitimate place in social existence it is necessary to recall the origins and development of these kinds of public health discourses. Concerns about the health of populations have always primarily been concerns about how these populations can be managed, controlled and put to productive use. The collection of data about the physical conditions of life, and the deployment of interventions to improve those conditions, coincided with the demand for an industrial workforce capable of sustained disciplined effort in the factory and an army equal to the rigours of industrialized warfare. In the era of empire, health was promoted in the interests of national efficiency. At the beginning, these interventions operated from above, at the level of society as a whole, or at the level of a particular class within society, for example through the provision of universal sewerage systems or the licensing of alcohol sales to reduce working-class absenteeism from the factories.[9] With the establishment of the National Health Service in the United Kingdom and other medical infrastructures elsewhere, these broad initiatives were supplemented by a system that could respond to illness on an individual basis, although not necessarily to the needs of individuals. Over time, the sophistication of epidemiological interventions, and the range of conditions treated, grew exponentially but the same basic idea prevailed – that health systems dealt with population-wide issues and responded to specific manifestations of disease as they arose.

In recent years the assumption that health is the default state and that the population can largely be left to get on with being healthy until some organic malaise leads them to seek treatment has been swept away by a new, positive conception of health. Health has now become an activity with its own onerous regimes and moral imperatives where the individual is given direct and total responsibility for their own well-being, and, by implication, their own illnesses. This transformation in the way health is understood can be linked to the discrediting of all narratives of social progress and the retreat from collective endeavour that followed the collapse of communism, and to the concomitant rise of individualism and laissez-faire economics. To be healthy now is to be both knowledgeable about and proficient in the complex tasks of self-monitoring required to optimize bodily performance and longevity through diet, exercise, screening and forms of holistic awareness. Failure in any of these areas signals moral turpitude, ignorance and a loss of status that warrants either coercive intervention or the denial of services that in future will be increasingly reserved for the worthy and compliant. As responsibility for the health of the population has now been devolved to the individual citizen, if that citizen fails to optimize their own health they now risk standing accused of threatening the health of society as a whole. This establishes health as a moral duty enforced by rigorous social sanctions rather than it being a problem of physical capabilities and their effective management. For example, that banning smoking in public places is a moral rather than a health measure is confirmed by the paucity of evidence that passive smoking poses any meaningful risk to health and by the cynical manipulation and exaggeration of the evidence that does supposedly justify these forms of social exclusion and segregation.[10] The smoker has become a figure of revulsion and contempt not only because they refuse their own responsibilities in relation to their health but also because they may prevent others, including innocent children, from achieving a state of health that is fully optimized. Smoking is now classified as a transmissible disease and the smoker as a wilful carrier of contagion.

Ideas about health and how it should be improved and maintained have then undergone dramatic changes in western society over the last two hundred years. From being a matter of fate, health became first a problem of managing populations, then of responding to particular disease states, and now it has become a social and moral duty. As different as these phases are, they have in common that they view the body as a material resource to be husbanded and put to use, even if it is now to be put to use simply in its own maintenance.

As a result of these health discourses, which dominate our conception of what it means to be healthy, it is a virtually unquestioned and unquestionable belief in our society that activities which are likely to increase the length of our life are, by definition, healthy, while activities that might decrease the length of our life are, by definition, unhealthy. If human health is simply equated with functional efficiency and longevity in this way then intoxication, as a state of being that has little to contribute to this end, should either be minimized or better still avoided altogether. However, if a different definition of health is employed then merely to survive and retain functional competence may actually be associated with a lack of health, or even with the presence of an underlying pathology. For Deleuze and Guattari a healthy organism is one that is able to make new reciprocal connections with its environment and with other organisms and an unhealthy organism is one that has ceased to make such new connections.[11] From this perspective, which measures health in terms of an organism's vigour in expanding its connections, rather than in years of survival and relative functional capacity, the use of intoxicant drugs could be a sign of either health or of an absence of health. For example, a repetitive relationship with a single substance that established no new connections between the individual, their environment and others would be defined as unhealthy, even if the individual lived to an exceptional age and retained all their faculties and capacities intact. Conversely, an individual who expended their energies in making new connections through the use of intoxicant drugs could be seen as healthy, even if they suffered physical side effects that had consequences for their longevity. Even more radically, a drug user who suffered a premature death as a result of their choices may have lived more and been healthier than a person who carefully husbanded their physical resources but at the expense of making new reciprocal connections with the world and with others. In other words, to prioritize the prolongation of life over living itself may be to confuse survival with health. This way of thinking about what it means to be healthy implies that health is not something fixed by objective coordinates but a point somewhere between expenditure and conservation that is difficult or perhaps even impossible to determine.

This is a definition of health that does not simply view it as an absence of disease and death, but positively as a capacity for living that is manifested in reciprocal interactions with the world and with others. As Peta Malins has suggested, when evaluating whether drug use is healthy or not: 'What becomes important is that bodies are able to go on connecting with other bodies, creating new flows of desire and undertaking new becomings.'[12]

Klein endorses this positive definition of health but takes it further still by suggesting that disease and decay are the very condition of human existence and that there is only one possible cure for this condition and that cure is death.[13] This means that the desire for health, understood as an absence of disease and decay, actually equates to a desire for death, since it is only through death that this kind of stasis could ever be achieved. The prospect of a life without disease or decay, in which death is indefinitely postponed, is nothing more than a fantasy at present – but it is a fantasy that would have the character of a nightmare were this ambition ever realized in practice. The moment that disease and death are finally conquered will actually be the moment of our collective death as a species, since the very meaning of human life resides in our mortality. At the point when death and disease are consigned to history, our attunement to a rationally ordered society will be complete because we will, finally, have become machines. But if we are, for the time being at least, as William Burroughs puts it, just dying animals on a doomed planet, then perhaps we require a definition of health that affirms our capacity for living rather than pursuing an ideal of physical stasis and perfectibility that ignores our evident and unavoidable decay. The problem is that our society has difficulty acknowledging the existence or value of anything that cannot be measured and quantified so we are left with an impoverished definition of health that can do no more than count the number of years we survive and list the practical tasks we can accomplish during those years.

Finding a place for intoxication in modern society

If health implies something more than the body's preservation and productive use, this raises further questions about the place of non-rational experiences such as intoxication in a rationally ordered society. As we grow ever more confident that we know what the body is and how it should function, for example, by mapping the human genome or scanning the brain in real time, we grow ever more confused about how to respond to desires that lie beyond these new certainties and to experiences that they cannot account for. As a society, we seem uncertain whether we should punish, attempt to cure or simply abandon to the forces of the market individuals who flout the injunction to make rational and productive use of their bodies at all times and instead seek intoxication. The deleterious consequences of this ambivalence for individuals and for society as a whole are easily enumerated.

By attempting to outlaw rather than integrate the desire for intoxication western societies have stigmatized and criminalized their own citizens, undermined civil rights, sponsored the development of international criminal networks, encouraged the spread of HIV, helped to fund terrorism, caused extensive environmental damage and created corrupt and unstable narco-states such as Afghanistan.[14] In addition, the war on drugs, which began as a metaphor, rapidly degenerated into a real shooting war with annual casualties numbered in the thousands.[15] In forty years this war has done nothing to reduce the supply of proscribed substances but has led to the diversion of vast resources and the wholesale incarceration of mainly black, Hispanic and poor white young men for committing 'crimes' that have no obvious victims. As well as these global impacts, confusion about the social role and meaning of intoxicant drug use finds expression in the selective system of prohibitions and regulations we have devised for the control of intoxicant drugs, which are an affront to both common sense and natural justice. The dignity and human rights of some drug users are violated with impunity on a routine basis simply because the drugs they happen to choose are subject to arbitrary proscription. Even those who frame these laws often freely admit that there is no rational basis for them but are happy to enforce them, and to repeat the superstitious beliefs that supposedly justify them, for reasons of political expediency.[16] This situation has led some enlightened campaigners to call for a charter of rights for drug users to bring an end to the abuse and ostracism many of them routinely endure in society. The reasoning behind this call is that drug users constitute an oppressed minority who suffer the same kinds of stigma and discrimination that other minorities have suffered in the past because of their race, gender, religion or sexual orientation and therefore should be afforded the same rights and protections.[17]

In the absence of such basic rights individuals are left either to discover their own meanings for the experiences of intoxication they have, sometimes with disastrous consequences, or are obliged to accept socially generated meanings that are damaging because they are based on irrational fears and misconceptions about intoxicant drug use. Faced with hysterical and hyperbolic claims about the destructive and enslaving properties of particular substances individuals may ignore or underestimate the actual risks involved in substance use, including, or especially, those substances that enjoy a degree of social toleration such as alcohol. Unable to reconcile their own experiences with available public discourses, individuals are forced to obtain information about intoxicant drugs from a variety of informal sources that may be equally unreliable such as peer groups, the Internet, media stories and urban myths. Even if drug users are able to locate reliable information about a particular substance and its effects there is no guarantee that it will apply to the substances they are actually using because the purity, potency and composition of drugs obtained through a black market economy is often unknown and highly variable. The consequences of this ignorance combined with routine exposure to adulterated substances can be seen in the deaths through overdose of the young and naive and in the gangrenous and amputated limbs of older injecting users. Perhaps the greatest risk to drug and alcohol users, however, does not come from ignoring dominant discourses about intoxication and finding their own forms of knowledge and meaning but in accepting the validity of some of these dominant discourses. Drug and alcohol users may embrace, or be forced to embrace, meanings for their experiences that are dis-empowering and highly stigmatizing, such as those provided by the construction of drug use as addiction. Told they are helpless victims yet punished for their behaviour individuals who have limited power and resources may be locked into a downward cycle of incarceration and failed rehabilitation with a spoiled identity that marks them as being at once deviant and diseased.

A charter of rights for drug users would certainly be a step in the right direction, and would have the obvious benefit that those who do encounter problems with their drug or alcohol use would be encouraged to come forward at an early stage for help and support, but the analysis of this book suggests that this still does not go far enough. What is really required to address the problems faced by drug users, and the problems caused by drug use in society, is the integration of non-rational experiences such as intoxication into the wider rhythms of social existence. What is required for this to happen is that the importance of non-rational experience, even in a society committed to a rational world view, must be fully acknowledged and accepted by the wider community. The persistence or even increase in the use of intoxicant drugs suggests that there are human needs and desires that remain unfulfilled by participation in the rational projects of a modern society. If we continue to dismiss these needs and desires, and the behaviours they give rise to, as the products of deviance, disease or hedonistic indulgence, rather than finding a legitimate space for them and acknowledging their real significance and value, the problems they cause for individuals and society are likely to continue unabated.

In many cultures that we think of as other, the body has not only been seen as an object that must be put to use, but also as a gateway to the dangerous and renewing forces of the sacred. In these older cultures, encounters with the uncoded energies of the sacred are alternated with the demands of everyday existence in a regulated and ritually guarded context. This endows such encounters with a recognized and agreed significance. In contemporary society, contact with the uncoded forces released by intoxicant drugs, like so many other aspects of social existence, has effectively been privatized and deregulated. While contact with the sacred through intoxication can never be without risks or consequences these are massively compounded in a situation where individuals must find their own way and attribute their own meanings to the experiences they have or accept the meanings that are given to them by the discourses that are dominant in society. The question is, how can a rationally ordered society ever acknowledge and accommodate a desire for non-rational experiences, such as intoxication, and accept that we are just human after all.

Schizophrenia, incitement and intoxication

At the dawn of the latest 'war on drugs' in the early 1970s, the celebrated science fiction author Philip K. Dick, imagined, with characteristic prescience, a future (that he set in the present) where society's ambivalent attitude to the use of intoxicant drugs would reach its logical and absurd conclusion. In *A Scanner Darkly* the main protagonist, a character named Bob Arctor, is a committed drug fiend whose day job happens to be that of an undercover police agent. As part of his police work, Arctor is assigned the task of gathering evidence against a committed drug fiend and his associates who turn out to be none other than Bob Arctor and his friends.[18] This paranoia-inducing and schizophrenic scenario is played out until one day Arctor suffers a breakdown, but also has a kind of epiphany, while addressing a citizens' meeting about the evils of the drug trade and the vile pushers who profit from it. The realization he comes to is that his own excessive drug use is a direct response to a society that has imposed this intolerable dual life on him. It would be difficult to conceive of a more perfect metaphor for a society that is at war with itself and incapable of admitting either to its own desires or to the futility of trying to eradicate these desires, and the psychic and social consequences of this. In seeking to deny intoxication a legitimate place in society, by regulating and prohibiting the substances and practices associated with it, and by stigmatizing and criminalizing its spontaneous irruptions we may simply be inciting and amplifying the desire for these states. It may be more than a coincidence that those countries with the strictest prohibitionist regimes, such as the United States, also have some of the highest levels of problematic drug use, while countries that are more tolerant and accepting of these desires and seek to normalize and integrate them, such as Portugal or the Netherlands, have seen stable or falling rates of problematic drug use.

Discourses about intoxication, like all discourses, are generative and productive, bringing into existence the phenomena they purport merely to describe. If we look for deviance, disease, addiction and threats to the social order then that is precisely what we will discover, and the harder we look and the more we try to understand and ameliorate these problems the larger they will become. Michel Foucault analysed the same processes at work when he traced the emergence of sexuality as a distinct object of enquiry and social concern, showing how it was not simply uncovered or explained but rather created by the discourses that surround it.[19] If we really want to do something meaningful about the real problems associated with drug and alcohol use all that is required is to look without preconceptions for long enough to see that the monster we fear is actually just us. Not certainly our everyday selves, but us enjoying a brief sabbatical from the necessary and the useful to get reacquainted with a world that is normally saturated in discursive meanings, and to encounter the other beyond the 'statuses, roles and offices' of everyday life. If we can embrace the monster rather than shunning it we may discover that it is no monster at all but a valuable and renewing possibility. As society succumbs to ever more intensive forms of rationalization, surveillance and control the need for sacrificial and transgressive experience has never been greater. Rather than pursuing the utopian fantasy that we can live without such experiences we should instead be working to find a place for them in a properly balanced social order.

Appendix A

How the interviews were conducted and interpreted: methodological and epistemological issues

To borrow a term used by the French philosopher Jean-Luc Nancy, the body can be implicated in its own *unmaking*.[1] As well as being a site where manifold social forces find corporeal expression the body can also be understood as a site where these same forces meet their limit and can suffer reversals. These limit points and reversals can take many forms, but for our purposes the phenomenon of voluntary intoxication can be taken as a paradigmatic case for investigating the *unmaking* of the socially constituted body.[2]

Intoxication is '*learned* in a social context',[3] as Giles and a number of other theorists have pointed out. Intoxication can also open on to realms of experience that are excessive of social context and learned behaviour. Intoxication offers an ideal focus for exploring the relationship between the body understood as a product of social forces and the body understood as a socially productive force.

If the body is to be understood as a source of meaning and social change then it is desirable to get as close to the realities of lived experience as the barrier of language will permit. One way of doing this is by seeking the meaning of specific embodied experiences as they are conveyed in personal narratives. However, if we are to arrive at these meanings we need to do more than simply listen to what people say about the experiences they have had. In order to reveal the phenomenal realities embedded in these stories it is necessary to place them within a clear interpretive framework. To construct this interpretive framework, and begin theorizing a productive role for the body, has involved establishing a dialogue between, on the one hand, a range of texts relating to the body, and on the other, the contributions made by the people I interviewed. The rationale, at an epistemological level, for adopting this approach stems from a belief that while the application of theory can help to reveal meanings in social existence that might otherwise remain obscure, equally importantly, the resistance to neat categorization which empirical data display can rescue theory from some of the excesses of abstraction and generalization for which it has potential.[4] By employing different levels of analysis and allowing them to inform one another the aim of my approach was to avoid the pitfalls both of theoreticism and also of a naive empiricism that too readily accepts empirical data as self-evidently veridical.

In the next section, the basic features of the interview process will be outlined, before each element of the process is discussed in greater detail under individual headings.

Methodology

The substantive element of this book is based on a series of sixteen semi-structured individual interviews that were conducted between 12 April 2002 and 11 December 2002. These interviews were carried out specifically for the book in order to gather new data relating to the phenomenon of voluntary intoxication in contemporary society. Each interview was recorded and the resulting audio tapes were transcribed in full before being analysed and interpreted from a phenomenological perspective. In the following sections, the methodological procedures and epistemological assumptions which governed the process of gathering and analysing the interview material will be described, and some of the issues and difficulties that arose in the course of this process will be discussed.

Sampling strategy and recruitment

The sampling criterion employed is known as 'intensity sampling' and involves locating 'information rich cases that manifest the phenomenon intensely but not extremely'.[5] As the book is concerned with meaning rather than the manipulation of variables the exact composition of the sample was less important than the quality of the responses obtained. The priority was to recruit individuals who had significant experience of intoxication and were willing to relate their experiences in an open manner. Having said that the composition of the sample was not a key priority, efforts were made to achieve a reasonably mixed sample, by purposively selecting the individuals who would take part.[6] The final sample included both males and females drawn from a range of different social backgrounds, and of differing ages (see Appendix B for a breakdown of the sample by age, sex and occupation).

It was initially intended that individuals who defined themselves, or were defined by others, as 'problematic' or 'dependent' drug or alcohol users would be excluded on both theoretical and ethical grounds but this proved to be a far more complex and ambiguous issue than anticipated. As the interviews progressed the usefulness of the terms 'problematic' and 'dependent', and the viability of the assumptions that underpin these terms, seemed increasingly untenable and the rationale of the sampling strategy had to be modified accordingly. The issues involved in this change in sampling criteria will be discussed more fully in the section which deals with the role of the interviewer.

Participants were recruited mainly through a process of 'snowballing' which relies on inviting those who take part to suggest the names of others with relevant experience who might be willing to participate. The recruitment process commenced with an individual who was a work colleague. Of those who were initially approached all agreed to be interviewed although one individual withdrew before the interview could take place, giving as their reason that they did not feel comfortable with the idea of being audiotaped. One other interview also had to be abandoned because it proved to be impossible to find a time to conduct it that was mutually convenient due to work commitments.

It is always a difficult issue in this type of research to decide when sufficient material has been collected and the point of effective 'saturation' reached. There is a balance to be struck between the concern that further interviews might yield new and valuable material and the danger of the '1000 page transcript' that Kvale has warned of – the problem that there is potentially an inverse relationship between the quantity of transcripts generated and the quality of the analysis that can be undertaken.[7] As the ratio of new material appeared to be declining sharply towards the end of the interview cycle it was decided to conclude after completing two additional interviews in order to confirm the trend, with the assumption in mind that additional material could be gathered at a later stage if required.

While the sample that was obtained is certainly not representative of any particular population or of the population in general, in any strict statistical sense, equally, there are no obvious grounds for believing that it is particularly eccentric in any way. In order to confirm this point, a limited survey of the Erowid (http://www.erowid.org) and Lycaeum (http://www.lycaeum.org) archives, where individuals post anonymous accounts of their experiences with a range of intoxicant substances, was carried out. Despite the great diversity of the contributors to these sites and the wide array of substances that they reported using, themes could be readily identified in their accounts that were broadly comparable to those appearing in the interviews conducted for the book. Although this survey was not systematic it did provide some reassurance that the findings are unlikely to be unique to the sample obtained. However, it is important to stress that this material was consulted only as a heuristic device and that no definite claims can be made about the generalizability of the book's findings based on this survey.

Data collection

The aims of the book were also reflected in the method of data collection that was employed. Individual interviews and open questions were preferred for their ability to elicit personal narratives.[8] As a number of researchers have suggested, individual narratives are both closer to the life world than other forms of discourse and a fundamental means by which human experience is organized.[9] These features, which are inherent to the narrative form, make individual narratives particularly fruitful for an analysis conducted from a phenomenological perspective. Rather than conducting individual interviews it would perhaps have been more straightforward to gather material by interviewing with a recognized group. Focus group interviews could have been arranged with, for example, a group of clubbers who had used the drug ecstasy, or a student rugby team who drank beer together, but it was felt that this would have been likely to produce a homogeneous set of responses that was dominated by public discourses. For the purposes of this book a heterogeneous set of responses rich in particular biographical material was desirable, and this, on the whole, is what was obtained.

Conducting the interviews

The interviews ranged in length from approximately twenty minutes to around ninety minutes and were mainly conducted in people's homes, although two were conducted at my home and one in an art gallery. The choice of venue was left entirely to the people I interviewed as was the timing and length of the interviews; although it was suggested at the time the interviews were arranged that their likely duration would be around one hour. All the interviews were audiotaped in full.

The interviews were semi-structured through the use of a topic list consisting of only six fairly short open-ended questions which were generally asked in the same order, and mainly took the form: 'Can you tell me about the first/last/best/worst/ experience you have had with drink or drugs?' (see Appendix C for a full list of the questions used). The questions referred mainly to very general temporal or evaluative categories that would be universally recognized. Efforts were made to balance each question so that accounts of good experiences, for example, were contrasted with accounts of negative experiences. The reasons for using this very general and balanced interview format were twofold. First, it encouraged people to give accounts of the widest possible range of experiences. Second, it avoided giving the impression that I had specific expectations or interests in mind beyond hearing the people's stories in the form they chose to tell them. This was an important consideration because, as a number of qualitative researchers have noted, interviewees are typically expert at divining an interviewer's underlying concerns and framing their answers accordingly.[10] In addition to the topic list non-directive probes and supplementary questions were also used to encourage people to expand on the accounts they had provided. Although the questions were focused as to topic they were intended to function as open 'story-telling invitations', designed to elicit narratives that were rich in indexical statements, that is, related to concrete events and specific times.[11] This emphasis on eliciting accounts of particular events, rather than exploring, for example, people's attitudes and opinions, reflected a preoccupation with the phenomenal significance of embodied experiences. However, since the representation of events in discourse is always highly mediated and constructed, assigning meaning to the experiences described remained a complex interpretive task. The issues involved in performing this task will be discussed in greater detail in the section that deals with the analysis and interpretation of the data.

Transcribing the data

The audio recordings obtained were generally of a very high quality but there is an inevitable degradation of the material in the process of transcription. There are some passages that remain ambiguous or obscure either because the recording itself is not clear or, more often, because the expressions or references used by people are unfamiliar to the interviewer and the meaning consequently unclear. A reduction in quality also occurs through the loss of context and because of the impossibility of rendering the many nuances of expression, intonation, accent, body language, etc. that were available in the original interview setting. For these reasons the analysis was conducted by listening to the original audio recordings while annotating the transcripts in order to evoke as fully as possible the original setting in which they occurred. In addition, memos were used to note ideas and connections that were suggested by the data as the analysis progressed.

Ethical considerations

Every effort was made to ensure that the research complied fully with all aspects of the 'Statement of Ethical Practice' produced by the British Sociological Association (as available from the BSA website at 16 March 2002). The purpose and nature of the research were explained before the interviews were conducted and assurances of confidentiality and anonymity were given.

In addition to these minimal requirements for informed consent, the general ethical orientation that has guided the research process is based on the principle of 'respect for the autonomy of persons'.[12] This ethical orientation is reflected in the format of the interviews, which were designed to encourage individuals to tell their own stories in their own words and with the assumption in mind that interviewing is a 'form of discourse between two people' in which both contribute to the production of meaning.[13] As a number of researchers have testified, this approach is potentially empowering for those who are interviewed.[14] While gathering these narrative accounts care was taken to ensure that a neutral demeanour was maintained at all times so that no judgement was expressed or implied on people's contributions. All the people I interviewed were assured at the end of the interviews that their contribution was valued and invited to ask any questions they might have. Most of the people interviewed seemed to feel that taking part had been an enjoyable and interesting experience. All the tapes and transcripts were anonymized and securely stored. The tapes were erased at the end of the project and transcripts retained in a safe place to maintain the confidentiality of the interviewees.

A basic risk assessment of the research plan was carried out and some rudimentary precautions were taken, such as ensuring that someone was informed of the time and location of the interviews.

Analysing and interpreting the data

To analyse and interpret the data gathered for this book posed a significant challenge. The relationship between the interview material and the subject of the study is not at all straightforward. At the most obvious level, the study is concerned with the meaning of embodied experiences while the material that was analysed to gain insights into these experiences took the form of retrospective *accounts* of such experiences, often at a considerable distance in time. This discontinuity between the topic of the book and the data gathered for the book posed questions both about the ontological status of narratives and about the epistemological assumptions that allow for their interpretation. Ultimately, these questions about what can be learnt of embodied experience from the things people say in interviews are questions concerning the possibilities of language itself. From a strong constructivist perspective, for example, the analysis of narratives could provide knowledge about the cultural *representation* of embodied experience but would not warrant claims about the phenomenal basis of experience.[15] Conversely, a realist might argue that while events may be available for direct observation and description, without corroborating evidence there is no way of knowing whether the events described in these particular narratives actually occurred in the form suggested. In contrast to the above perspectives the assumption was made, following Holstein and Gubrium, that narratives have the 'ability to convey situated experiential realities'[16] using a 'substantial repertoire of interpretive methods and stock of experiential materials'.[17] In other words, narratives may be understood as simultaneously constructed and as giving access to 'real' events, in the sense that they can evoke the realities of lived experience. As Hollway and Jefferson have suggested, 'though it is far from transparent, there is a relationship between people's ambiguous representations and their experiences' which the researcher can, in principle, explore.[18]

In addition to the fundamental difficulties posed by attempting to assign a definite evidential status to the interview material, the problem of distinguishing between public discourses and personal biographical elements within the interview material also had to be addressed. The term 'public discourse', in this context, refers to any widely disseminated set of beliefs or opinions that are current in everyday life, whether these emanate from governmental, media or other sources.[19] By contrast, 'personal biographical elements' are the unique events that go to make up an individual history. If a person, for example, says that they are aware that they should drink less than x number of units of alcohol per day, because of their health, and they then go on to relate the story of a recent incident where they drank a very much larger quantity of alcohol and fell down some stairs, then it is relatively easy to distinguish between public discourse and personal biography. The notion of a healthy limit for the consumption of alcohol that is measured in units is recognizably drawn from recent widely reported public health initiatives, whereas the drinking bout that ends in a fall clearly refers to a specific event in a person's life. However, very few cases are as clear-cut as this fictitious example, and the form in which an individual history is presented is often profoundly influenced by the way in which widely available discourses have been appropriated or internalized by people. Unravelling these disparate elements and assessing their implications for the way reported events should be interpreted is very far from being an exact science.

As well as being filtered through a variety of public discourses the telling of a personal history is also of course modified by the setting in which it is told.[20] Although Kvale has suggested that we now live in an 'interview society'[21] in which people are both familiar with and ready to participate in this form of discourse, it remains a contrived encounter that can impose particular roles and elicit particular kinds of responses. People may feel constrained to present their story in a specific way based on the real or imagined expectations of the interviewer. Equally, the interviewer may feel that certain things are expected of them which can in turn influence the final form in which the narratives are presented. However, it would be wrong to overstate the degree to which formal interviews are more problematic in these respects than other discursive contexts. All narratives of past events are recounted with a strategic eye to self-presentation and are delivered under the influence of a myriad of confounding factors, including those that occur in so-called *natural* settings. As Miller and Glassner point out:

> While naturally occurring talk and interaction may appear to be more spontaneous, less 'staged' than an interview, this is true only in the sense that such interaction is staged by persons other than an interviewer. Resulting conversations are not necessarily more 'realistic' or 'authentic'.[22]

Bearing in mind these considerations the interpretations that are offered in this book should be read as both provisional and perspectival rather than as laying claim to being in any sense definitive. By adopting a different standpoint these same interviews could, quite legitimately, yield entirely different conclusions. This does not imply that the particular interpretations offered here are therefore arbitrary, but that all interpretations are inevitably conditioned by the assumptions they operate within and the point of view they adopt. All that is required for the interpretations to be valid is that a reader who has adopted the same standpoint as the author can see what they saw in the interview material.[23] What is sought, then, is not the truth in any transcendent sense but the more modest and pragmatic objective of producing an account that provides 'useful knowledge'.[24]

The interview transcripts were analysed by hand using a thematic approach. The themes selected were not designed to act as hypotheses that would be tested but simply as broad categories that would help to begin the process of differentiating and analysing the material. These themes could be equated roughly to the questions: 'What is happening when intoxication occurs?' 'When does intoxication occur?' and 'Where does intoxication occur?' As the analysis was undertaken from a phenomenological perspective it was important to approach the data with categories that imposed as few existing meanings as possible and excluded as little as possible from consideration. It was also vital to begin with categories of the highest generality and inclusiveness because the argument of the book is developed, in part, by drawing parallels between embodied experiences in different social and historical contexts. By using these inclusive categories the connections between culturally disparate experiences could be explored; a relationship to time, location and activity are common to human experience in all situations. The book attempts to make these connections, and so answer the above questions, by analysing in turn the particular form of exchange which is characteristic of intoxication, the temporal dimensions of the experience of intoxication and the relationship between the experience of intoxication and the formation of liminal communities.

While assigning elements of the data provisionally to the broad categories 'what' 'when' and 'where' was a useful starting point, in order to complete the analysis a lengthy process of repeated readings was required to gradually refine concepts, locate and account for disconfirming instances and ensure that all the material had been given equal weight. In early readings, all data that referred to the theme being considered, however tangentially, were collected together. As the readings progressed this mass of material was gradually reduced and organized into sub-themes using terms present in the data to label the newly differentiated elements. At this stage care was taken to ensure that sub-themes actually were present in the data rather than being imposed on it and that material was not being excluded simply because it contradicted these emergent patterns. This initial coding was then gradually amalgamated into groups with similar properties and 'coded', that is labelled, in more general terms before finally being related to the theoretical concerns of the book. The quotes that were eventually presented in the book were not selected for their typicality but instead because they point to key issues that emerged in the analysis of the interviews. Some of the quotes were very lightly edited to make them more readable but only where this did not alter in any way the sense of what was being said.

The relationship between researcher and participants in qualitative research

In quantitative studies the role of the researcher is unambiguously prescribed. Their sole task is to act as a neutral conduit for information with a straightforward duty to report the objective facts and guard against anything that might contaminate the data or introduce bias into the analysis of the data. To this end, quantitative studies are carefully designed to minimize, or eliminate, the impact of the researcher on the findings. By contrast, qualitative approaches that embrace an interpretive model of knowledge production tend to deny that this ideal of absolute detachment is either attainable or desirable.[25] The re-evaluation of the researcher's role, which this scepticism about the possibility of objectivity through method expresses, has been driven by post-structuralist, post-modern and feminist critiques of the realist epistemological assumptions that have dominated western thought since the Enlightenment.[26] Instead of striving for an objective detachment that is viewed as illusory, qualitative approaches often seek instead to acknowledge and account for the input of the researcher. From being understood in purely negative terms, as a potential source of error or contamination of the data, the role of the researcher is transformed when seen as part of a context that actively shapes and constructs the data obtained.

This change in perspective, it is argued, opens the way to a reduction in the asymmetrical power relations that have often characterized the research encounter, and a greater flexibility in defining the part played by the researcher.[27] A new emphasis on the collaborative nature of the enterprise, which has both an epistemological and an ethical dimension, comes to the fore when designing studies.[28] This concern with redefining the research relationship is also reflected in debates about the relative merits of 'insider' research designs, where personal involvement with participants is seen to enhance understanding, as opposed to 'outsider' research designs, where such involvement is deemed to be, at best, an irrelevance. In this context, Miller and Glassner have suggested that social distance between researchers and participants can both reduce the quality of data obtained and pose real problems for its sound interpretation.[29]

The potential benefits of reduced social distance between researchers and participants have also been stressed in feminist and ethnographic studies. Devault, for example, writing from a feminist standpoint, has drawn attention to the importance that a background of experiences, shared by interviewer and interviewee, can have in overcoming the limitations inherent in the way gender is constructed linguistically in a patriarchal culture.[30] The idea that researcher involvement and empathy assists rather than obstructs interpretation and understanding has also been taken up in ethnographic work by, for example, Ots.[31] While conducting a study of Chinese cathartic healing Ots noted that it was only after seven or eight informal interviews that he was able to get past public discourses and elicit the kind of personal responses he was seeking. In the light of this experience, Ots has called for researchers to go beyond even participant observation as a mode of social investigation, and move towards a genuine engagement with their subject, removing all barriers to direct understanding. While this kind of total involvement could perhaps work for some topics it is difficult to see how it could be applied successfully to a study of say street-level prostitution or, as is the case with some of the people interviewed for this book, intravenous drug use.

At a more general level, approaches that call for a high level of researcher involvement risk elevating claims of authenticity or advocacy above the demands of analysis. This could lead to a situation where the issue of who conducts a study, or what they have experienced, is deemed to be more significant than what the study is able to discover. Conversely, to equate direct experience with validity seems to suggest that researchers could be debarred from investigating areas that they have no direct knowledge of which would mark an unacceptable and impractical restriction of intellectual freedom. As Butler has pointed out, in response to such suggestions, identification with the object of research is no guarantee of quality and can lead to somewhat naive notions of giving direct voice to the excluded simply by uncritically recording their perspective.[32] While taking up the role of advocate or 'going native' by fully identifying with the situation and lifestyle of participants may be ill-advised, there are good grounds for believing that a limited form of empathetic engagement is both ethically desirable and theoretically useful. Indeed, a phenomenological analysis, such as that employed in this book, that did not seek to enter into the perspective of the people interviewed at some level would almost seem to be a contradiction in terms. As Becker has argued, unless researchers are able to present the reality that engages the people they are studying they 'will not have achieved full sociological understanding of the phenomenon [they] seek to explain'.[33]

In writing this book, walking a tightrope between empathetic identification and analytic detachment in order to try to present the reality which engaged the participants proved to be a tricky balancing act. To take one example, as already indicated the sampling criteria had to be modified as the study progressed. Categories such as 'problematic' and 'dependent' substance use that seemed serviceable before the study commenced were cast into doubt by encountering some of the lived realities that these terms supposedly encompass. Entering into the participant's perspective made it clear that such terms do not refer to objective states but rather operate as contested objectifications. Again Becker, in a discussion of deviance, clarifies the point when he notes that 'deviant behaviour is behaviour that people so label … [d]eviance is not a quality that lies in behaviour itself'.[34]

It is a key task of the researcher concerned with the meaning of lived experience to call into question the dominant social categories that serve to contain and delimit experience. One of the ways this task can be accomplished is by identifying with the perspective of those who are subject to these categories. However, if their perspective is adopted uncritically the result may simply be to replace one set of doxic categories with another rather than uncovering the underlying meaning of the experiences being investigated. It is incumbent upon the researcher in the type of qualitative research that has been undertaken for this book to 'articulate the pre-reflective level of lived meanings, to make the invisible visible'.[35] To achieve this involves going beyond both the dominant social categories that seek to define the phenomenon under investigation, *and* the self-understandings of the participants.

Appendix B

Who was interviewed

Participants	*Age*	*Gender*	*Occupation*
Participant 1	45	M	Musician
Participant 2	34	M	Chef
Participant 3	39	M	IT trainer
Participant 4	40	F	Teacher
Participant 5	38	M	Caretaker
Participant 6	30	F	Licensee
Participant 7	32	M	Shop manager
Participant 8	34	M	Homemaker
Participant 9	31	M	Delivery driver
Participant 10	27	M	IT sales
Participant 11	36	F	Teaching assistant
Participant 12	30	M	Satellite engineer
Participant 13	27	M	Graphic artist
Participant 14	36	M	Assistant hotel manager
Participant 15	33	M	Club promoter
Participant 16	47	F	Homemaker

Appendix C

Interview schedule

1. Can you tell me about your first real experience with drink or drugs?
2. Can you tell me about your best experience with drink or drugs?
3. Can you tell me about your worst experience with drink or drugs?
4. Can you describe any situations you have been in where you wanted to take drugs or drink but for whatever reason decided not to?
5. Can you describe any situations where you drank or took some drugs but the situation made it difficult?
6. Can you tell me about your most recent experience with drink or drugs?

Notes

1 Introduction

1 M. Jay, *High society: Mind-altering drugs in history and culture,* London: Thames & Hudson, 2010, p. 10.

2 See, for example, HM Government drug strategy 2010, *Reducing demand, restricting supply, building recovery: Supporting people to live a drug free life*: http://www.homeoffice.gov.uk/publications/alcohol-drugs/drugs/drug-strategy/drug-strategy-2010?view=Binary (accessed 8 February 2012).

3 M. Weber, 'Power and bureaucracy', in K. Thompson and J. Tunstall (eds.) *Sociological perspectives,* Penguin: Harmondsworth, 1971 (1922). F. Tonnies, *Community and association (Gemeinschaft und gesellschaft),* London: Routledge & Kegan Paul, 1955 (1887).

4 E. Dunning, *Sport matters: Sociological studies of sport, violence and civilisation,* London: Routledge, 1999.

5 P. Falk, *The consuming body,* London: Sage, 1994.

6 A.Giddens, *Modernity and self-identity: Self and society in the late modern age,* Cambridge: Polity Press, 1991.

7 N. Elias, *The civilizing process: The history of manners and state formation and civilization,* Oxford: Blackwell, 1989 (1939).

8 P. Bourdieu, *Distinction: A social critique of the judgement of taste,* London: Routledge & Kegan Paul, 1984. P. Bourdieu, *Outline of a theory of practice,* Cambridge: Cambridge University Press, 2000 (1997). P. Bourdieu, *Practical reason,* Cambridge: Polity Press, 2001.

9 J. Baudrillard, *Symbolic exchange and death,* London: Sage, 1993 (1976).

10 W. Watts Miller, 'Durkheimian time', *Time & Society* 9 (1), 2000, 5–20.

11 Bataille cited in C. Jenks, *Transgression,* London: Routledge, 2003, p. 102.

12 Baudrillard, op. cit.

13 W.J. Ong, *Orality and literacy: The technologizing of the word,* London: Methuen, 1982.

14 For a subtle analysis of related processes see W. Benjamin, *The work of art in the age of mechanical reproduction,* London: Penguin Books, 2008.

15 P. Clastres, *Society against the state,* New York: Zone Books, 1987.

16 Bourdieu, 1984, op. cit.

17 G. Simmel, 'The metropolis and mental life', 1903, in D. Levine (ed.) *Georg Simmel: On individuality and social forms,* Chicago: University of Chicago Press, 1971.

18 C. Auge, *Non-places: Introduction to an anthropology of supermodernity,* London: Verso, 1995.

19 V.W. Turner, *The ritual process: Structure and anti-structure,* New York: Aldine, 1969.

20 Ibid., p. 96.
21 Ibid., p. 97.
22 V. Turner and E.L.B. Turner, *Image and pilgrimage in Christian culture,* New York: Columbia University Press, 1978. See also H. Schmalenbach, *On society and experience: Selected papers,* Chicago: Chicago University Press, 1977.

2 Sacrificing the rational body: the transgressive economy of intoxication

1 M. Mauss, *The gift: Forms and functions of exchange in archaic societies,* London: Cohen & West, 1966 (1950).
2 Suleiman cited in C. Jenks, *Transgression,* London: Routledge, 2003, p. 100.
3 I. Burkitt, *Social selves: Theories of self and society* (second edition), London: Sage, 2008.
4 G. Bataille, *Georges Bataille: Essential writings,* M. Richardson (ed.), London: Sage, 1998. G. Bataille, *Eroticism,* Harmondsworth: Penguin Books, 2001 (1962).
5 G. Deleuze and F. Guattari, *A thousand plateaus: Capitalism and schizophrenia,* London: Athlone Press, 1988, p. 181.
6 Bataille, 1998, op. cit.
7 J.C. Alexander, 'The dialectic of individuation and domination: Weber's rationalization theory and beyond', in S. Whimster and S. Lash (eds) *Max Weber, rationality and modernity,* London: Routledge, 1987, pp. 185–206.
8 J. Baudrillard, *Symbolic exchange and death,* London: Sage, 1993, (1976), p. 14.
9 Ibid., p. 126. See also M. Csikszentmihalyi, *Flow: The psychology of optimal experience,* New York: Harper & Row, 1990, for a positive account of the psychology and phenomenology of absorbed activity.
10 Baudrillard, op. cit.
11 A. Lingis, *Foreign bodies,* London: Routledge, 1994, p. 10.
12 P.E.S. Freund, 'The expressive body: a common ground for the sociology of the emotions, health and illness', *Sociology of Health and Illness* 12, 1990, 452–77.
13 G. Bataille, *Visions of excess: Selected writings, 1927–1939,* Minneapolis: University of Minnesota Press, 1985.
14 M. Shildrick, *Leaky bodies and boundaries: Feminism, postmodernism and (bio) ethics,* London: Routledge, 1997.
15 M. Merleau-Ponty, *The structure of behaviour,* London: Methuen, 1963.
16 M. Heidegger, *Being and time,* Oxford: Blackwell, 2000 (1962), p. 95.
17 Ibid., p. 47.
18 Deleuze and Guattari, op. cit., p. 159.
19 Bataille, 1998, op. cit.
20 Bataille, 1985, op. cit., p. 129.
21 B. Wilshire, *Wild hunger: The primal roots of modern addiction,* Oxford: Rowman & Littlefield, 1998.
22 C. Shilling, 'Embodiment, experience and theory: In defence of the sociological tradition', *Sociological Review* 49 (3), 2001, 327–44.
23 Bataille, 2001 (1962), op. cit.
24 Bataille cited in Jenks, op. cit., p. 102.
25 Baudrillard, op. cit.
26 Ibid., p. 95.
27 Bataille, 1998, op. cit.
28 R. Klein, *Cigarettes are sublime,* Durham, NC: Duke University Press, 1993, p. 184.
29 P. Bourdieu, *Distinction: A social critique of the judgement of taste,* London: Routledge & Kegan Paul, 1984. P. Bourdieu, *Outline of a theory of practice,* Cambridge: Cambridge University Press, 2000 (1972).

30 Deleuze and Guattari, op. cit., p. 11.
31 A. Ronnel, *The telephone book: Technology, schizophrenia, electric speech,* Lincoln: University of Nebraska Press, 1989, p. 29.
32 Bataille, 1998, op. cit.
33 Bataille, 2001 (1962), op. cit.
34 C. Levi-Strauss, *Introduction to the work of Marcel Mauss,* London: Routledge & Kegan Paul, 1987 (1950).
35 J. Huizinga, *Homo ludens: A study of the play element in culture,* Boston: Beacon Press, 1950, p. 82.
36 P. Bourdieu, *Practical reason,* Cambridge: Polity Press, 2001, p. 94.
37 J. Derrida, *Given time 1: Counterfeit money,* Chicago: University of Chicago Press, 1992, p. 8.
38 Bataille, op. cit., p. 68.
39 J. Derrida, *The gift of death,* Chicago: University of Chicago Press, 1995, p. 112.
40 Ibid., p. 107.
41 Derrida, 1992, op. cit., p. 12.
42 Ibid.
43 Bataille, 1998, op. cit.
44 G. Mars, and Y. Altman, 'Alternative mechanisms of distribution in a Soviet economy', in M. Douglas (ed.) *Constructive drinking: Perspectives on drinking from anthropology,* Cambridge: Cambridge University Press, 1987, pp. 270–9.
45 G. Bennington, 'Introduction to economics 1: Because the world is round', in C. Bailey-Gill (ed.) *Bataille: Writing the sacred,* London: Routledge, 1995, pp. 46–57.
46 F. Rehfisch, 'Competitive beer drinking among the Mambila', in Douglas, op. cit., pp. 135–45.
47 Jenks, op. cit., p. 7.
48 J. Lowell Lewis, 'Sex and violence in Brazil: *Carnival, caporeira,* and the problem of everyday life', *American Ethnologist* 26 (3), 2000, 539–57.
49 G. Bataille, *The impossible,* San Francisco: City Lights Books, 1991. Bataille, 1998, op. cit.
50 Deleuze and Guattari, 1988, op. cit., p. 162.
51 The function of these discourses of power, according to Bryan Turner, is fourfold – the reproduction of populations in time, the regulation of bodies in space, the disciplining of the 'interior' body, and the representation of the 'exterior' body in social relations. See B.S. Turner, *The body and society,* London: Sage, 1996.
52 J. Gil, *Metamorphosis of the body,* Minneapolis: University of Minnesota Press, 1998, p. 90.
53 Klein, op. cit., p. 105.
54 Deleuze and Guattari, op. cit., p. 190.
55 Klein, op. cit., p. 88.
56 Foucault cited in Jenks, op. cit., p. 92.

3 Seeking the *impossible*: expenditure beyond necessity

1 G. Bataille, *Georges Bataille: Essential writings,* M. Richardson (ed.), London: Sage, 1998.
2 J. Baudrillard, *Symbolic exchange and death,* London: Sage, 1993 (1976).
3 M. Weber, *The Protestant ethic and the spirit of capitalism,* London: Routledge, 2001 (1904).
4 P. Bourdieu, *Distinction: A social critique of the judgement of taste,* London: Routledge & Kegan Paul, 1984.
5 M. Featherstone, 'The body in consumer culture', *Theory, Culture and Society* 1, 1995, 18–33.

6 G. Deleuze and F. Guattari, *A thousand plateaus: Capitalism and schizophrenia,* London: Athlone Press, 1988, p. 204.
7 J. Gil, *Metamorphosis of the body,* Minneapolis: University of Minnesota Press, 1998, p. x.
8 For a discussion of the discursive construction of the idea of addiction see A. Bancroft, *Drugs, intoxication and society,* Cambridge: Polity Press, 2009.
9 R. Klein, *Cigarettes are sublime,* Durham, NC: Duke University Press, 1993, p. 43.
10 Deleuze and Guattari, op. cit.
11 On the importance of planning in modernity see N. Elias, *The civilizing process: The history of manners and state formation and civilization,* Oxford: Blackwell, 1994 (1939). A. Giddens, *Modernity and self-identity: Self and society in the late modern age,* Cambridge: Polity Press, 1991.
12 J.P. Carse, *Finite and infinite games: A vision of life as play and possibility,* New York: Free Press, 1986.
13 Deleuze and Guattari, op. cit., p. 397.
14 Gil, op. cit., p. 91.
15 Baudrillard, op. cit. W. Benjamin, *Illuminations,* London: Pimlico, 1999 (1955).
16 Bataille, op. cit.
17 J. Derrida, *Dissemination,* London: Athlone Press, 1981.
18 C. Jenks, *Transgression,* London: Routledge, 2003.
19 J. Butler, *Bodies that matter: On the discursive limits of sex,* London: Routledge, 1993, p. 94.
20 Deleuze and Guattari, op. cit., p. 198.
21 Jenks, op. cit., p. 2.
22 J. Derrida, *Politics of friendship,* London: Verso, 1997.

4 Traditional time and modern time

1 G.Deleuze and F. Guattari, *A thousand plateaus: Capitalism and schizophrenia,* London: Athlone Press, 1988.
2 J. Gil, *Metamorphosis of the body,* Minneapolis: University of Minnesota Press, 1998.
3 J. Subrt, 'The problem of time from the perspective of the social sciences' (Abstract), *Czech Sociological Review* 9 (2), 2001, 211–24: http://www.ibss.ac.uk (accessed 11 October 2002).
4 See, for example, E. Durkheim, *The elementary forms of religious life,* New York: Free Press, 1995 (1914). J. Baudrillard, *Symbolic exchange and death,* London: Sage, 1993 (1976). P.A. Mellor and C. Shilling, *Re-forming the body: Religion, community and modernity,* London: Sage, 1997. A. Giddens, *Modernity and self-identity: Self and society in the late modern age,* Cambridge: Polity Press, 1991. J. Brannen and A. Nilsen, 'Young people's time perspectives: From youth to adulthood', *Sociology* 36 (3), 2002, 513–37. S. Segre, 'A Weberian theory of time', *Time & Society* 9 (2–3), 2000, 147–70.
5 G. Jordan, 'Flight from modernity: Time, the other and the discourse of primitivism', *Time & Society* 4 (3), 1995, 281–303, p. 289.
6 Mauss cited in W. Watts Miller, 'Durkheimian time', *Time & Society* 9 (1), 2000, 5–20.
7 A. van Gennep, *The rites of passage,* London: Routledge & Kegan Paul, 1960 (1908).
8 Gil, op. cit., p. 79.
9 Durkheim, op. cit., p. 382.
10 Ibid., p. 378.
11 P. Baert, *Time, self and social being: Temporality within a sociological context,* Aldershot: Avebury, 1992, p. 33.

12 Hubert cited in Watts Miller, op. cit., p. 8.
13 Durkheim, op. cit., p. 327.
14 Gil, op. cit.
15 E. Leach, *Culture and communication: The logic by which symbols are connected,* Cambridge: Cambridge University Press, 1976, p. 41.
16 Gil, op. cit., p. 79.
17 J. Derrida, *Given time 1: Counterfeit money,* Chicago: University of Chicago Press, 1992.
18 Gil, op. cit. Leach, op. cit.
19 W.J. Ong, *Orality and literacy: The technologising of the word,* London: Methuen, 1982.
20 Ibid., p. 32.
21 Ibid., p. 160.
22 Gil, op. cit., p. 83.
23 Baudrillard, op. cit.
24 Gil, op. cit., p. 54.
25 Baudrillard, op. cit., p. 126.
26 Ibid.
27 Gil, op. cit., p. 53.
28 See, for example, F. Tonnies, *Community and association (Gemeinschaft und gesellschaft),* London: Routledge & Kegan Paul, 1955 (1887). G. Simmel, 'The metropolis and mental life', in D. Levine (ed.) *Georg Simmel: On individuality and social forms,* Chicago: University of Chicago Press, 1971 (1903). S. Tabboni, 'The idea of social time in Norbert Elias', *Time & Society* 10 (1), 2001, 5–27. Baudrillard, op. cit. Gil, op. cit. Giddens, op. cit. Mellor and Shilling, op. cit.
29 Giddens, op. cit., p. 17.
30 J.P. Carse, *Finite and infinite games: A vision of life as play and possibility,* New York: Free Press, 1986.
31 Baudrillard, op. cit.
32 M. Foucault, *The birth of the clinic: An archaeology of medical perception,* London: Tavistock, 1973. M. Foucault, *Discipline and punish: The birth of the prison,* London: Penguin, 1977.
33 Gil, op. cit., p. 208.
34 D. Inglis and M. Holmes, 'Toiletry time: Defecation, temporal strategies and the dilemmas of modernity', *Time & Society* 9 (2–3), 2000, 223–45.
35 Gil, op. cit.
36 Baudrillard, op. cit., p. 146.
37 Derrida, op. cit.
38 M. Heidegger, *Being and time,* Oxford: Backwell, 2000 (1962), p. 302.
39 R. Kugelman, 'Relational approach to health' (unpublished draft), 2001. B.S. Turner, *The body and society,* London: Sage, 1996.
40 Simmel, 1971 (1903), op. cit.
41 M. Merleau-Ponty, *The structure of behaviour,* London: Methuen, 1963.
42 B. Wilshire, *Wild hunger: The primal roots of modern addiction,* Oxford: Rowman & Littlefield, 1998.
43 Gluckman cited in Gil, op. cit., p. 68.
44 Daily cited in Brannen and Nilsen, op. cit., p. 517.
45 Nowotney cited in Brannen and Nilsen, op. cit., p. 517.
46 Mellor and Shilling, op. cit.
47 M.L. Davies, 'Shattered assumptions: Time and the experience of long term HIV positivity', *Social Science & Medicine* 44 (5), 1997, 561–71, p. 561.
48 W. Benjamin, *Illuminations,* London: Pimlico, 1999 (1955), p. 92.
49 Baudrillard, op. cit., p. 17.
50 A. Ahmadi, 'On the indispensability of youth for experience: Time and experience in Paul Valery and Walter Benjamin', *Time & Society* 10 (2–3), 2001, 191–212.

51 Ibid. Brannen and Nilsen, op. cit.
52 M.S. Santos, 'Memory and narrative in social theory: The contributions of Jacques Derrida and Walter Benjamin', *Time & Society* 10 (2–3), 2001, 163–89. p. 167.
53 Baert, op. cit., p. 40.
54 Beck-Gernsheim cited in Brannen and Nilsen, op. cit., p. 515.
55 Giddens, op. cit., p. 71.
56 Ibid., p. 5. For an alternative perspective on leaving the past behind see also Z. Bauman, 'Time and space reunited', *Time & Society* 9 (2–3), 2000, 171–85.
57 Gil, op. cit.
58 G. Jordan, 'Flight from modernity: Time, the other and the discourse of primitivism', *Time & Society* 4 (3), 1995, 281–303. H.H. Bash, 'A sense of time: Temporality and historicity in sociological enquiry', *Time & Society* 9 (2–3), 2000, 187–204.
59 Deleuze and Guattari, op. cit.
60 Ibid., p. 262.
61 Ibid., p. 262.
62 Gil, op. cit., p. 154.
63 Ibid., p. 153.
64 R. Twine, 'Physiognomy, phrenology and the temporality of the body', *Body & Society* 8 (1), 2002, 67–88. p. 83.
65 D. Leder, 'A tale of two bodies: The Cartesian corpse and the lived body', in D. Welton (ed.) *Body and flesh: A philosophical reader,* Oxford: Blackwell, 1998, pp. 117–29. See also Foucault on the role of the cadaver in the development of modern medicine, 1973, op. cit.

5 From bodies in time to time in the body

1 A. Schutz, *Collected papers 1: The problem of social reality,* New York: Humanities Press, 1962.
2 G. Deleuze and F. Guattari, *A thousand plateaus: Capitalism and schizophrenia,* London: Athlone Press, 1988.
3 On the importance of a predictable future see, for example, N. Elias, *The civilizing process: The history of manners and state formation and civilization,* Oxford: Blackwell, 1994 (1939).
4 J. Gil, *Metamorphosis of the body,* Minneapolis: University of Minnesota Press, 1998.
5 J.P. Carse, *Finite and infinite games: A vision of life as play and possibility,* New York: Free Press, 1986.
6 A. Ronell, *The telephone book: Technology, schizophrenia, electric speech,* Lincoln: University of Nebraska Press, 1989.
7 For a subtle analysis of similar processes see W. Benjamin, *The work of art in the age of mechanical reproduction,* London: Penguin Books, 2008.
8 Schutz, op. cit., p. xxxii.
9 D. Carr, *Time, narrative and history,* Bloomington: Indiana University Press, 1986. G. Reith, 'In search of lost time: Recall, projection and the phenomenology of addiction', *Time & Society* 8 (1), 2000, 99–117.
10 J. Derrida, *Given time 1: Counterfeit money,* Chicago: University of Chicago Press, 1992.
11 Carse, op. cit.
12 Deleuze and Guattari, op. cit.
13 L.J. Kirmayer, 'The body's insistence on meaning: Metaphor as presentation and representation in illness experience', *Medical Anthropology Quarterly* 6 (4), 1992, 323–46.
14 Levi-Strauss cited in E. Leach, *Culture and communication: The logic by which symbols are connected,* Cambridge: Cambridge University Press, 1976, p. 44.

15 Gil, op. cit., p. 175.
16 M. Heidegger, *Being and time,* Oxford: Blackwell, 2000 (1962).
17 Schutz, op. cit., p. xxxii.
18 M. Blanchot, *The unavowable community,* Barrytown, NY: Station Hill Press, 1988, p. 25.
19 P.A. Mellor and C. Shilling, *Re-forming the body: Religion, community and modernity,* London: Sage, 1997.
20 On issues around life course and lifestyle see K.C. Backett and C. Davison, 'Lifecourse and lifestyle: The social and cultural location of health behaviours', *Social Science & Medicine* 40 (5), 1995, 629–38.

6 Theorizing community

1 S. Brint, '*Gemeinschaft* revisited: A critique and reconstruction of the community concept', *Sociological Theory* 19 (1), 2001, 1–23.
2 C.J. Calhoun, 'Community: Toward a variable conceptualization for comparative research', *Social History* 5 (1), 1980, 105–29.
3 Brint, op. cit.
4 P.A. Mellor and C. Shilling, *Re-forming the body: Religion, community and modernity,* London: Sage, 1997.
5 V.W. Turner, *The ritual process: Structure and anti-structure,* New York: Aldine, 1969, p. 126.
6 F. Tonnies, *Community and association (Gemeinschaft und gesellschaft),* London: Routledge & Kegan Paul, 1955 (1887).
7 M. Maffesoli, *The time of the tribes: The decline of individualism in mass society,* London: Sage, 1996a.
8 L.J. Kirmayer, 'The body's insistence on meaning: Metaphor as presentation and representation in illness experience', *Medical Anthropology Quarterly* 6 (4), 1992, 323–46. p. 324.
9 Tonnies, op. cit.
10 Brint, op. cit.
11 G. Simmel, '*The metropolis and mental life',* in D. Levine (ed.) *Georg Simmel: On individuality and social forms,* Chicago: University of Chicago Press, 1971 (1903).
12 L. Wirth, *On cities and social life,* Chicago: University of Chicago Press, 1964.
13 Mellor and Shilling, op. cit.
14 R.J. Antonio, 'Nietzsche's antisociology: Subjectified culture and the end of history', *American Journal of Sociology* 101 (1), 1995, 1–43, p. 9.
15 A. Giddens, *Modernity and self-identity: Self and society in the late modern age,* Cambridge: Polity Press, 1991.
16 Z. Bauman, *Community: Seeking safety in an insecure world,* Cambridge: Polity Press, 2001.
17 C.S. Fischer, 'The subcultural theory of urbanism: A twentieth-year assessment', *American Journal of Sociology* 101 (3), 1995, 543–77.
18 A. Maryanski, 'The last ancestor: An ecological network model on the origins of human sociality', *Advances in Human Ecology* 1, 1992, 1–32.
19 Brint, op. cit., p. 6.
20 Fischer, op. cit.
21 Maffesoli, 1996a, op. cit. Antonio, op. cit.
22 R. Schmitt and T.E. Moody (eds) *Alienation and social criticism,* Atlantic Highlands, NJ: Humanities Press, 1994. C. Lasch, *The culture of narcissism: American life in an age of diminishing expectations,* New York: Warner Books, 1979.
23 Maffesoli, 1996a, op. cit., p. 11.
24 Ibid., p. 21 (original emphasis).

25 Ibid., p. 43.
26 D. Evans, 'Michel Maffesoli's sociology of modernity and postmodernity: An introduction and critical assessment', *Sociological Review* 45, 1997, 221–43.
27 M. Warnock, Introduction to J.P. Sartre, *Being and nothingness: An essay on phenomenological ontology,* London: Methuen, 1972 (1958), pp. xvi.
28 Brint, op. cit.
29 Ibid., p. 8 (original emphasis).
30 Calhoun, op. cit.
31 M. Mauss, *The gift: Forms and functions of exchange in archaic societies,* London: Cohen & West, 1966 (1950).
32 G. Simmel, 'Sociability', in K. Wolff (ed.) *The sociology of Georg Simmel,* New York: Free Press, 1950.
33 Ibid., p. 44.
34 E. Canetti, *Crowds and power,* London: Phoenix Press, 2000 (1965), pp. 17–19 (original emphasis).
35 Turner, op. cit.
36 Ibid., p. 96.
37 Ibid., p. 131.
38 Martin Buber cited in Turner, op. cit., p. 136.
39 Ibid., p. 138.
40 Ibid., p. 138.
41 J. Gil, *Metamorphosis of the body,* Minneapolis: University of Minnesota Press, 1998, p. 100.
42 Ibid., p. 81.
43 Ibid., p.100.
44 M. Bakhtin, *Rabelais and his world,* Bloomington: Indiana University Press, 1984 (1965), p. 10.
45 G. Bataille, *Eroticism,* Harmondsworth: Penguin Books, 2001 (1962).
46 T.S. Smith, *Strong interaction,* Chicago: University of Chicago Press, 1992.
47 Bakhtin, op. cit.
48 B. Wilshire, *Wild hunger: The primal roots of modern addiction,* Oxford: Rowman & Littlefield, 1998.
49 P. Clastres, *Society against the state,* New York: Zone Books, 1987, p. 188.
50 Bakhtin, op. cit., p. 87.
51 For a critique of Bakhtin's analysis of carnival see C. Lindahl, 'Bakhtin's carnival laughter and the Cajun Country Mardi Gras', *Folklore* 107, 1996, 57–70.
52 Durand's term cited in M. Maffesoli, *Ordinary knowledge: An introduction to interpretive sociology,* Cambridge: Polity Press, 1996b.
53 Gil, op. cit., p. 109.
54 Turner, op. cit., p. 137.
55 I. Burkitt, *Bodies of thought: Embodiment, identity and modernity,* London: Sage, 1999.
56 Mellor and Shilling, op. cit.
57 M. Featherstone, 'The body in consumer culture', *Theory, Culture & Society* 1, 1995, 18–33.
58 M. Shildrick, *Embodying the monster: Encounters with the vulnerable self,* London: Sage, 2002, p. 5.
59 Gil, op. cit., p. 90.
60 Deleuze and Guattari, op. cit.
61 J. Derrida, *The gift of death,* Chicago: University of Chicago Press, 1995.
62 Lasch, op. cit., p. 132.
63 G. Agamben, *The coming community,* Minneapolis: University of Minnesota Press, 1990, p. 50.

7 Intoxication liminality and community formation

1 J. Gil, *Metamorphosis of the body,* Minneapolis: University of Minnesota Press, 1998, p. 81.
2 Simmel cited in E. Probyn, 'Beyond food/sex: Eating and the ethics of existence', in V. Bell (ed.) *Performativity and belonging,* London: Sage, 1999, 215–28, p. 216.
3 G. Deleuze and F. Guattari, *Anti-Oedipus: Capitalism and schizophrenia,* London: Athlone Press, 1984.
4 E. Canetti, *Crowds and power,* London: Phoenix Press, 2000 (1965), p. 191.
5 P. Falk, *The consuming body,* London: Sage, 1994, p. 21.
6 Ibid., p. 21.
7 P. Clastres, *Society against the state,* New York: Zone Books, 1987.
8 G. Deleuze and F. Guattari, *A thousand plateaus: Capitalism and schizophrenia,* London: Athlone Press, 1988, p. 29 (original emphasis).
9 Canetti, op. cit., p.17 (original emphasis).
10 G. Pearson, *The new heroin users,* Oxford: Blackwell, 1987.
11 M. Shildrick, *Embodying the monster: Encounters with the vulnerable self,* London: Sage, 2002, p. 4.
12 G. Agamben, *The coming community,* Minneapolis: University of Minnesota Press, 1990.
13 D.M. Massey, 'A brief history of human society: The origin and role of emotion in social life', *American Sociological Review* 67 (1), 2002, 1–29.
14 Deleuze and Guattari, 1988, op. cit. J.M. Barbalet, *Emotion, social theory and social structure,* Cambridge: Cambridge University Press, 2001.
15 I. Burkitt, *Bodies of thought: Embodiment, identity and modernity,* London: Sage, 1999, p. 55.
16 Deleuze and Guattari, 1988, op. cit., p. 151.
17 M. Bakhtin, *Rabelais and his world,* Bloomington: Indiana University Press, 1984 (1965), p. 88.
18 Ibid., p. 20.
19 Gil, op. cit.
20 M. Merleau-Ponty, *The structure of behaviour,* London: Methuen, 1963.
21 E. Goffman, *Stigma: Notes on the management of spoiled identity,* Harmondsworth: Penguin, 1968. See also C. Britton, '"Feeling letdown": An exploration of an embodied sensation associated with breast feeding', in S. Nettleton and J. Watson (eds) *The body in everyday life,* London: Routledge, 1998, 64–81. B. Williams and H.A. Barlow, 'Falling out with my shadow: Lay perceptions of the body in the context of arthritis', in Nettleton and Watson, op. cit., 124–41.
22 Canetti, op. cit., p. 223.
23 Ibid., p. 393.
24 Shildrick, op. cit., p. 54.
25 C. Shilling, 'Toward an embodied understanding of the structure/agency relationship', *British Journal of Sociology,* 50 (4), 1999, 543–62.
26 Deleuze and Guattari, 1988, op. cit.
27 D. Lupton, *The imperative of health: Public health and the regulated body,* London: Sage, 1995.
28 J. Baudrillard, *Symbolic exchange and death,* London: Sage, 1993 (1976).
29 Ibid. See also R. Klein, *Cigarettes are sublime* Durham, NC: Duke University Press, 1993.
30 A. Bancroft, *Drugs, intoxication and society,* Cambridge: Polity Press, 2009, p. 185.
31 M. Douglas (ed.) *Constructive drinking: Perspectives on drink from anthropology,* Cambridge: Cambridge University Press, 1987, p. 12.
32 C. Auge, *Non-places: Introduction to an anthropology of supermodernity,* London: Verso, 1995.

33 J. Derrida, *Politics of friendship,* London: Verso, 1997.
34 L.J. Kirmayer, 'The body's insistence on meaning: Metaphor as presentation and representation in illness experience', *Medical Anthropology Quarterly* 6 (4), 1992, 323–46, p. 324.
35 C.J. Calhoun, 'Community: Toward a variable conceptualisation for comparative research', *Social History* 5 (1), 1980, 105–29, p. 114.
36 Agamben, op. cit., p. 86.
37 Bakhtin, op. cit., p. 90.

8 Conclusion

1 A. Bancroft, *Drugs, intoxication and society,* Cambridge: Polity Press, 2009.
2 P. Bourdieu, *Distinction: A social critique of the judgement of taste,* London: Routledge & Kegan Paul, 1984.
3 W. Benjamin, *The arcades project,* Cambridge, MA: Belknap Press, 2002.
4 N. Elias, *The civilizing process: The history of manners and state formation and civilization,* Oxford: Blackwell, 1994 (1939).
5 J. Butler, *Bodies that matter: On the discursive limits of sex,* London: Routledge, 1993. See also J. Butler, 'Gender as performance: An interview with Judith Butler', *Radical Philosophy* 67, Summer, 1994, 32–9.
6 Butler, 1993, op. cit., p. 231.
7 J. Gil, *Metamorphosis of the body,* Minneapolis: University of Minnesota Press, 1998.
8 A. Schutz, *Collected papers 1: The problem of social reality,* New York: Humanities Press, 1962.
9 M. Foucault, *The birth of the clinic: An archaeology of medical perception,* London: Tavistock, 1973.
10 M. Fitzpatrick, *The tyranny of health: Doctors and the regulation of lifestyle,* London: Routledge, 2001.
11 I. Buchanan, 'The problem of the body in Deleuze and Guattari, or, what can a body do?', *Body & Society* 3 (3), 1997, 73–91.
12 P. Malins, 'Machinic assemblages: Deleuze, Guattari and an ethico-aesthetics of drug use', *Janus Head* 7 (1), 2004, 84–104, pp. 97–8.
13 R. Klein, *Cigarettes are sublime,* Durham, NC: Duke University Press, 1993.
14 Count the costs: 50 years of the war on drugs, http://www.countthecosts.org/ (accessed 9 May 2011).
15 D. Boothroyd, *Culture on drugs: Narco-cultural studies of high modernity,* Manchester: Manchester University Press, 2006.
16 Bancroft, op. cit.
17 R. Newcombe, 'Second class citizens: Discrimination against drug users'. Paper presented at the Seventh International Conference on Diversity in Communities, Organisations and Nations; Amsterdam, Netherlands, 2007.
18 P.K. Dick, *A scanner darkly,* London: Victor Gollancz, 1977.
19 M. Foucault, *The history of sexuality: The will to knowledge, vol. 1,* London: Penguin, 1998.

Appendix A: How the interviews were conducted and interpreted: methodological and epistemological issues

1 J.-L. Nancy, *The inoperative community,* Minneapolis: University of Minnesota Press, 1991.
2 On the *unmaking* of the body through pain see E. Scarry, *The body in pain,* Oxford: Oxford University Press, 1985.

3 D. Giles, 'Retrospective accounts of drunken behaviour: Implications for theories of self, memory and the discursive construction of memory', *Discourse Studies* 1 (4), 1999, 387–403, p. 389. H.S. Becker, *Outsiders: Studies in the sociology of deviance,* New York: Free Press, 1963. M. Douglas (ed.) *Constructive drinking: Perspectives on drink from anthropology,* Cambridge: Cambridge University Press, 1987. M. Jay, *Emperors of dreams: Drugs in the nineteenth century,* Sawtry, Cambs: Dedalus, 2000. M. Jay, *High society: Mind-altering drugs in history and culture,* London: Thames & Hudson, 2010.

4 M. Maffesoli, *Ordinary knowledge: An introduction to interpretive sociology,* Cambridge: Polity Press, 1996. S. Nettleton and J. Watson, 'Introduction: The body in everyday life', in S. Nettleton and J. Watson (eds) *The body in everyday life,* London: Routledge, 1998, pp. 1–23. L. Kontos, 'The uncanny and the sublime in human experience: On the relevance of critical philosophy and psychoanalysis for sociological interpretation', *Sheffield Online Papers in Social Research* 3, 2001, http:/www.shef.ac.uk/uni/R-Z/socst/shop/3.html (accessed 10 June 2002).

5 K.F. Punch, *Developing effective research proposals,* London: Sage, 2000, p. 56.

6 C. Robson, *Real world research: A resource for social scientists and practitioner-research,* Oxford: Blackwell, 2000.

7 S. Kvale, *Interviews: An introduction to qualitative research,* London: Sage, 1996.

8 E.G. Mishler, *Research interviewing: Context and narrative,* Cambridge, MA: Harvard University Press, 1986.

9 M. Freeman, *Rewriting the self: History, memory, narrative,* London: Routledge, 1973. Mishler, op. cit. W. Hollway and T. Jefferson, *Doing qualitative research differently: Free association, narrative and the interview method,* London: Sage, 2000.

10 H. Arksey and P. Knight (eds) *Interviewing for social scientists,* London: Sage, 1999. Mishler, op. cit.

11 Hollway and Jefferson, op. cit., p. 35.

12 J.H. Reiman, 'Research subjects, political subjects, human subjects', in C.B. Klockars and W.O. O'Connor, *Deviance and decency: The ethics of research with human subjects,* London: Sage, 1979, p. 47.

13 Mishler, op. cit., p. 65.

14 See, for example, Hollway and Jefferson, op. cit. C.K. Riessman, *Narrative analysis,* London: Sage, 1993. Kitson *et al.* 1996 cited in Arksey and Knight, op. cit., p. 114.

15 Giles, op. cit.

16 J.A. Holstein and J.F. Gubrium, 'Active interviewing', in D. Silverman (ed.) *Qualitative research: Theory, method and practice,* London: Sage, 1997, pp. 113–29, p. 117.

17 Ibid., p. 122.

18 Hollway and Jefferson, op. cit., p. 3.

19 T. Ots, 'The silenced body – the expressive *Leib:* On the dialectic of mind and life in Chinese cathartic healing', in T.J. Csordas (ed.) *Embodiment and experience: The existential ground of culture and self,* Cambridge: Cambridge University Press, 1994.

20 Mishler, op. cit.

21 Kvale, op. cit.

22 J. Miller and B. Glassner, 'The 'Inside' and the 'Outside': Finding realities in interviews', in Silverman, op. cit., p. 106.

23 Giogi cited in Kvale, op. cit., p., 209.

24 Ibid., p. 42.

25 Mishler, op. cit. Reiman, op. cit. Holstein and Gubrium, op. cit.

26 K.J. Gergen, *The saturated self: Dilemmas of identity in contemporary life,* New York: Basic Books, 1991.

27 Oakley cited in Mishler, op. cit., p. 58.

28 Hollway and Jefferson, op. cit.
29 Miller and Glassner, op. cit.
30 M.L. Devault, 'Talking and listening from women's standpoint: Feminist strategies for interviewing and analysis', *Social Problems* 37 (1), 1990, 96–116.
31 Ots, op. cit.
32 J. Butler, *Bodies that matter: On the discursive limits of sex,* London: Routledge, 1993.
33 Becker, op. cit., p. 174.
34 Ibid., p. 14.
35 Kvale, op. cit., p. 53.

Select bibliography

Agamben, G. *The coming community,* Minneapolis: University of Minnesota Press, 1990.

Ahmadi, A. 'On the indispensability of youth for experience: Time and experience in Paul Valery and Walter Benjamin', *Time & Society* 10 (2–3), 2001.

Alexander, J.C. 'The dialectic of individuation and domination: Weber's rationalization theory and beyond', in Whimster, S. and Lash, S. (eds) *Max Weber, rationality and modernity,* London: Routledge, 1987.

Antonio, R.J. 'Nietzsche's antisociology: Subjectified culture and the end of history', *American Journal of Sociology* 101 (1), 1995.

Arksey, H. and Knight, P. (eds) *Interviewing for social scientists,* London: Sage, 1999.

Auge, C. *Non-places: Introduction to an anthropology of supermodernity,* London: Verso, 1995.

Backett, K.C. and Davison, C. 'Lifecourse and lifestyle: The social and cultural location of health behaviours', *Social Science & Medicine* 40 (5), 1995, 629–38.

Baert, P. *Time, self and social being: Temporality within a sociological context,* Aldershot: Avebury, 1992.

Bakhtin, M. *Rabelais and his world,* Bloomington: Indiana University Press, 1984 (1965).

Bancroft, A. *Drugs, intoxication and society,* Cambridge: Polity Press, 2009.

Barbalet, J.M. *Emotion, social theory and social structure,* Cambridge: Cambridge University Press, 2001.

Bash, H.H. 'A sense of time: Temporality and historicity in sociological enquiry', *Time* & Society 9 (2–3), 2000, 187–204.

Bataille, G. *Visions of excess: Selected writings, 1927–1939,* Minneapolis: University of Minnesota Press, 1985.

Bataille, G. *The impossible,* San Francisco, CA: City Lights Books, 1991.

Bataille, G. *Georges Bataille: Essential writings,* Michael Richardson (ed.), London: Sage, 1998.

Bataille, G. *Eroticism,* Harmondsworth: Penguin Books, 2001 (1962).

Baudrillard, J. *Symbolic exchange and death,* London: Sage, 1993 (1976).

Bauman, Z. 'Time and space reunited', *Time & Society* 9 (2–3), 2000, 171–85.

Bauman, Z. *Community: Seeking safety in an insecure world,* Cambridge: Polity Press, 2001.

Becker, H.S. *Outsiders: Studies in the sociology of deviance,* New York: Free Press, 1963.

Bendelow, G. and Williams, S.J. (eds) *Emotions in social life: Critical themes and contemporary issues,* London: Routledge, 1998.

Benjamin, W. *Illuminations,* London: Pimlico, 1999 (1955).

Bennington, G. 'Introduction to economics 1: Because the world is round', in Bailey-Gill, C. (ed.) *Bataille: Writing the sacred,* London: Routledge, 1995, 46–57.

Berger, P.L. *Redeeming laughter: The comic dimension of human experience,* New York: Walter de Gruyter, 1997.

Berridge, V. *Opium and the people: Opiate use and drug control policy in nineteenth century and early twentieth century England,* London: Free Association Books, 1981.

Blanchot, M. *The unavowable community,* Barrytown, NY: Station Hill Press, 1988.

Bloor, M., Monaghan, L., Dobash, R.P. and Dobash, R.E. 'The body as a chemistry experiement: Steroid use among South Wales bodybuilders', in Nettleton, S. and Watson, J. (eds) *The body in everyday life,* London: Routledge, 1998.

Boothroyd, D. *Culture on drugs: Narco-cultural studies of high modernity,* Manchester: Manchester University Press, 2006.

Bourdieu, P. *Distinction: A social critique of the judgement of taste,* London: Routledge & Kegan Paul, 1984.

Bourdieu, P. 'Concluding remarks: For a sociogenetic understanding of intellectual works', in Calhoun, C., LiPuma, E. and Postone, M. *Bourdieu: Critical perspectives,* Cambridge: Polity Press, 1995.

Bourdieu, P. *Outline of a theory of practice,* Cambridge: Cambridge University Press, 2000 (1972).

Bourdieu, P. *Practical reason,* Cambridge: Polity Press, 2001.

Brannen, J. and Nilsen, A. 'Young people's time perspectives: From youth to adulthood', *Sociology* 36 (3), 2002, 513–37.

Brint, S. '*Gemeinschaft* revisited: A critique and reconstruction of the community concept', *Sociological Theory* 19 (1), 2001, 1–23.

Britton, C. '"Feeling letdown": An exploration of an embodied sensation associated with breast feeding', in Nettleton, S. and Watson, J. (eds) *The body in everyday life,* London: Routledge, 1998, 64–81.

Buchanan, I. 'The problem of the body in Deleuze and Guattari, or, what can a body do?', *Body & Society* 3 (3), 1997, 73–91.

Budgeon, S. 'Identity as an embodied event', *Body & Society* 9 (1), 2003, 35–55.

Burkitt, I. *Bodies of thought: Embodiment, identity and modernity,* London: Sage, 1999.

Butler, J. *Bodies that matter: On the discursive limits of sex,* London: Routledge, 1993.

Butler, J. 'Gender as performance: An interview with Judith Butler', *Radical Philosophy* 67, Summer, 1994, 32–39.

Calhoun, C.J. 'Community: Toward a variable conceptualization for comparative research', *Social History* 5 (1), 1980, 105–129.

Canetti, E. *Crowds and power,* London: Phoenix Press, 2000 (1965).

Carr, D. *Time, narrative and history,* Bloomington: Indiana University Press, 1986.

Carse, J.P. *Finite and infinite games: A vision of life as play and possibility,* New York: Free Press, 1986.

Clastres, P. *Society against the state,* New York: Zone Books, 1987.

Crossley, N. *The Social body: Habit, identity and desire,* London: Sage, 2001.

Crossley, N. 'Embodiment and social structure: A response to Howson and Inglis', *Sociological Review* 49 (3), 2001, 318–326.

Csikszentmihalyi, M. *Flow: The psychology of optimal experience,* New York: Harper & Row, 1990.
Davies, M.L. 'Shattered assumptions: Time and the experience of long term HIV positivity', *Social Science & Medicine* 44 (5), 1997, 561–571.
Deleuze, G. and Guattari, F. *Anti-Oedipus: Capitalism and schizophrenia,* London: Athlone Press, 1984.
Deleuze, G. and Guattari, F. *A thousand plateaus: Capitalism and schizophrenia,* London: Athlone Press, 1988.
Derrida, J. *Given time 1: Counterfeit money,* Chicago, IL: University of Chicago Press, 1992.
Derrida, J. *The gift of death,* Chicago, IL: University of Chicago Press, 1995.
Derrida, J. *Politics of friendship,* London: Verso, 1997.
Devault, M.L. 'Talking and listening from women's standpoint: Feminist strategies for interviewing and analysis', *Social Problems* 37 (1), 1990, 96–116.
Dick, P.K. *A scanner darkly,* London: Victor Gollancz, 1977.
Douglas, M. (ed.) *Constructive drinking: Perspectives on drink from anthropology,* Cambridge: Cambridge University Press, 1987.
Dunning, E. *Sport matters: Sociological studies of sport, violence and civilization,* London: Routledge, 1999.
Durkheim, E. *The elementary forms of religious life,* New York: Free Press, 1995 (1912).
Elias, N. *The civilizing process: The history of manners and state formation and civilization,* Oxford: Blackwell, 1994 (1939).
Elias, N. 'The symbol theory: An introduction, part one', *Theory Culture & Society* 6, 1989, 169–217.
Evans, D. 'Michel Maffesoli's sociology of modernity and postmodernity: An introduction and critical assessment', *Sociological Review* 45, 1997, 221–43.
Falk, P. *The consuming body,* London Sage, 1994.
Featherstone, M. and Burrows, R. (eds) *Cyberspace/cyberbodies/cyberpunk: Cultures of technological embodiment,* London: Sage, 1995.
Featherstone, M. 'The body in consumer culture', *Theory Culture & Society* 1, 1995, 18–33.
Fischer, C.S. 'The subcultural theory of urbanism: A twentieth-year assessment', *American Journal of Sociology* 101 (3), 1995, 543–77.
Fitzpatrick, M. *The tyranny of health: Doctors and the regulation of lifestyle,* London: Routledge, 2001.
Foucault, M. *The birth of the clinic: An archaeology of medical perception,* London: Tavistock, 1973.
Foucault, M. *Discipline and punish: The birth of the prison,* London: Penguin, 1977.
Frank, A. 'For a sociology of the body: An analytical review', in Featherstone, M., Hepworth, M. and Turner, B.S. (eds) *The body: Social process and cultural theory,* London: Sage, 1991.
Freeman, M. *Rewriting the self: History, memory, narrative,* London: Routledge, 1973.
Freund, P.E.S. 'The expressive body: A common ground for the sociology of the emotions, health and illness', *Sociology of Health and Illness* 12, 1990, 452–77.
Gergen, K.J. *The saturated self: Dilemmas of identity in contemporary life,* New York: Basic Books, 1991.
Giddens, A. *Modernity and self-identity: Self and society in the late modern age,* Cambridge: Polity Press, 1991.

Gil, J. *Metamorphosis of the body,* Minneapolis: University of Minnesota Press, 1998.
Giles, D. 'Retrospective accounts of drunken behaviour: Implications for theories of self, memory and the discursive construction of memory', *Discourse Studies* 1 (4), 1999, 387–403.
Goffman, E. *Stigma: Notes on the management of spoiled identity,* Harmondsworth: Penguin, 1968.
Grosz, E. *Space, time, and perversion,* London: Routledge, 1995.
Heidegger, M. *Being and time,* Oxford: Blackwell, 2000 (1962).
Hepworth, M. and Featherstone, M. 'The male menopause: Lay accounts and the cultural reconstruction of midlife', in Nettleton, S. and Watson, J. (eds) *The body in everyday life,* London: Routledge, 1998, 276–301.
Hollway, W. and Jefferson, T. *Doing qualitative research differently: Free association, narrative and the interview method,* London: Sage, 2000.
Holstein, J.A. and Gubrium, J.F. 'Active interviewing', in Silverman, D. (ed.) *Qualitative research: Theory, method and practice,* London: Sage, 1997, 113–29.
Howson, A. 'Embodied obligation: The female body and health surveillance', in Nettleton, S. and Watson, J. (eds) *The body in everyday life,* London: Routledge, 1998, 218–40.
Howson, A. and Inglis, D. 'The body in sociology: Tensions inside and outside sociological thought', *Sociological Review* 49 (3), 2001, 297–317.
Huizinga, J. *Homo ludens: A study of the play element in culture,* Boston, MA: Beacon Press, 1950.
Inglis, D. and Holmes, M. 'Toiletry time: Defecation, temporal strategies and the dilemmas of modernity', *Time & Society* 9 (2–3), 2000, 223–45.
Jay, M. *Emperors of dreams: Drugs in the nineteenth century,* Sawtry, Cambs: Dedalus, 2000.
Jay, M. *High society: Mind-altering drugs in history and culture,* London: Thames & Hudson, 2010.
Jenks, C. *Transgression,* London: Routledge, 2003.
Jordan, G. 'Flight from modernity: Time, the other and the discourse of primitivism', *Time & Society* 4 (3), 1995, 281–303.
Keane, H. *What's wrong with addiction?* Victoria: Melbourne University Press, 2002.
Kirmayer, L.J. 'The body's insistence on meaning: Metaphor as presentation and representation in illness experience', *Medical Anthropology Quarterly* 6 (4), 1992, 323–46.
Klein, R. *Cigarettes are sublime,* Durham, NC: Duke University Press, 1993.
Kontos, L. 'The uncanny and the sublime in human experience: On the relevance of critical philosophy and psychoanalysis for sociological interpretation', *Sheffield Online Papers in Social Research* 3, 2001: http:/www.shef.ac.uk/uni/R-Z/socst/shop/3.html
Kvale, S. *Interviews: An introduction to qualitative research,* London: Sage, 1996.
Lasch, C. *The culture of narcissism: American life in an age of diminishing expectations,* New York: Warner Books, 1979.
Leach, E. *Culture and communication: The logic by which symbols are connected,* Cambridge: Cambridge University Press, 1976.
Leder, D. *The absent body,* Chicago, IL: University of Chicago Press, 1990.
Leder, D. 'A tale of two bodies: The Cartesian corpse and the lived body', in Welton, D. (ed.) *Body and flesh: A philosophical reader,* Oxford: Blackwell, 1998, 117–29.
Levi-Strauss, C. *Introduction to the work of Marcel Mauss,* London: Routledge & Kegan Paul, 1987 (1950).

Lindahl, C. 'Bakhtin's carnival laughter and the Cajun Country Mardi Gras', *Folklore* 107, 1996, 57–70.

Lingis, A. *Foreign bodies,* London: Routledge, 1994.

Lowell Lewis, J. 'Sex and violence in Brazil: Carnaval, capoeira, and the problem of everyday life', *American Ethnologist* 26 (3), 2000 539–57.

Lupton, D. *The imperative of health: Public health and the regulated body,* London: Sage, 1995.

Lupton, D. 'Going with the flow: Some central discourses in conceptualising and articulating the embodiment of emotional states', in Nettleton, S. and Watson, J. (eds) *The body in everyday life,* London: Routledge, 1998, 82–99.

Lyon, M.L. and Barbalet, J.M. 'Society's body: Emotion and the "somatization" of social theory', in Csordas, T.J. (ed.) *Embodiment and experience: The existential ground of culture and self,* Cambridge: Cambridge University Press, 1994.

Maffesoli, M. *The time of the tribes: The decline of individualism in mass society,* London: Sage, 1996.

Maffesoli, M. *Ordinary knowledge: An introduction to interpretive sociology,* Cambridge: Polity Press, 1996.

Malins, P. 'Machinic assemblages: Deleuze, Guattari and an ethico-aesthetics of drug use', *Janus Head* 7 (1), 2004, 84–104.

Mars, G. and Altman, Y. 'Alternative mechanism of distribution in a Soviet economy', in Douglas, M. (ed.) *Constructive drinking: Perspectives on drink from anthropology,* Cambridge: Cambridge University Press, 1987, 270–9.

Maryanski, A. 'The last ancestor: An ecological network model on the origins of human sociality', *Advances in Human Ecology* 1, 1992, 1–32.

Massey, D.M. 'A brief history of human society: The origin and role of emotion in social life', *American Sociological Review* 67 (1), 2002, 1–29.

Maturana, H.R. and Varela, F.J. *The tree of knowledge: The biological roots of human understanding,* Boston, MA: Shambhala Publications, 1992.

Mauss, M. *The gift: Forms and functions of exchange in archaic societies,* London: Cohen & West, 1966 (1950).

Mellor, P.A. and Shilling, C. *Re-forming the body: Religion, community and modernity,* London: Sage, 1997.

Merleau-Ponty, M. *The structure of behaviour,* London: Methuen, 1963.

Miller, J. and Glassner, B. 'The "Inside" and the "Outside": Finding realities in interviews', in Silverman, D. (ed.) *Qualitative research: Theory, method and practice,* London: Sage, 1997, 99–112.

Mishler, E.G. *Research interviewing: Context and narrative,* Cambridge, MA: Harvard University Press, 1986.

Mommsen, W.J. *The age of bureaucracy: Perspectives on the political sociology of Max Weber,* Oxford: Blackwell, 1974.

Nancy, J-L. *The inoperative community,* Minneapolis: University of Minnesota Press, 1991.

Nettleton, S. and Watson, J. 'Introduction: The body in everyday life', in Nettleton, S. and Watson, J. (eds) *The body in everyday life,* London: Routledge, 1998, 1–23.

O'Malley, P. and Valverde, M. 'Pleasure, freedom and drugs: The uses of "pleasure" in liberal governance of drug and alcohol consumption', *Sociology* 38 (1), 2004, 25–42.

Ong, W.J. *Orality and literacy: The technologising of the word,* London: Methuen, 1982.

Ots, T. 'The silenced body – the expressive *Leib:* On the dialectic of mind and life in Chinese cathartic healing', in Csordas, T.J. (ed.) *Embodiment and experience: The existential ground of culture and self,* Cambridge: Cambridge University Press, 1994.

Pearson, G. *The new heroin users,* Oxford: Blackwell, 1987.

Probyn, E. 'Beyond food/sex: Eating and the ethics of existence', in Bell, V. (ed.) *Performativity and belonging,* London: Sage, 1999, 215–28.

Punch, K.F. *Developing effective research proposals,* London: Sage, 2000.

Race, K. *Pleasure consuming medicine: The queer politics of drugs,* Durham, NC: Duke University Press, 2009.

Refisch, F. 'Competitive beer drinking among the Mambila', in Douglas, M. (ed.) *Constructive drinking: Perspectives on drink from anthropology,* Cambridge: Cambridge University Press, 1987, 135–45.

Reiman, J.H. 'Research subjects, political subjects, human subjects', in Klockars, C.B. and O'Connor, W.O. *Deviance and decency: The ethics of research with human subjects,* London: Sage, 1979.

Reith, G. 'In search of lost time: Recall, projection and the phenomenology of addiction', *Time & Society* 8 (1), 2000, 99–117.

Riessman, C.K. *Narrative analysis,* London: Sage, 1993.

Robson, C. *Real world research: A resource for social scientists and practitioner-research,* Oxford: Blackwell, 2000.

Ronell, A. *The telephone book: Technology, schizophrenia, electric speech,* Lincoln: University of Nebraska Press, 1989.

Ronell, A. *Crack wars: Literature addiction mania,* Lincoln: University of Nebraska Press, 1992.

Santos, M.S. 'Memory and narrative in social theory: The contributions of Jacques Derrida and Walter Benjamin', *Time & Society* 10 (2–3), 2001, 163–89.

Sartre, J.P. *Sketch for a theory of the emotions,* London: Methuen, 1971 (1962).

Scarry, E. *The body in pain,* Oxford: Oxford University Press, 1985.

Schmalenbach, H. *On society and experience: Selected papers,* Chicago, IL: University of Chicago Press, 1977.

Schmitt, R. and Moody, T.E. (eds) *Alienation and social criticism,* Atlantic Highlands, NJ: Humanities Press, 1994.

Schutz, A. *Collected papers 1: The problem of social reality,* New York: Humanities Press, 1962.

Segre, S. 'A Weberian theory of time', *Time & Society* 9 (2–3), 2000, 147–70.

Shewan, D. and Dalgarno, P. 'Evidence for controlled heroin use? Low levels of negative health and social outcomes among non-treatment users in Glasgow (Scotland)', *British Journal of Health Psychology* 10, 2005, 33–48.

Shildrick, M. *Leaky bodies and boundaries: Feminism, postmodernism and (bio)ethics,* London: Routledge, 1997.

Shildrick, M. *Embodying the monster: Encounters with the vulnerable self,* London: Sage, 2002.

Shilling, C. *The body and social theory,* London: Sage, 1993.

Shilling, C. 'Toward an embodied understanding of the structure/agency relationship', *British Journal of Sociology* 50 (4), 1999, 543–62.

Shilling, C. 'Embodiment, experience and theory: In defence of the sociological tradition', *Sociological Review* 49 (3), 2001, 327–44.

Shilling, C. *The body and social theory,* second edn, London: Sage, 2003.

Shilling, C. *The body in culture, technology and society,* London: Sage, 2005.

Simmel, G. 'Sociability', in Wolff, K. (ed.) *The sociology of Georg Simmel,* New York: Free Press, 1950.

Simmel, G. 'The metropolis and mental life', in Levine, D. (ed.) *Georg Simmel: On individuality and social forms,* Chicago, IL: University of Chicago Press, 1971 (1903).

Smith, T.S. *Strong interaction,* Chicago, IL: University of Chicago Press, 1992.

Sobchack, V. 'Beating the meat/Surviving the text, or how to get out of this century alive', in Featherstone, M. and Burrows, R. (eds) *Cyberspace/cyberbodies/cyberpunk: Cultures of technological embodiment,* London: Sage, 1995, 205–14.

Southgate, E. and Hopwood, M. 'Mardi Gras says, "be drug free": Accounting for resistance, pleasure and the demand for illicit drugs', *Health* 3 (3), 1999, 303–16.

Subrt, J. 'The problem of time from the perspective of the social sciences',*Czech Sociological Review* 9 (2), 2001, 211–24.

Tabboni, S. 'The idea of social time in Norbert Elias', *Time & Society* 10 (1), 2001, 5–27.

Tarde, G. *Gabriel Tarde: On communication and social influence,* Clark. T.N. (ed.), Chicago, IL: University of Chicago Press, 1969.

Tonnies, F. *Community and association (Gemeinschaft und gesellschaft),* London: Routledge & Kegan Paul, 1955 (1887).

Turner, B.S. 'The rationalization of the body: Reflections on modernity and discipline', in Whimster, S. and Lash, S. (eds) *Max Weber, rationality and modernity,* London: Routledge, 1987, 222–41.

Turner, B.S. *The body and society,* London: Sage, 1996.

Turner, V.W. *The ritual process: Structure and anti-structure,* New York: Aldine, 1969.

Turner, V. and Turner, E.L.B. *Image and pilgrimage in Christian culture,* New York: Columbia University Press, 1978.

Twine, R. 'Physiognomy, phrenology and the temporality of the body', *Body & Society* 8 (1), 2002, 67–88.

Van Gennep, A. *The rites of passage,* London: Routledge & Kegan Paul, 1960 (1908).

Warnock, M. 'Introduction' to J. P. Sartre, *Being and nothingness: An essay on phenomenological ontology,* London: Methuen, 1972 (1958), *XVI.*

Watts Miller, W. 'Durkheimian time', *Time & Society* 9 (1), 2000, 5–20.

Weber, M. 'Power and bureaucracy', in Thomson, K. and Tunstall, J. (eds) *Sociological perspectives,* Penguin: Harmondsworth, 1971 (1922).

Weber, M. *The Protestant ethic and the spirit of capitalism,* London: Routledge, 2001 (1904).

Williams, B. and Barlow, H.A. 'Falling out with my shadow: lay perceptions of the body in the context of arthritis', in Nettleton, S. and Watson, J. (eds) *The body in everyday life,* London: Routledge, 1998, 124–41.

Williams, S.J. 'Modernity and the emotions: corporeal reflections on the (ir)rational', *Sociology* 32 (4), 1998, 747–69.

Wilshire, B. *Wild hunger: The primal roots of modern addiction,* Oxford: Rowman & Littlefield, 1998.

Wirth, L. *On cities and social life,* Chicago, IL: University of Chicago Press, 1964.

Index

Page numbers in *Italics* represent tables; Page numbers followed by n represent endnotes; Page numbers followed by a represent appendix.

accumulation processes 25–6, 110
acid *see* LSD
addiction 26, 29, 64, 128, 146n; anti-addiction drugs 29
Aeon 42, 54–6
Afghanistan 127
Agamben, G. 89, 116
agonistic competition 19, 20
agrarian societies 6–7, 79–80
Ahmadi, A. 51
alcohol 31–2, 62–4, 68–70, 94, 96, 101, 106, 109, 110, 114, 128, 134a; healthy limit 136a
Altman, Y.: and Mars, G. 19
amphetamine 26–7, 39, 110–11
amyl nitrate 70
ancestors 45, 47; 'ancestral body' 87, 112, 117
arborescent structures 107
Auge, C. 112
autonomy 96–8; surrender 97

Bakhtin, M. 76, 86, 87, 90–1, 92, 100, 103, 116, 150n
Bancroft, A. 112
Bataille, G. 4, 12–15, 18, 20–1, 24, 86
Baudrillard, J. 11–12, 14, 49, 110
Bauman, Z. 79, 90, 92
Becker, H. 140a
'becoming' state 55–6, 58, 60
behaviour 64; 'deviant' 140a; norms 120; rationality 11–12; unacceptable 16
Benjamin, W. 51, 119
Blanchot, M. 68
the body 33, 43, 46–8, 53, 74–6, 78, 87–9, 93; control 12; de-temporalized 52; failures 106–7; grotesque body 88, 101–2, 117, 118; ideal 120; modern 2–4, 9–23, 42, 89, 98–100, 118; playful 102–7; relinquishing the rational 98–100; sacrificing 9–23; self-destruction 22; time 53–6, 57–73; unmaking 9–23, 24, 131a, *see also* rational body sacrifice
the body and time 57–73; activities 64–5; embodying the past 71–2; forgetting 60–4; non-linear time 65–8; sacrificing the future 58–60; sharing the present 68–71
boundary-crossing 4, 109
Bourdieu, P. 15–17, 25
Brazilian carnival 21
Brint, S. 76, 80, 83–4, 90, 92
British Sociological Association (BSA) 135
Burkitt, I. 101
Burroughs, W. 127
Butler, J. 37, 119–20, 140a

calculation transcending 33–5
Calhoun, C. 115
Canetti, E. 85, 91, 94, 98, 105
cannabis 26, 31–2, 64, 94, 100, 110, 114, 124
capital 25
carnival 21, 88, 103, 150n
cathartic healing 139a
Chinese healing 139a
Christian pilgrimage 7
'chronographic body' 67
Chronos 42, 54–6

cigarette smoking 22–3, 29–30; moral condemnation 125; prayer comparison 22
Clastres, P. 87
clocks 49, 65–6, 67, 73, 120–1; immunity 66; universal language 66–7
co-presence 70, 81
cocaine 39, 62–4, 68, 97–8, 109, 111
collective activities 44
collective effervescence 45
communication 59–60, 68–9, 78, 101–2, 104, 108; desire 81; oral 6, 46–7
communion 95
communitas 7, 88–9, 93, 97–8, 105, 109, 114, 117, 122; paradox 114–16
community 74–91, 92–117; alternative concepts 83; concepts 74–91; definition 75; formation 6–8, 82, 92–117; liminal 74–91, 121–2, 138a; obligations 84; positives 112; ties 7, 80; underground centrality 81
Community and Association (Tonnies) 76
community theorizing 74–91; community of everyone 81–2; concept embodying 87–9; concept limits 75–6; different conceptualizing approach 83; *gemeinschaft* definition 77; *gesellschaft* definition 78–9; Maffesoli's concept implications 82; modernity's closed body 89; social structures 83–7; structure and community 76; Tonnies's model limits 79–81; total community 76–7
Constructive Drinking (Douglas) 19
constructivist perspective 136a
contemporary society 55, 71, 73, 74–91; allowing intoxication 127–9; communal ties 7; community experience 74–117; drug users position 122–3; industrial ethic 25; isolation 121; lifestyle 3; time 5–6, 47–50, 57–73
corporeal irruption 100
criminalisation 127
crowd forms 85
cultural representation 136a
cultural transmission 46
culture 1, 43, 48, 50–1, 115; consumer 81–2; Eskimo 4, 44; oral 46–7; other 129; post-Enlightenment 48; traditional 44; urban 3; western 1, 123

dance 66–8, 69, 121
Dasein (rational animal) 13
Davies, M. 51
deferred gratification 25
Deleuze, G.: and Guattari, F. 11, 13, 15, 21–2, 25, 30, 38, 54, 98, 102, 107, 126
Derrida, J. 17–19, 40, 63
desires 24, 30, 81; social conflict 129–30
Devault, M. 139a
Dick, P. 129
disease 126
disembedding mechanisms 52
dosage 34
Douglas, M. 112
drinking customs 19
drug policies 124
drug use 2, 128; forgetting 33–6; health question 124; social acceptance 127–9; unreliable information 128; users rationale 126; users social position 122–4, *see also* experiences
drugs: context 138a; unpredictability 128
Durkheim, E. 44–5
Durkheimian view 45–7, 82
dyadic relationships 79

economy 18; sacrificial 42, 54, 74
ecstasy 27, 68, 96, 101, 108, 109, 111, 113, 124, 134a
empathetic engagement 140a
engagement modes 9–15, 64
environmental conditions 35
environmental cues 50
ephemeral communities 113
ephemeral utopias 110–12, 117
epidemiological interventions 124
equality 84–5, 87, 94–5, 121–2; illusions 85; symbolism 94–5
erotic activity 15, 66, 69
Erowid archive 133a
Eskimo culture 4, 44
evanescent activities 54, 60
evanescent experiences 68
evanescent reality 64, 66–7
exchange values 14
existence 48, 72; accelerated pace 48; the body 48; corporeal 122; time relatives 65–6
expenditure 119–20; beyond necessity 24–41; free 13, 23–4, 26–30, 110; sacrificial 9–23, 25; wasteful 25–30
experiences 13, 24, 51; collective 97; communal 106; embodied 53–4, 57–8, 60–1, 66–7, 87, 92, 131a, 134a, 136a, 138a; free expenditures 26–30; inside 95, 105; negative 106–7, 123; outside

95, 105; rituals 92–117; time 42; unpredictability 33, *see also* temporal experiences
experiential communication 88
experiential level 57–8, 61, 63, 72, 94, 100, 110
experimentation 30–1, 40

Falk, P. 95
feminism 139a
Fischer, C. 80
floating energies 28
forgetting 33–6, 39, 59–64
Foucault, M. 23, 49, 130
free action 31
free experimentation logic 30
Freund, P. 12
friendship 113–14
the future 58–9; open 51–3; sacrificing 58–60; unknown 45–6, 57, 71, 121

gemeinschaft 75–6, 78, 80, 82, 90; definition 77
Georgian feasts 19–20; 'Tamada' 19–20
gesellschaft 75–7, 80, 90, 117; definition 78–9
Giddens, A. 48, 52, 78–9, 90, 92
The Gift: Forms and Functions of Exchange in Archaic Societies (Mauss) 16
gift-form 19–21, 33, 37; concept 9; economy 18; possibility conditions 15–19; reciprocity 17
Gil, J. 28, 32, 46–7, 55, 67, 86–9, 94
Giles, D. 131a
Glassner, B.: and Miller, J. 137a, 139a
glue 110
Goffman, E. 105
Guattari, F.: and Deleuze, G. 11, 13, 15, 21–2, 25, 30, 38, 54, 98, 102, 107, 126
Gubrium, J.: and Holstein, J. 136a

habitus concept 15
haltung 12
health 2, 29, 118, 122–3, 136a; discourses 125; irrational arguments 123–4; meaning 123–7; policies 124
Heidegger, M. 12–13, 49, 67
heroin 26–7, 62, 66–7, 100; health evidence 124
hierarchy 107, 122; inversion 88
Hillery, G. 75
Hollway, W.: and Jefferson, T. 136a
Holstein, J.: and Gubrium, J. 136a
human desires 24, 30, 81, 129–30
human energies 9–23, 24–30
human needs 3–4, 10–11, 14
human rights 127–8

identity 7, 34, 45, 105, 112–13, 116, 119, 128
immersion 61, 96–8
'the impossible' 21, 24–41; forgetting 33–6; labour to play 30–3; surplus energies disposal 25–30; transgression limits 36–41
incitement 129–30
individualism 89, 125
informed consent 135a
'insider' research designs 140a
intensity sampling 132a
interactions 90; order 105; play form 85; reciprocal 126; rhizomic 107–9, 122; social 119; spontaneous 109
internet 5–6, 59; chat rooms 84
interview format 134–5a
interview process 131–40a; analysis and interpretation 136–8a; conducting interviews 134a; data collection 133–4a; data transcription 135a; ethical considerations 135a; methodology 132a; questions *142*; recruitment 132–3a; research and participant relationship 138–40a; sampling strategy 132–3a
interview society 137a
interviewees *141*; Amanda 95, 113; Brian 33; David 39, 69, 71, 99, 101, 111, 114; Edward 27, 70, 97, 113, 115; Geoff 26–7, 31–2, 38, 60, 64–5, 68, 99, 103, 108; George 28, 32, 38, 68, 96, 100, 109, 113; Jenny 33; Joanna 36, 61, 63, 71, 97, 108; Karen 33, 38, 62, 64, 68–70, 72, 99, 100, 106, 107, 108, 109, 113, 114; Linda 38; Michael 34, 36, 39, 61, 67, 72, 113; Peter 62, 69–70, 104, 106, 109, 111; Philip 26–7, 34, 37, 62, 100, 106; Robert 27, 62, 64, 66, 99, 100, 104, 106; Roger 68, 94, 102, 111; Sally 66, 104; Simon 27–8, 36, 62, 99, 100, 111; Steven 29–32, 39, 62, 67, 103, 104, 108, 113; Tony 34, 35, 62–4, 69–70, 96, 99, 102, 103, 114
intoxication: characteristics 14, 64–5; eventful quality 65; learned intoxication 131a; social acceptance 127–9

intoxication liminality and community formation 92–117; communitas paradox 114–16; ephemeral utopias 110–12; immersion and autonomy 96–8; inhabiting the playful body 102–7; language 101–2; rational body relinquishing 98–100; rhizomic interactions 107–9; rituals 93–6; social ties 112–14

Jefferson, T.: and Hollway, W. 136a
Jenks, C. 21, 38

Kabyle society 16
ketamine 31–2, 34, 60–1, 99
Kirmayer, L. 76, 115
Klein, R. 14, 22, 30, 110, 126
Kvale, S. 133a, 137a

labour 11–12, 25, 51, 89; transition to play 30–3
landscapification 11
language 32, 78, 101–2, 131a; body use 102; embodied use 101; intoxicated imagery 100–1; possibilities 136a
Largactil 38–9
Lasch, C. 89
laughter 66, 69, 102–7, 121
Lavater, J. 55
laws 127
Leach, E. 45
Levi-Strauss, C. 16–17, 66
Lewis, L. 21
liberated energies 28
life cycles 43–4, 49, 72, 121
liminal communities 121–2, 138a; formation 74–91
Lingis, A. 12
lived event 66
lived experience 2, 131a, 140a
lived present 5–6, 13, 45–6, 52, 54, 58–60, 62–3, 67, 69–72, 120–2; immersion 61, *see also* the present
lived reality 45–6, 140a
'lower stratum' 103
LSD 28, 32, 35, 36, 39, 61–3, 65, 66–8, 70–1, 108, 110, 111
Lycaeum archive 133a

Maffesoli, M. 75–6, 81–2, 90, 92, 114, 117; community concept implications 82
magic mushrooms 34, 39, 61, 66–7, 94–5, 114
magico-religious ceremonies 44–6
Malins, P. 126
Mambila people 20
Mars, G.: and Altman, Y. 19
Maryanski, A. 80
material reality 122–3
Mauss, M. 4, 9, 16–18, 44
Mead, G. 52
medicine 55
medieval society 86, 88, 103
Mellor, P.: and Shilling, C. 78
memory 33–6, 38–9, 59–64, *see also* forgetting
Merleau-Ponty, M. 12, 50
Miller, J.: and Glassner, B. 137a, 139a
misconceptions 128
modernity 5–6, 57, 73, 81, 92, 118, 123, 146n; the body 89; conditions 78–9, 115; ideal 1; time 42–56; transition 79
moral responsibility 113
morphine 106
mortality 68–9, 110, 126–7
music 66–8, 69, 121; events 64, 101, 111
mutual acknowledgement 122
mutual recognition 86–7
myths 46, 80

Nancy, J. 131a
narratives 136a
National Health Service (NHS) 124
natural time 44
'natural will' 77–8
necessities: existence 39; primordial 40; remembered 36; social 36, 39, 40
The Netherlands 130
nicotine 29
Nietzsche, F. 81
normality 27
nostalgia 61

Ong, W. 46
organic human interconnectedness 76, 79
organic temporality 57
ostracism of users 127–8
the other 85, 129
Ots, T. 139a
'outsider' research designs 139a

the past 57–8; embodying 71–2
pathognomy 55
patriarchy 77
Pearson, G. 100
personal biographical elements 136–7a

pharmakon 34
phenomenological perspective 57, 72, 76
phrenology 55
physiognomy 55
Politics of Friendship (Derrida) 40
population health 124–5
Portugal 130
potlatch 16, 18–20
practical appropriation 10–13
practical needs 9
the present 59–60, 64, 66, 72; immersion 59, 61; luxurious 66; sharing 68–71, *see also* lived present
primate society studies 80
the profane: order of existence 46; time 44–5; world 40, 61
prohibition consequences 127
projective activities 52, 116–17
Protestant ethic 25
public discourse 136–7a, 139a
public health initiatives 136–7a
purposeful activities 13–15, 21, 27, 30

qualitative research 138–40a; researcher's role 139a
quantitative studies 138a; critique 139a

rational activities 11–12, 14
rational animal 13
rational appropriations 9, 10–13
rational body sacrifice 9–23; gift form 15–21; gift form possibility conditions 15–19; practical appropriation engagement 10; practical to rational appropriations 10–13; rationality and experience 13; sacrificial expenditure engagement 13–15; transgression 21–2
'rational will' 78
rationalist ontology 48
realist perspective 136a
reality 122–3
regulated reciprocity 19
Rehfisch, F. 20
relationships 74–91, 122; creation importance 126; dyadic 79
researcher's role 139a
resource expenditure 119–20
retrospective accounts 136a
rhizome 107
rights: charter of 128
rituals 46, 86, 92–117; collective 44–5; contemporary society 92–117; eating 94–5; inclusion 97; performance 44–6, 57; rites of passage 87; sensual immersion 86
romanticism 90
Ronnel, A. 15

the sacred 45–6, 48, 57, 70, 72, 118–19, 129; lived reality 45–6; time 44; world 37, 40, 44, 61
sacrifice 37; economy 9–23, 42, 54, 74; expenditure 9–23, 25; the future 58–60; gesture 118–20; time 121
A Scanner Darkly (Dick) 129
schizophrenia 129–30
Schutz, A. 60, 69
self-awareness 38
sensual engagement 86, 95–6
settlements: small-scale 79–80
shared states 7
Shildrick, M. 12, 100
Shilling, C. 105; and Mellor, P. 78
side effects 31
Simmel, G. 14, 51, 78, 84–5, 87, 91, 94
Smith, T. 86
sobriety 118
sociability 84–5, 87
social boundaries 109
social consequences 105
social interaction 119
social organization 74–91
social spaces 7, 85
social structures 76, 83–7, 107, 122
social ties 112–14, 121
social time 44
social value 119
sociality: empathetic 81; origins 80
society 6–7, 24, 45, 74–91; conflicts 75; drugs overview 1; expectations 119; 'finite games' 48–9; historical development 2–7; interactions 25; mass 82; time 5–6, 42–56; understanding sacrifice 19, *see also* contemporary society; traditional societies
sociological theorizing 75
sociology 76
space 67; liminal 7–8, 93, 102, 116, 122; shared 102
spontaneity 65, 109
Star Trek 101
Statement of Ethical Practice (BSA) 135
stigma issues 127–8, 130
Suleiman 10
'surveyor-body' 67

technology 5–6, 48–9, 59
television 5, 50, 59
temazepam 34, 62
temporal experience 42–56, 57, 59, 72; diachronic elements 43, 45, 55; dichotomization 53; embodied 66–7; machinic 49–50; synchronic elements 43, 45, 55; traditional societies 43–7
temporality 120–1; dimensions 42; reality 66; reversibility 47; schemas 42, 58
Tess of the D'Urbervilles (Hardy) 49
A Thousand Plateaus (Deleuze and Guattari) 98
threat perception 123–4
time 5–6, 42–56, 120–1; *Aeon* 42, 54–6; the body 57–73; *Chronos* 42, 54–6; devices 48–9, 65–6; gift-giving 17; linear 53–4, 57–8, 64, 67, 72, 121; model 42–56; modernity 47–9; non-linear 65–8; perceptions 58; sociological 53; traditional 42–56, *see also* clocks
time in societies 42–56; the body 53–6; filling and emptying time 50–1; machinic temporality 49–50; modernity 47–9; open future promise 51–3; sociological time antinomies 53; temporality and recurrence 43–5; traditional societies experience 43; traditional societies temporality and change 45–7
tobacco 29
Tonnies, F. 75–81, 83–4, 88, 90, 92, 112, 114, 117; community mode limits 79–81
traditional societies 42, 57, 87; rituals 86; role of the dead 45, 47; temporality 43–7; temporality and change 45–7; time experience 43; tribal 3, 6, 84, 86, 95
transgression 21–2; limits 36–41
transgressive economy 9–23
Trobriand Islanders 16
Turner, E.: and Turner, V. 7
Turner, V. 7, 76, 85–8, 90–1, 92, 97–8, 122; and Turner, E. 7
Twine, R. 55

United Kingdom (UK) 124; North West England 100
United States of America (USA) 130
urbanism 79–80
use value 10–11, 14

valium 106
venues 107–8, 122
vivid simultaneity 68–9

war on drugs 127, 129
wasteful activities 24–41
Weber, M. 11
Wirth, L. 78
writing inability 68

youths 71–2

Zyban 29